Praise for *Kingdom F*

As someone who is absolutely (............................ king that
is going to advance the cause of .... .il that my
friends Jeff and Mac have worked to deepen our understanding on this crucial topic. *Kingdom First* is a very useful and practical guide in order to get
it right up front.

> ~ Alan Hirsch, author on the dynamics of missional movements and
> founder of Forge Missional Training Network and Future Travelers

Jeff Christopherson is one of the foremost thinkers, practitioners, and influencers in the field of church planting today. I can't imagine planting a church
without first reading this book.

> ~ Richard Blackaby, president of Blackaby Ministries International,
> author of *Spiritual Leadership* and *Unlimiting God*

If I could recommend only one book on how to start a church, this would be
it! I loved it. It is comprehensive, biblical, and holistic. Jeff Christopherson
is someone who has lived the principles of which he has written.

> ~ Bob Roberts, author of *Bold as Love* and senior pastor,
> NorthWood Church

Before I had finished reading the two pages of the introduction, I could see
that Jeff Christopherson is a church planter who "gets it." As I read on, that
impression was only confirmed. He gets that church planting isn't a career
path, it's a calling. It's not about building the church, but about building the
Kingdom of God. It's not about a checklist, but about character tested by the
real world. So read and take to heart the sometimes surprising wisdom from
someone who has lived it.

> ~ Bob Logan, author of *The Missional Journey*

Kingdom First is not just another book on church planting. It's an in-depth,
principle-based handbook on participating in the advancement of God's
Kingdom. I particularly found the section on multiplication helpful as defining the standard for what we are starting.

> ~ Keith E. Webb, author of *The COACH Model for Christian Leaders*

Jeff Christopherson was an early voice in the emerging Kingdom conversation. In *Kingdom First* he makes another wonderful contribution to the discussion, particularly with his emphasis on developing a Kingdom-centric church approach. Though written specifically for church planters, this volume has practical insight for every church leader, no matter their ministry assignment.

~ Reggie McNeal, author of *Kingdom Come: Why We Must Quit Our Obsession Over Fixing the Church—And What We Should Do Instead*

From only a few times collaborating in the same room with Jeff, his heart for taking the gospel to every man, woman, and child was clearly apparent to me. In *Kingdom First* Jeff takes his Kingdom-driven approach to mission, leadership, and church planting to the next level. If your heart is to saturate cities with the gospel through Kingdom-driven, missionary leaders, then *Kingdom First* is an essential tool for your toolbox.

~ Neal McGlohon, lead visionary of The Cypress Project

So thankful for this necessary resource written by my two good friends, Jeff Christopherson and Mac Lake. Church planting is not the goal. The Kingdom of God being expanded to the ends of the earth is the goal. This book exemplifies this principle and provides practical insights to live it out. Every church planter needs to read *Kingdom First*!

~ Vance Pitman, senior pastor of Hope Church, Las Vegas

When I wrote *Planting Growing Churches for the 21st Century* in 1992, there was little material available for the aspiring church planter. I could count the number of books on one hand. Since then, there has been an explosion of books on the topic. Some that are good, and some that are not. Jeff and Mac's Kingdom First is must reading for anyone who has any interest in church planting.

~ Aubrey Malphurs, author of *Advanced Strategic Planning* and senior professor of Leadership and Pastoral Ministry, Dallas Theological Seminary

With more than 267 million people in North America that have no relationship with Christ, the Great Commission task to push back lostness on our continent is more challenging than ever. This important book has potential to reshape how the church sees and fulfills that mission. I'm excited to see

what will happen as more church leaders catch Jeff Christopherson's vision to start Kingdom-centered churches with the potential to multiply at unprecedented rates. Every pastor and church planter needs to read this book!
~ Kevin Ezell, president of the North American Mission Board

I am thrilled to recommend Jeff Christopherson's book to you. *Kingdom First* is an important book for church planters and church planting network leaders to read, particularly in the Canadian landscape. The chapters on the character of a church planter and contextualization are worth the price of the book alone. This book is required reading for all Canadian church planters!
~ Gord Fleming, national director of C2C Network

The Western world is desperately in need of a multiplying movement of evangelistically effective churches. Jeff Christopherson helps us understand this in *Kingdom First* and then points us to a path that leads to that end. I hope that every church planter reads this book and then puts it into practice.
~ Darrin Patrick, lead pastor of The Journey, a church in St. Louis, and vice president of Acts 29 and author of *Church Planter*

Kingdom First is a profound win for pastors, church planters, missionaries, and all church leaders. Jeff Christopherson's passion will not only set your heart on fire with vision, but also practically equip you to see your vision through into reality. Forward your future at an accelerated pace by reading personally and sharing *Kingdom First* with others. Let this movement begin with you!
~ Ronnie Floyd, president of the Southern Baptist Convention and senior pastor of Cross Church, Springdale, Arkansas

Kingdom First is an excellent rubric church planters *must* employ during the calibration process of aligning their heart with God's. Christopherson nails down the biblical definition of God's Kingdom and unpacks how its implications create a life-altering impact on how church planters live on mission both in private and public.
~ D. A. Horton, author of *DNA: Foundations of the Faith* and *G.O.S.P.E.L.*

In our own attempts to plant churches, we have understood how primary a proper understanding of the Kingdom of God must be. I so appreciate Jeff

Christopherson's clarion call to lead us all in that direction. I hope you will read this book.

— Archbishop Emeritus Bob Duncan, Anglican Church in North America

There will always be a deep relationship between churches embracing the gospel and churches multiplying and planting new churches. In this great book, Jeff Christopherson entreats us to embrace a call to Kingdom-focused church planting. You should read it and share it with your team.

— Matt Chandler, pastor of The Village Church, president of Acts 29, and author of *The Explicit Gospel*

Church planting has become an endeavor many pursue but few accomplish well. To the average man, planting a church seems unattainable, encumbered with insurmountable challenges and obstacles. *Kingdom First* reinforces disciple-making and church planting principles for indigenous planters who have a passion to overcome obstacles in order to reach their communities. The eight principles in this book restore hope to the practitioner and serve as a great resource to guide church planting movements in North America.

— Dhati Lewis, founder of Rebuild Network

Jeff Christopherson not only clearly understands the biblical truth of seeking God's Kingdom first, but also has the rare ability to communicate deep truths in a practical way that touches every area of ministry. *Kingdom First* should be required reading for everyone hoping to plant a church or enter into ministry. I truly believe that health and longevity of our ministries will flow from the foundational truths captured in this book.

— Brian Bloye, founder and senior pastor of West Ridge Church, Dallas, Georgia, and founder of the Multiply Group

Jeff Christopherson has had successful church planting experience in a very tough area. I love his focus on reaching the lost from the beginning of a plant, including those new to the faith on your launch team, and prioritizing church multiplication. Jeff will stretch your mind, challenge your motivations, and redirect your heart toward Kingdom purposes.

— John Worcester, church planting specialist

When you are flying in an airplane through turbulent air, you want experienced pilots. In *Kingdom First*, Jeff Christopherson and Mac Lake are your experienced pilots that will fly you through the turbulent air of church planting. Learn well from these experienced church-planting navigators.

~ Derwin L. Gray, lead pastor of Transformation Church, and author of *The High-Definition Leader: Building Multi-Ethnic Churches in a Multi-Ethnic World*

If you are planning to start a new church and want to explore the issues associated with that challenge, I cannot think of a better book.

~ Neil Cole, Director of Church Multiplication Associates and author of *Organic Church, Organic Leadership, Church 3.0,* and *Primal Fire*

When churches are planted and people are discipled, believers are able to bring the touch of Jesus to a spiritually confused community. This power is so clearly displayed as God gathers His people into newly formed congregations that effectively engage their diverse contexts. In *Kingdom First,* Jeff Christopherson does the Kingdom a great service by calling us back to that encouraging truth.

~ Alton Garrison, assistant general superintendent of Assemblies of God and author of *The 360 Degree Disciple*

In *Kingdom First,* Jeff Christopherson and Mac Lake have combined their significant experience as practitioners/thought leaders in church planting and leadership into a practical and accessible guide for any leader. I have had a front-row seat as this material has been developed, and I am thrilled it is now in written form so anyone can access it.

~ Geoff Surratt, author of *A Multi-Site Church Roadtrip* and *The Multi-Site Church Revolution*

JEFF CHRISTOPHERSON

WITH MAC LAKE

FOREWORD BY ED STETZER

KINGDOM
FIRST

STARTING CHURCHES THAT
SHAPE MOVEMENTS

B&H
PUBLISHING GROUP

NASHVILLE, TENNESSEE

978-1-4336-8883-6

Published by B&H Publishing Group
Nashville, Tennessee

Dewey Decimal Classification: 254.1
Subject Heading: EVANGELISTIC WORK \ KINGDOM OF GOD \
CHURCH PLANTING

Unless otherwise noted, all Scripture is taken from the English Standard
Version® (ESV®), copyright © 2001 by Crossway, a publishing ministry of
Good News Publishers. Used by permission. All rights reserved.

Also used: Holman Christian Standard Bible (HCSB) Copyright © 1999,
2000, 2002, 2003, 2009 by Holman Bible Publishers. Used by permission.

Also used: New International Version®, NIV® Copyright © 1973, 1978,
1984, 2011 by Biblica, Inc.® Used by permission. All rights reserved.

1 2 3 4 5 6 7 8 • 20 19 18 17 16 15

DEDICATION

For Laura, who lives unwaveringly yielded to her King.
Thank you for all the unseen sacrifices.

ACKNOWLEDGMENTS

I am grateful to an army of Kingdom warriors across the nations who are right now laying down their lives in order to establish new communities of Christ. Any benefit from this book will be directed to them.

I am grateful for their leaders who have long paid the price of Kingdom advancement in the midst of a more selfish era of ecclesiastical self-interest. Daniel Morgan, Gary Irby, Mark Custalow, Barry Whitworth, Hal Haller, and David Jackson, thank you for your guiding voices in this project.

I am so grateful to work in an uncommon environment of bold faith and courageous leadership at the North American Mission Board. Thank you Kevin for your audacious vision and fortitude to follow it through. Thank you Dino Senesi, Ryan West, Mark Clifton, and Mac Lake for your significant lifting. To quote Randy Bachman, "We ain't seen nothing yet."

I am grateful for Devin Maddox and Kim Stanford at B&H for believing in this idea and seeing it through. It was wonderful working with you.

And King Jesus, words cannot express the depth of gratitude that swells in this heart for the measureless grace that you have heaped on my life. Undeserved. Indebted. Thank you.

CONTENTS

Part 5: Teamwork (written by Mac Lake)

Part 6: Making a Difference

Part 7: Making Disciples

Part 8: Multiplication

FOREWORD

Church movements are tricky things, but the phrase has never been more popular. People keep referring to themselves as "a movement for global change" or "a church planting movement."

If we're honest, however, that's usually not the case.

Why do so many people classify themselves as a movement? People want to be a part of one. I recognize that desire because I share it. I am a seeker of movements. I want one. We need one.

Yet, only God can create a movement—it takes His divine and sovereign work. But, based on my observations in history and around the world today, there do seem to be some patterns related to such movements.

The obvious question is, "What will it take for a church movement to start now?"

Here are just a few ideas of many:

We need unreasonable men and women. The comfortable do not create movements. Instead, they originate with those who are desperate, demanding something different. Movements come from those who become more committed than they are now.

George Bernard Shaw, Irish dramatist and socialist, once said, "The reasonable man adapts himself to the world; the unreasonable one persists in trying to adapt the world to himself. Therefore all progress depends on the unreasonable man."

He's right, in a way.

I'd say that when women and men allow their faith to be tamed by the world, they end up with a "nice religion" uninterested in the big issues like global evangelization, world poverty, and injustice. That's why I love passionate people. We need more, not less of them.

Christianity needs unreasonable people who are uncomfortable with the status quo and unwilling to be content with the current mode of life and church. We all need a cause bigger than ourselves, which can drive us to action with a holy dissatisfaction.

We need churches that are willing to sacrifice. Seeing the Kingdom as more important than an individual church will take sacrifice, but that's what a movement is about. For so many churches that are simply trying to get by, however, that is an odd thing. Instead of a vision for the Kingdom, they have a vision for survival.

A movement takes churches that so believe in their mission and cause that they are willing to sacrifice for it—financially, congregationally, and corporately. They are willing to give *and* go. Movement churches will sacrifice people to send out missionaries around the world and church planters across the nation.

Everyone loves a movement, as long as it looks great but costs them little. A true movement will have a steep price, but those who are a part of it will recognize the immeasurable value.

We need multiplying disciples. That's so basic it is easy to miss, but it cannot be more essential. The fact is, no disciples are willing to be unreasonable and no churches are willing to sacrifice unless deeply committed disciples are involved.

Discipleship is the DNA of "movemental Christianity." It is the basic building block of anything Jesus calls us to do, which is why it is central to the mission of God. Disciples are unreasonable because they want the world to know of Jesus and to live as those who are changed by the gospel's power. Disciples demand their churches sacrifice for greater gospel good.

Paul explained that when we become new creations in Christ, we are drafted into service. We go out on God's behalf and offer reconciliation to the people in our lives. We don't replace Christ, but we do join Him in the grand plan of redemption. We join churches and sacrifice for the good of the Kingdom.

On multiple occasions Jesus challenged the faith development of His disciples. As time went on, He expected them to step out in faith and believe with more consistency. He expected them to step out of boats with greater confidence. He expected them to be *unsatisfied.*

No Christian movement can be birthed without discipleship. It is impossible.

So, what needs to happen and what needs to change?

This book, *Kingdom First: Starting Churches that Shape Movements,* by Jeff Christopherson, is a helpful tool to answer that very question. Throughout this text, Jeff walks the reader through the various necessities required for a real movement of the church, focused on the kingdom, powered by discipleship.

All sorts of factors play into church movements: leadership, purpose, communication, teamwork, and so much more. I am thankful for the ways in which Jeff has addressed all of these topics because each one of them plays an important role in real, effective Kingdom-centric movements of the global church.

I hope that as you read and engage with Jeff's book, you would be inspired to take the steps necessary to focus your discipleship-fueled multiplication on the good of the universal Kingdom of God.

—Ed Stetzer, LifeWay Research, www.edstetzer.com

Seek the Kingdom of God first.

—King Jesus

INTRODUCTION

Before we dive in, I think it would be helpful if I declared four big ecclesio-logical biases up front. These will be apparent throughout the book and will dramatically impact my approach to seemingly familiar matters. If these are new and unfamiliar, stay with me.

The Means, Not the End

For too long, in my opinion, the local church has unwittingly seen her-self as the end and ultimate good. If we were quizzed, we might correctly answer that the Kingdom of God has supremacy, and the local church is a God-ordained and instituted instrument to advance that eternal reality—but our actions would often contradict our impressive theological answers. We too often design churches as if they were the "end" in and of themselves. Inherent in that idolatrous design is a deviant, sacred darkness that the har-vest finds entirely repelling. This book is about crafting a new church for the Kingdom of God.

Principle Based, Model Neutral

Based upon our experiences and personality types, most of us have a church-planting model of preference. Those who have serially planted in multiple contexts have discovered that rigidly clinging to our favorite model usually brings depreciating results. Moreover, if our model is dependent upon a readily accessible preevangelized team to build upon, that seems to be an increasingly implausible presumption in many of our most unharvested contexts. Therefore, the ideas in this book will not presuppose a model/ models but will reflect larger principles that will help us think through contextual approaches. The companion guidebook to this book will help a potential planter with the application of more specific model approaches to his assignment.

Intentionally Bivocationally Germane

You will not see the words *bivocational* or *intentionally vocational* very often in this book. Not because it is unimportant but because this approach is of such importance that everything has been written with a filter of bivocational accessibility. Even though I give some leadership to one of the largest church-planting instruments in North America, I still am painfully aware that there are not enough resources available for true movements of God. Further, attempting to penetrate the places of greatest lostness with a singular and traditional focus of "funded planter," we will guarantee ineffectiveness. Intentionally bivocational church-planting teams are as indispensable to today's required movements as they were in the first century.

From Evangelism, Not for Evangelism

Finally, it is comforting to find common agreement that church planting is about evangelism. It's not uncommon to hear the famed and oft-quoted rationale that church planting is "the single most effective evangelistic methodology under heaven."[1] But is that really the case? In some cases absolutely. But in most cases only in comparison to the relative evangelistic impotence that has become normal to our evangelical culture. When churches are planted *for* evangelism, they often find themselves culturally mismatched and fail to gain an indigenous foothold. When churches are started *from* evangelism, they seem instinctively to know how to move forward, with great credibility, in a sea of networks and relationships. The art of planting from evangelism needs to be quickly rediscovered for the sake of a waiting harvest.

So we are about to go on a journey from crucial theological underpinnings to strategic missiological application. Our first stop will be to gain a practical understanding of what Jesus might have meant for His church to be *Kingdom first*. Perhaps it is a concept that is not front of mind in most ecclesiological discussions but certainly dominated the teaching ministry of Jesus and guided the actions of first-century church planters.

From there we will take an unexpected turn and delve into a practical look at the *character* of a leader that is necessary for Kingdom advancement.

Since the Kingdom of God is often more about *who* than *what*, we will attempt to describe the character of a potential church planter that is well positioned for Kingdom advancement. This may seem a bit unusual in a church-planting discussion, but from many years of observation, many have agreed that this singular subject is the strongest determiner of potential success or failure.

Third, with an underpinning of Kingdom and character, we will begin to understand the impact of context. Obviously *contexts* radically differ, not only from region to region but also from neighborhood to neighborhood. What is a Kingdom-first approach that is both respectful to the communities we will serve and strategic in effectively winning the harvest?

Fourth, we will examine the subject of *communication* and gain an appreciation for what "grace" and "truth" might sound like to our varied audiences. Our communication prowess is often the limiting window to which others see and understand the gospel; therefore growing in dexterity becomes crucial. We will tackle a seldom-considered subject and seek to differentiate between preaching and effective church-planting preaching.

Fifth, we will investigate the kind of *teamwork* necessary for effective Kingdom collaboration. What do these teams look like? How does a leader maintain team health, and how does a leader effectively lead leaders?

Sixth, we will seek perspective on how a church should *make a difference* in the geography it occupies and beyond. Learning the lessons of the recent past, we will attempt to describe a balanced picture of what it truly means for a church to be gospel centered. The implications of this gospel-centeredness extend far beyond the familiarity of the pulpit and actually take us to the nations.

Seventh, from the fruit of community transformation, we will begin building a Kingdomesque road map for *disciple making*. We will attempt to put great distance between our prevalent evangelical understanding of discipleship and the simple picture we see in the New Testament. With a biblical understanding of what we quantify as "fruit," we will focus on a process of discipling the harvest into harvesters.

Finally, we will reflect on the corollaries implicit in Jesus' assignment of Kingdom multiplication. We will explore what it means for the church itself to become a *multiplication* system. We will debunk several myths and highlight several common and painful missteps to avoid.

The whole process becomes a practical application of what it might mean to plant a church that is truly Kingdom first. In navigating this process, we might often find ourselves positioned as countercultural to our sacred subculture but, at the same time, moving affably with the rhythms of a biblical Kingdom.

So let's get started.

Part 1: **Kingdom First**

Few dreams are more spiritually intoxicating than the dream of being used by God to start a new community of Christ that skillfully brings the restorative gospel to a lost and broken city. What wouldn't you sacrifice to be a part of something that only could be described as a God-honoring, gospel movement? Something which feels like a spiritual landslide that starts with lostness and ends in an avalanche of new congregations multiplying and transforming community after community into which they unmistakably seep. A movement that vividly remembers the insubstantial days of a mustard seed with a sense of awe and wonder when looking at the indescribable harvest that stands all around.

Imagine that this was your dream and you are now ten full years into fleshing it out. It began and was propelled with the planting of a single church that you would later describe as Kingdom first. It was a vision that was realized by a selfless church that was not consumed with its religious reputation but instead was obsessed with a singular passion for the Kingdom of God. Your leaders did not see Jesus' abounding teachings on the Kingdom as abstract metaphors but as instructional marching orders. Men, women, boys, and girls reached beyond their comfort zones in order to become stretched into the instruments God could use to bring the Kingdom of heaven down to earth.

But possibly the strangest and most unexpected outcome of all, the Word of God had a new and dazzling crispness to it. When reading the Acts of the Apostles, there was inexplicable and yet comforting familiarity to it. No longer did it seem like Luke should have introduced his account with, "Once upon a time," as if it were a fable designed to impart a spiritual moral. The acts of the Holy Spirit in this contemporary Kingdom adventure seem remarkably reminiscent of days of old.

And then the penny drops; first-century results rarely come from twenty-first-century priorities. What made the first-century church so potent was its absolute disinterest in itself. It saw its reason to be as a catalyst for the Kingdom, emulating the pattern lived out by its founders (who followed the standard set by the Founder).

Kingdom first.

It would seem that the church of Jesus Christ is only observed in power when she sees herself as the King's instrument to advance His eternal goal and not as the end itself. The staggering differences are described in my earlier book, *Kingdom Matrix: Designing a Church for the Kingdom of God.*[2]

So the logical question follows, "If I am a church planter, how can this noble Kingdomesque notion be implemented with any degree of practicality?" More than likely you have limited resources and a limited time line to move things from an ethereal concept to a self-sustaining reality. The burden you feel seems as if you're standing in a bathtub of hard-won resources and the minute you start someone pulls the rubber stopper. The pressure is on your shoulders to get this church to a place of self-sustainability before you hear that hideous gurgly-shlurp sound of the final resources swirling down the drain. It is a lot of pressure.

Add to that the burden of personal competency. If you have ever given sincere consideration to starting a new church, you have likely had more than a few moments of second-guessing. "Do I have what it takes? Do I have the ability to gather resources? Can I effectively cast a compelling, God-inspired vision?"

The good news is that when you move past the threshold of your competency and comfort, you find yourself in the spot where God can use you like no other. You, by force of circumstances, find yourself in the most vulnerable intersection of weakness and lack. Perhaps for the first time in a long time, you are uniquely positioned and ready to experience the authority found in Kingdom first.

Remember those strange and counterculture words of our King: "Do not be anxious, saying, 'What shall we eat?' or 'What shall we drink?' or 'What shall we wear?' For the Gentiles seek after all these things, and your heavenly Father knows that you need them all. *But seek first the kingdom of God and his righteousness, and all these things will be added to you*" (Matt. 6:31–33, emphasis added).

Chapter 1

What Is the Kingdom?

If the church of Jesus Christ is God's primary vehicle to advance His Kingdom, it might be wise to gain a better understanding of what the Kingdom of God actually is, what it prefers, and how to rightly behave as loyal citizens.

Definitions are wide and varied, ranging from simplistic and somewhat missing the point to enormously complex, accommodating numerous historical and theological nuances. For our purposes let's understand the Kingdom of God (or Kingdom of heaven) to be Gods active and sovereign reign through history bringing about His purposes in the world through Christ Jesus. In the simplest of terms, the Kingdom of God is what the world looks like when King Jesus gets His way.

How important is it to have an informed understanding of the Kingdom of God? Think about this. Jesus had just spent a little more than three years in almost constant contact with His disciples. He taught them amazing things about how the universe works. It seemed like most of the time His friends just didn't get it. Then came the gruesome and stomach-turning Roman execution. His friends didn't see that coming either. And then the really big surprise—Jesus, their friend, became completely undead! It was an outrageous week to say the least. The Gospels close and the stage is set for an unprecedented unleashing of God's power through this cast of baffled and emotionally ragged troupers (as recorded by Doctor Luke in his Acts of the Apostles).

The volume we call Acts is uncapped with the briefest of introductions before we are immediately ushered into an often overlooked, yet theologically momentous verse: "He presented himself alive to them after his suffering by many proofs, appearing to them during forty days and speaking about the kingdom of God" (Acts 1:3).

Now picture this: The recently dead and now alive Jesus bends over backward to convince His friends that He was indeed physically alive and well in the state of Judea. From there He had everyone's attention. Better than that, they had His attention. For forty days Jesus and His friends hung out. Jesus taught. They believed. Who wouldn't believe every word that comes from this man's lips? And what did Jesus single out as the most significant reality in the universe for His friends to understand and master? Discipleship? Evangelism? Leadership? Missions? Church planting? How to be a better apostle?

No.

The subject on Jesus' postresurrection syllabus was curiously analogous to his precrucifixion teaching: the Kingdom of God. Days one through forty were all on this singular focus. Luke devotes the subsequent twenty-eight chapters to chronicle the sermons and actions of these disciples as they skillfully walked and talked as their Master had instructed. These Kingdom-centric deeds were the acts of the apostles.

The book closes in its final chapter with the last known activities of one of history's most influential leaders, Saul of Tarsus. How did this terrorist turned apostle fill his last days on earth? Precisely as his Master had done, he gave firsthand testimony of the transformational power of the Kingdom of God.

> From morning till evening he expounded to them, testifying to the kingdom of God and trying to convince them about Jesus both from the Law of Moses and from the Prophets. . . . He lived there two whole years at his own expense, and welcomed all who came to him, proclaiming the kingdom of God and teaching about the Lord Jesus Christ with all boldness and without hindrance. (Acts 28:23, 30–31)

Though the apostle Paul devoted his life, after his conversion, to the planting and encouraging of new churches, he understood that the starting and nourishing of churches could never be the goal; it was simply the means to the goal.

If the church were the goal, then sustaining that church would logically be the priority of the highest order. But if the Kingdom of God was the goal, then the Kingdom-building instrument would gladly self-sacrifice for the eternal prize. Saul's conversion on the road to Damascus included a radical death to his former fallen compulsion to "save himself." The DNA of this Kingdom conversion rippled through every spiritual priority in the churches he led in establishing.

Though Paul would never make it to Rome in the way he had longed, his conclusion to his epistle to the Roman churches (see Rom. 16:1–23) gives us insight into the tremendous Kingdom impact this imprisoned church planter had on the new Roman church. Scores of Kingdom leaders had ascended from the numerous points of light he had helped inaugurate. These leaders formed the gospel leadership to serve earth's most significant city. Soon the selfless, countercultural Kingdom influence these leaders had on Rome (as recorded by contemporaneous historians such as Josephus) would be the impetus for the great Jesus movement that would sweep throughout the Roman Empire.

The history of the world was eternally changed by an uncredentialed (see Acts 4:13; 17:6) band of church planters who were far less infatuated by the church they would plant than they were by the Kingdom fruit their new churches would produce. Function trumped form as these new churches poured into the deepest fissures of collective brokenness with a mandate and spiritual obligation of self-abandonment. The gospel message lived by its messengers produced the multidimensional harvest of the gospel—the restoration of personhood, family, society, and land. The good news didn't need to be cleverly argued as if this were merely a battle of words and ideas. The Kingdom of God was fully, convincingly, and unmistakably on display for all to see.

Propping up our kingdoms that are erected in our own image demands much more of our time and devotion.

So, what does the Kingdom of God look like? What does it prefer, and what does it reject? Jesus gave us two pictures of His Kingdom when He asked and answered His rhetorical questions recorded in Luke 13.

He said therefore, "What is the kingdom of God like? And to what shall I compare it? It is like a grain of mustard seed that a man took and sowed in his garden, and it grew and became a tree, and the birds of the air made nests in its branches." And again he said, "To what shall I compare the kingdom of God? It is like leaven that a woman took and hid in three measures of flour, until it was all leavened." (Luke 13:18–21)

Jesus the incarnate Christ, stepping out of eternity into time, had, like no one before Him, the perfect perspective on the passions of His Father. From His eternal station with the Father, He entered earth as the singularly qualified voice to speak on the realities of the universe. As the cause of creation, Jesus alone had the ability to teach humanity how a whole person thinks and lives. And consistent with the humility of our King, He takes an inexhaustible subject and simplifies it into two relatable down-to-earth metaphors: a mustard seed and yeast. From Jesus' explanation of the Kingdom, we can internalize several principles that should inspire and revolutionize our approach to church planting.

In the Kingdom of God, Small Is Formidable

To introduce His Kingdom to His disciples and the world, Jesus chose the most improbable object to illustrate great power. A single seed of black mustard was known by His much more agrarian audience as a seed that resembled a speck of dust. It was likely the smallest article with which these first-century disciples were familiar. Obviously, Jesus had a point to make. This seemingly insignificant particle of life, when planted, could lay dormant in the soil for a number of years waiting for the right conditions to be achieved. When the exact combination of temperature and moisture intersect, a miracle of life occurs swelling this speck of dust into one of the Middle East's greatest plants—a virtual tree towering over the other plants of the garden at a stature of nine feet.

Jesus' Kingdom point should not be missed by those of us intoxicated by the desire to boldly follow Christ while at the same time paralyzed by a long list of personal inadequacies. It speaks to a familiar theme throughout both Testaments with few exceptions. God chooses the people the world dismisses as unnecessary. "Small" is the consistent value of the Kingdom of God. God chooses the weakest, the youngest, the lowest, and the least in terms of pedigree, nationality, giftedness, education, or past reputation. First Corinthians 1:18–31 is a summation of this Kingdom principle being observed by Paul and offered up as a teachable moment for the fleshly Corinthian church inebriated with a culture of celebrity and reputation.

Our smallness is actually the place where God demonstrates His grandeur and infinite might. The impossible task that awaits any church planter is not a task well suited for human strength. Human strength can build a fine religious organization but can never substitute for what can happen through a lowly mustard seed fully submitted to an omnipotent King.

Shaping a transformational movement requires a humility of spirit that understands and embraces the impossibilities of faith.

In the Kingdom of God, an Uninvested Faith Is Desertion

Jesus continued His revelation of the Kingdom and the mustard seed by adding, "That a man took and sowed in his garden" (Luke 13:19). The central figure and activity in Jesus' lesson was a farmer farming. Jesus did not identify the potential of the mustard seed apart from the effort of the laborer. The mustard seed carefully kept safe and dry on the appropriate seed shelf had zero probability of becoming the garden's greatest plant. Implicit in the farmer's assignment of farming was the responsibility of removing the seed from its safe storage and losing it in the dark, damp furrows of soil. Only in this process of risk and loss can the seed's potential ever be realized. The pseudo-security of the seed shelf can only make deceptive promises of sanctuary and safekeeping. For the farmer the call for safety is actually an appeal for certain disappointment. The farmer's faith step of losing his seed is the only possible way he can ever experience his dream of a harvest.

This principle of the stewardship of faith has great ramifications for a church planter. The Kingdom assignment we are called to is always an assignment of faith. Seldom are the resources available in advance for what God places on our hearts. Seldom is the whole road seen, understood, and prepared for in advance. Our assignment is to invest what God puts in our hands and continue to walk in the direction of His voice. Those who refuse to follow because of the uncertainty of the road miss out on the highest adventures and the greatest movements. In Jesus' parable of the talents (see Matt. 25:14–30), we see a stronger warning against an uninvested faith; we are counted among the deserters. As with the farmer, so with the Kingdom citizen, playing it safe is the most dangerous game of all.

So the task of the church planter is to learn to recognize his King's voice and to quickly obey. We don't "wrestle with Him." We don't "struggle with Him." We do the only thing a subject is able to do in responding to his sovereignty: "We obey him." Smooth-sounding, evangelical easy-speak cannot adequately disguise a fearful heart, nor can it replace the joy found in a well-planted faith.

In the Kingdom of God, Grace Extends beyond the Graced

Jesus finished His image of the Kingdom through the mustard seed with an unexpected picture, "And it grew and became a tree, and the birds of the air made nests in its branches" (Luke 13:19). We were tracking with the illustration so far; the Kingdom of God does not require big, but it does require faith. But now Jesus adds an addendum to the story about branches and nesting birds. Do you suppose this is significant?

As we unpack the illustration, we quickly grasp that the primary recipient of Kingdom grace was the farmer. He exercised a modicum of faith by giving up his seed to the soil. The result of his faith was a grace gift that was totally out of proportion to his actions and for which he had no personal power to produce. From his investment of the most insignificant of seeds came the most impressive plant within his garden. The picture of grace. If the illustration ended here, we would have already had a revolutionary understanding of the Kingdom of God. But Jesus wasn't finished.

The primary recipient of grace was the farmer, but the secondary recipients of grace were homeless wild birds. The grace made available to the farmer increased his harvest, but that same grace afforded shelter, safety, and a home for the often-exposed birds. The farmer's invested faith produced a grace harvest well out of proportion to his actions, and the blessing of that grace harvest overflowed to God's creation that was outside of the process. What was Jesus teaching us about His Kingdom?

To be beneficiaries of God's grace automatically makes us distributors of that same grace. Sometimes this happens unintentionally as a by-product of God's goodness; at other times it happens through carefully executed Kingdom priorities. The blessings of God in the lives of His grateful children extend beyond His children to those outside the family of faith.

The husband who faithfully and sacrificially loves his wife over a lifetime not only receives the personal blessing of a joyous marriage, but further, the Kingdom ripples of that union emanate through generations. For example, a broken marriage is not useful for the benefit of neighbors. However, when a marriage is free of strife, it is free to bless, encourage, and inspire the lives that surround them. Children, grandchildren, colleagues, friends, and neighbors are all secondary recipients of the grace experienced in a godly marriage.

As time passes, that same couple receives promotions at their places of work because they are recognized as workmen of integrity. While many of their colleagues enter into larger mortgages for more impressive homes, this couple doubles-down their payments on their current residence. Much sooner than they could have imagined, they find themselves debt free. The grace they experience as a couple is a life free from the tyranny of obligation. This couple continues to live a lifestyle much the same as they always had, but now they have disposable income to invest in others' lives and ministries. The secondary recipients of God's grace are legion and are being multiplied around the world.

In Christ's Kingdom grace extends well beyond the graced.

In the Kingdom of God, Status Is Irrelevant

As Jesus wraps up His imagery of the mustard seed, we can imagine that these early disciples were busy trying to index all they had heard. Before they could finish processing these unfathomable truths, Jesus hits them with another picture: "It is like leaven that a woman took" (Luke 13:21).

The audience of Jesus' day was familiar with status. The religious subculture had a hierarchy that was understood and observed by all. Stooping over on almost the bottom rung of that sacred status ladder was the pitiable station of women. On a good day women were prized somewhere between fine possessions and helpful slaves. Their rights were few and their responsibilities were many. It was not a glamorous life. This cultural blind spot was one Jesus confronted.

The fact that Jesus chose someone at the lower end of the societal hierarchy as the model for his illustration of the Kingdom should not go unnoticed. It follows in a long list of examples of Christ breaking down societal barriers in His countercultural Kingdom revolution. For the One who stepped out of the glories of heaven into the miseries of earth, our provincial pecking order must have seemed like a trivial thing indeed. Earthly status and Kingdom impact seemed to have little correlation in the mind of the lowly Galilean carpenter's son.

We know God does not show partiality (see Acts 10:34). We see abundant evidence in the Scriptures of God selecting the outsider over the one deemed with status to accomplish the amazing. We can see through history how God has set movements aflame through the most unlikely of disciples. The ongoing task of today's Kingdom expanders is to continually remove the status filters in which our world operates and instead look at people through the eyes of the Holy Spirit. The Kingdom potential that unfolds before us can be staggering.

So we ask some difficult questions: Does the Kingdom advance faster behind the pulpit or the barber's chair? Is the Kingdom impacted greater through the missionary or the musician? Are grander Kingdom lessons learned from the seminary professor or the coffee barista? If our reflexive answer comes too easily, we may miss out on the full force of Jesus' intention. In the Kingdom of God, status is irrelevant.

In the Kingdom of God, Influence Is Viral

In Jesus' two brief word pictures, we have noted several significant principles of the countercultural Kingdom of Christ. Small is formidable. An uninvested faith is desertion. Grace extends well beyond the graced. And societal status is irrelevant. What would happen through a leader and a spiritual community who lived these four principles well? The last words tell the story, "It is like leaven that a woman took and hid in three measures of flour, until it was all leavened" (Luke 13:21).

To a modern reader, the idea of "yeast" inspires an image of a can or a package filled with little dry beige kernels of some mysterious substance. To Jesus' audience yeast looked altogether different. It wasn't a separated substance carefully stored for use at a later time. It was dough that contained activated yeast. It was infected dough, and it would infect everything it touches. The task of the baker was to mix the infected dough with flour and other ingredients and then watch the virus do its magic.

Yeast is a funny thing: it appears to be invisible and innocuous; yet it radically transforms everything it comes in contact with. Dough sitting flat and lifeless in a baker's pan suddenly animates and springs to life growing by the minute with the introduction of the smallest amount of leavened dough. The two doughs may look the same, but they are not—one has a secret power.

What better picture could be painted about the Kingdom of God? Ordinary men and women, boys and girls, once lifeless and purposeless, now spirited and full of purpose. The recipients of this grace become the distributors of grace, and in this exchange the rule of God grows organically relationship by relationship. The transformational power of this Kingdom lived is unstoppable as it courses through networks and neighborhoods. Nothing can stay the same. Impossible cases become the everyday commonplace. Things that have been long broken and discarded are repaired and found useful once again.

God's Kingdom has come because God's will is being done in our neighborhood as it is in heaven.

Coaching Questions

1. What is your dream for the Kingdom?

2. What is your biggest concern about personal competency?

3. What is God saying to you now?

Chapter 2

The Kingdom
Is Beautiful

Perhaps one of the most intuitively problematic assignments pastors routinely ask their flock to do is to convince an emotionally healthy lost person that he needs to go to church. It is inherently difficult because we instinctively know that almost everything that happens on a Sunday morning would be of little interest to our unchurched friend.

For church planters this presents a problem of the highest order. If the assignment is both to start a church and not just to relocate church members from one church to another, how do we go about our task? If the lost in my community are as disinterested in church as you or I may be about taking membership in the Loyal Order of Moose Lodge, how in the world do we hook them?

The first tactic many planters employ is to design a hipper church. Brand your own custom variation of the formula—super casual dress, cool tech in every direction, and a laid-back dude talking with his bros while clutching the newest phablet. Get the buzz out that the band is rocking and the preacher is chill. Watch the lost rush in.

Except the lost don't seem to come. You end up gathering a crowd, but the pack seems eerily familiar to the deficient assembly you attended before you started the superchurch. Everyone loaded with smartphones and Bible apps and an insatiable appetite to devour all the goods and services you could ever sacrificially provide. The contract seems to be a one-way relationship. You provide; they consume. It's devastatingly simple.

And where are the lost? From the landslide of feedback you received after the band played an eight-year-old worship song, this gang has been feeding a long time from the provisions of numerous churches in your community that now hobble along, left with little more than melancholy memories. The gossip is that the last iteration of you got a bit lame, so the ravenous pack, as one, meandered off en masse. Apparently the worship pastor was way too sweaty. Superchurch 9.1 was next in line for feeding privileges. (The .1 came from old historic Trinity Baptist who, in a bold attempt to revision, changed its name to "Portico." It sounded so magnificently tantalizing, but in the end it was another colossal disappointment. They kept the handbells.)

So now you're up.

But where are the lost? Perhaps they were no more looking for a hipper church than you would ever look for a hipper Moose Lodge.

Dressing up the Sunday moose might make club members feel better, but it does little to inspire someone with no church memory to start up a new churchgoing habit. The more lipstick you put on the moose, the more desperate you look. The whole process can feel like you have sold your soul for trinkets and beads when you stop to recall your original intention for ministry. Your life was called out for the gospel. You were to be a fisher of men.

If cosmetically enhanced worship services aren't what the spiritually uninitiated are yearning for, what exactly is the object of their quest? What should we do? Who should we be?

By asking questions like these, we begin to scratch in the right spot. Answering these questions will give you the power to speak with integrity to the longing lives of the spiritually hungry that are living all around you. It is well worth the time.

Common Ground

In *Kingdom Matrix,* I devoted much attention to understanding the contrast between sacred darkness and secular light. Much of what the modern evangelical church does to occupy itself in the sacred space might be designated as "darkness" to many who are generationally unchurched. Priorities and practices that we routinely embrace (and never think too deeply about) can become major stumbling blocks for many outside of the church. Values we espouse and propagate as "biblical" seem to arouse an innate sense of anger among those who habitually walk past our sacred doors. Our self-justifying axiom that "darkness flees from light" doesn't really seem to answer the specifics of their spiritual objections. Reconciling the historic Jesus to what modern evangelical churches produce can be a problematic assignment for many.

As disquieting as these claims might be to our sacred sensibilities, we would do well to adopt a learning posture for the sake of the harvest. There are some significant questions to be asked and answered.

Have you every wondered why those whom we slate in the category of secular seem to have a more vigorous Kingdom pulse than many who have lived their entire lives seated comfortably on their sacred pew? Has it ever bothered you that while much of the church is amusing itself into extinction, one conference at a time, secular community groups are providing the muscle for Kingdom opportunities long neglected by the church?

Most troubling of all: why is it not unsettling to Christian leaders that the pursuits that occupy much of our time, energy, and nearly all of our resources are seen as immature and self-serving to Kingdom seekers?

What is a Kingdom seeker? There is a spiritual impulse in God's highest creation that longs for its Creator. This longing creature has been fashioned by the Creator and in the Creator's image for things that are wholly eternal. Ecclesiastes 3:11 describes this spiritual phenomenon: "He has also set eternity in the hearts of men; yet they cannot fathom what God has done from beginning to end" (NIV).

We yearn for our Maker, but our broken, sinful state precludes any ability to be in relationship with the Holy and Eternal One. This exclusion, however, does not wipe away the eternal stamp of God's creation. His thumbprint is on us. We are His image bearers.

We understand that mankind has always been created for eternity. We have responded to God before we have any heavenly status made possible through justification. But even in a fallen state, it is apparent to a casual observer that some respond to the eternal things of the Kingdom before they ever bow their knee to its kingly source. They are almost like homing pigeons responding to impulses of truth wherever they can see it. Prewired by their Heavenly Creator, they instinctively recognize the absence of mercy and justice in human affairs and personally seek to be, in themselves, a remedy.

While much of the evangelical church chooses to value temporal effects that bring more comfort or prestige to its cardholding constituency, Kingdom seekers believe people are of paramount importance and will personally sacrifice for the bona fide needs they discover. They look with suspicion at those who claim to speak for the Almighty but who live lives of perpetual unconcern with what any God of love should value. This persistent contradiction exemplified by the church has fueled much of the wariness of an increasingly secular culture to become involved in something as inconsequential as organized religion. Who can blame them?

PART 1: KINGDOM FIRST

Somehow those in this space have squarely connected to Kingdom causes before they have connected to their King.

Kingdom Sacrifice

We began this chapter with an admission that deep down, somewhere in the depths of our most honest soul, we instinctively know that most generationally unchurched people have little desire to attend our churches. They don't feel guilty for not coming. Their values and what they perceive as ours are well out of sync, and they have other things to do.

But what might happen if they could see that our values reflect the values of Jesus Christ? What if the church you plant began to tap in to the brokenness of your community as a source of both temporal and eternal hope. What if the gospel actually sounded like "good news" to those who might listen in? What if your new community welcomed and included Kingdom seekers as you traveled this new path humbly and honestly together. Would the unchurched be interested? Would they sacrifice their prejudices and stereotypes to count themselves numbered among the King's people?

What did Jesus say? "The kingdom of heaven is like treasure hidden in a field, which a man found and covered up. Then in his joy he goes and sells all that he has and buys that field" (Matt. 13:44).

The Kingdom of God is beautiful. Those who lead in this life of divine abandonment discover a priceless treasure that fashions deep attraction to the hearts of those not given to more mundane religious pursuits. With absolute joy Kingdom seekers will lay down their sacrosanct stereotypes, prior aspirations, and sacred misgivings to join you in history's most eternally significant countercultural revolution, the Kingdom of God.

It is a bargain at any price.

Coaching Questions

1. What area of brokenness in your community could your church plant address immediately?

2. How could you provide space for Kingdom seekers to join you?

3. What sacrifices are needed by your church plant to live out the values of Jesus?

Chapter 3

The Kingdom-centric Church Plant

If the goal of a new church is to be relevant, edgy, and, as quickly as possible, grow to a place of self-sufficiency, then a thoughtful discussion on "church" is all that is required. But, if the goal of a new church is to appeal to the spiritual cravings of the lost and in that process introduce them to their heart's desire in Jesus Christ, then a soul-searching, gut-wrenching discussion on "Kingdom" becomes absolutely essential.

Have you ever wondered what Jesus meant when He spoke of both light and darkness in the life of a person? And why did He follow up the light-and-darkness theme with a divine declaration that His followers can only serve one of two masters?

> The eye is the lamp of the body. If your eyes are good, your whole body will be full of light. But if your eyes are bad, your whole body will be full of darkness. If then the light within you is darkness, how great is that darkness! No one can serve two masters. Either he will hate the one and love the other, or he will be devoted to the one and despise the other. You cannot serve both God and Money. (Matt. 6:22–24 NIV)

For a church planter, as with every disciple, our actions and decisions are inspired by one of two spiritual sources and advance the spiritual realm of their origin. The masters to whom we pay allegiance clearly indicate the Kingdom we advance at any given moment. In the battle of good and evil, there clearly is no demilitarized zone. We are for Him or we are against Him. We are never undecided.

Undoubtedly, Jesus wanted these first church planters, and the ones who would follow throughout the generations, to grasp the significance of the kingdoms we occupy. To Jesus everything is light and darkness. Just because I claim to be a sacred spokesman for God does not mean I automatically advance the Kingdom of God. Just because the trendy church I am starting claims to be a community of Christ does not mean it is advancing the cause of Christ. Both the ancient pages of church history and the "religion section" of last week's newspapers are awash with examples of the church acting entirely un-Christlike. Apparently religious expression and "darkness" are not necessarily mutually exclusive concepts. Our sacred has no birthright to the Kingdom of God.

Evidently the Kingdom of God doesn't advance through religious assemblies, even a brand-new one, but advances only through the countercultural faith steps of allegiance from a grateful people to their Sovereign King. Sacred categories and institutions are no exception to the rule. The masters to whom the church pays allegiance clearly indicate the Kingdom it advances at any given moment.

And so every decision I make as a church planter, and every decision I lead a new church to corporately make, is actually a spiritual decision. Spiritual forces inspire us to pursue one of two diametrically opposed paths. These are not equal spiritual forces, but they are exclusive in their demands and in the directions they are moving.

Darkness persuades us to save ourselves by serving ourselves, even if only for a season. Light calls us to immediate faith. It reminds us of the essence of our relationship with God and inspires us to continue walking in the manner in which we began this relationship. Consolidation, even for a season, is a term without faith and, therefore, a season of dark spiritual disconnection.

Kingdom Expanders

The Kingdom-centric new church holds as its highest value the redemptive mission of God. It understands the difference between tools (worship services, buildings, staff) and purpose (becoming a rescuing and restoring community). It holds its sacred forms loosely and grips its eternal purpose tightly. It understands that every church, including the one that is just about to launch, has a determined life span. All churches have a start date and an expiration date. No local church is eternal. It also understands that actions it takes in participation with Kingdom expansion have eternal effect. A cup of cold water freely given in Jesus' name has a rippling effect throughout eternity.

So what does a Kingdom-focused church plant look like? There is so much to say to adequately describe this picture. The following chart[3] from my earlier book encapsulates the stark contrast between a church on a Kingdom mission and a church hell-bent on a mission to grow itself.

KINGDOM PRINCIPLES	KINGDOM SOURCE	
	DOMINION OF DARKNESS	KINGDOM OF GOD
CHURCH	**BRAND EXPANDERS**	**KINGDOM EXPANDERS**
Resources	Religious Consumerism	Sacrificial 'giving away'
Energy	Competiton	His Presence
Community	Group Isolation	Interdependence
Change	Conforming	Incarnation
Authority	Corporate Identity	THE KING
Obedience	Orthodoxy / No Orthopraxy	Orthodoxy / Orthopraxy
SECULAR	**SELF-SEEKERS**	**KINGDOM SEEKERS**
Resources	Materialism	Spiritual Reciprocity
Energy	Ego	Good Will
Community	Isolation	Support
Change	Manipulation	Transformation
Authority	Me	God as I understand Him
Obedience	No Orthodoxy / No Orthopraxy	No Orthodoxy / Orthopraxy

KINGDOM MATRIX   Kingdom Principles Reaching a Secular World

For the church planter Kingdom expansion should be the exclusive motivation for planting a new church. As the leader begins to ponder through all of the spiritual and practical implications involved in "Kingdom First," he begins to naturally drift away from the church being primarily an "event" to the church's being primarily an "influence." He begins to think from the perspective of the spiritually uninitiated and sympathizes with the reasons of their disenchantment with "organized religion."

He also begins to take note of the Kingdom impulse that he sees among many of his unchurched friends and neighbors. These observations start to shape the priorities that he envisions for the future church. The idea of "making disciples" no longer starts with church members and guided Bible studies but with neighbors and women's shelters and transparent conversations. His idea of church has exploded outside of its traditional form.

The mustard seed is lost in the soil, and the yeast is set loose in the dough. The King is fully in charge.

Coaching Questions

1. What are ways your new church can "appeal to the spiritual cravings of the lost"?

2. What needs to change for the four marks of a Kingdom-centric church to be your primary focus?

3. Which of the four marks will be your biggest challenge?

Chapter 4

Redefining Success

Church planters are a curiously goal-driven people. Give us a numerical goal worth pursuing, and we will focus the entirety of our energy toward it, considering no sacrifice too great. We will not give up. Goals give us a buzz. We know psychological help is available for us, but for now we will skip the therapy and enjoy being just a speck off balanced. It's what makes us, us. We're okay with that.

We goal lovers tend to have something in common: we love the refrain, "Those who fear numbers usually have none to report." What a beautiful mantra. It totally emasculates the namby-pamby voices that ask us to consider some deeper attributes. Wimps.

If that's not enough, we go on and become doggedly and profoundly theological: "You don't think God loves numbers? He loves them so much that He named the fourth book of the Bible after them!" Wham! What can you say to that stellar line of theological reasoning?

Yet sometimes an inflexible few still look at us goal-oriented people with a slight air of skepticism. Inconceivable. For those who still are not yet abundantly convinced, we bring out the big artilleries. To do this we must lower our voices, cast our glance downward, and declare in the most spiritually sounding tone we can muster, "But sister, every number represents a blessed soul God loves."

High five. Case closed. We have yet again validated, beyond a reasonable doubt, our neurosis with numbers.

Most church planters wouldn't want to confess this, but sometimes we can be a pretty insecure bunch. You gather a group of us in a conference room, start the timer app on your smartphone, and begin counting the seconds until the first conversation goes the way of, "So, how many are you running these days?" This of course has nothing to do with a cross-country jogging ministry designed for some physical benefit. No, this question is designed exclusively to serve our insecure egos. Somewhere in our thinking exists a belief that the quantity we have gathered in our rented sacred space is in direct correlation to the impact we are having on the Kingdom of God. How then do numbers and impact correlate? Remember Jesus' teaching on the mustard seed and the yeast? Numbers and influence correlate only to the extent of our participation in God's Kingdom agenda. Members of a band small in number and singular in Kingdom devotion have always been the ones who have changed the world. Size matters only in as much as it relates to the obedience of our faith.

So really, when we ask the question, "How many are you running?" in most cases we are simultaneously asking, "How many are you sitting?" Sitting in a sacred semicircle and extending the Kingdom of God can be two different activities. In fact, often they are polar opposites. If "running" involves listening to truth but not transforming our priorities, then we have missed out on the thrust of the Kingdom of God. "Do not merely listen to the word, and so deceive yourselves. Do what it says" (James 1:22 NIV).

What if a church planter owned, as his supreme goal, the advancement of the Kingdom of God, instead of the number of precious lives he has gathered and organized into a perfect geometric pattern at the high school gymnasium? How would his metrics for self-evaluation be transformed?

What are we really asking with the numbers question? The "how many are we sitting?" question might actually more accurately be asked as, "How many are we sidelining?" How many have been benched? How many have we kept off the Kingdom playing field in order to fill our stands and stroke our collective egos? If the sacred gathering is the exclusive and premier metric we track, we might want to rethink our motivation for planting a church. The radical idea of the body of Christ was eternally designed for far more than sitting and serving its sacred self. Her mission is far from passive.

How many members of the body of Christ need to be put on the disabled list in order for us to feel like we are being successful in our clerical pursuits? How many have we effectively convinced that their spectator-like attendance and their tithe are all God is ever going to hold them accountable for on the day of judgment?

And so we keep score; nickels and noses are the tokens that count. And so that is all that we count. All the while praying for better year-over-year returns. Our investors are restless.

But has a pesky question like this one ever nagged at your spirit, "Who can rent a high school gymnasium big enough to contain all God desires to do?" If it has, perhaps there is room for an alternative reality that leads toward a truly Kingdom-centric design.

Four Marks of a Kingdom-centric Church Plant

Rewiring our long-established hardwiring can be an exasperating procedure. All of our spiritual muscle memory has been dedicated to the objective of growing the sacred gathering; it is difficult to shake that off. Rethinking and recalibrating against this instinctive pattern can be a challenging assignment for those gutsy enough to attempt it. But for those who will, they discover that the sacred assembly becomes a natural by-product of four other Kingdom activities. But this new assembly may look and feel altogether different than they imagined. An ecclesiological upgrade that more resembles the first century than the twenty-first.

Doctors intuitively get this idea. They rarely look at a patient's stature and predict his level of health. To a physician, *tall* doesn't mean healthy, nor does *short* mean unhealthy. Instead, they have a handful of significant metrics they measure, which are commonly called "vital signs." Vital signs are significant to a physician in quickly ascertaining the general health and well-being of a patient. These are not a comprehensive picture of a person's health, but, if something is awry in any one of them, major health complications usually follow. In the same way the following four marks of a Kingdom-centric church plant do not describe every nuance of health, but the gaps can tell a troubling story of the road ahead.[4]

1. New Believers

If a new church plant moves into a neighborhood and manages to successfully grow at a rapid pace but baptisms are limited to children (from already believing families growing in their own commitment to Christ) and the previously evangelized transferring in (and submitting to a new mode of baptism), would this be considered a healthy plant? Certainly any measurements of health should include an evaluation to see if the lost are being found and added to the family of faith.

Consequently, the highest value measured is that of the gospel in the lives of those formerly far from Christ. The first and primary phase of any new church plant must be a concentrated and intense focus on effective evangelism. For most planters this will require careful spiritual reconnaissance of an area to determine patterns of resistance. Does this neighborhood or people group have emotional, intellectual, or volitional barriers to the message of Jesus? Accurately understanding the soil you are investing in will return great rewards when it is harvest time. We will take a much closer look at this later when we examine context.

The ability to successfully advance the subsequent three vital signs hinges directly on a church plant's effectiveness in engaging the lost. With new believers regularly discovering faith in Christ, a new church has the culture and raw materials necessary for tremendous Kingdom impact.

2. New Disciple Makers

The word *discipleship* has lost much of its punch over the past half century. For many, discipleship refers to a deeper-life process brought about through study courses and Bible studies. Jesus' call for the church to "go and make disciples" is too often artificially fulfilled with a godly leader and a small group of eager Bible students in a location that is well insulated from the lost sheep.

If disciple making (that is, helping the evangelized develop into being fishers of men themselves) is not a part of a new church's strategic processes, is that church plant obedient to the commission of Christ? A Kingdom-centric church plant will help shape this expectation in the disciple early on in the discipleship process. Evangelism is an unfinished task until those evangelized find themselves evangelizing.

A church plant that will have substantial Kingdom impact will regularly measure its effectiveness in engaging the breadth of its membership in the assignment of being fishers of men. To the church's leadership this metric is considered extremely valuable and is publicly celebrated with frequency. Pastors and worship services become support structures for a membership that understands its Kingdom assignment in disciple making.

3. New Communities of Faith

Any understanding of a church plant's health, that does not account for the normative reproduction of its Kingdom assignment in other geographies and cultural expressions, should be dismissed as a relic of a more self-serving era. A church plant with no plans or strategy in place to "give itself away" to populations and geographies with little or no access to an effective gospel-proclaiming church cannot consider itself whole.

There is likely a pretty intelligent reason why McDonalds does not construct a Super McDonald's restaurant in the epicenter of every city and insist that hamburger aficionados commute to its home turf where they can enjoy all the amusing embellishments that can be offered with a restaurant of dominant size. Instead they scattered a myriad of restaurants across every city, expressing themselves in different shapes and sizes and with different themes and appeal. Why? Because McDonald's number-one value is food sales, not customer assemblage. Franchises do not publicly appear to compete with one another for the longest lines or fullest dining rooms. They organize and cooperate together to effectively accomplish their primary value. They sell hamburgers.

What should be a new church's primary value? What on earth should it count as more precious than everything else? Should it not be the lost son or daughter being eternally united with his or her heavenly Father? If this is our highest value, then it follows that a church plant would behave somewhat McDonalds-like in its planning. It would become a facilitator for multiple movements of these "eternal reunions" to take place within diverse neighborhoods and people groups. The church plant operating in this way correctly sees itself as a tool for the assignment, not the reason of the assignment.

Developing metrics (or a road map) for a new church plant to sacrificially multiply (or partner with others in planting) new congregations as a normal part of its lifestyle is a vital sign of Kingdom health. Time and experience in that community will undoubtedly reveal "gospel gaps," whether they are affinity based, linguistic, or cultural. These gaps become troubling to your spirit, motivating you and your team to prayerfully seek solutions to this eternal problem.

By instilling (or not instilling) this value in the preassembly DNA of the church plant will determine the relative probability of a new church becoming a multiplying church. If it is calendared as a value to be adopted after achieving self-sustainability, it will never be a value at all. When it comes to determining future trajectory, actions always speak louder than words.

4. Transforming Communities

Finally, is it possible to consider a church plant to be healthy that has little or no transformative presence in the community in which it exists? Certainly Christ's notion of His unstoppable community would more closely resemble His own personal ministry than our best ideas on a well-polished worship experience.

Once again time and experience advise a Kingdom-centric church plant how to release its membership as selfless agents of transformation wherever they exist. The testimony of this health indicator can be observed as salt and light penetrating hidden places that a sacred service could never find. Metrics to qualify gained ground in this area become less objective and more anecdotal. The church in which I am a leader has a goal of three thousand "Kingdom imprints" over the next five years. We define *Kingdom imprint* as "a documented occasion when a believer meets a physical need in the community and attaches the credit to the grace of Jesus Christ." Good works and good news on display in the context of Christian community become a potent testimony of our faith. Again we will devote an entire section to this Kingdom mark when we look together at "making a difference."

Four distinct Kingdom characteristics, all reproducing by nature and all expressing our King's desires for His creation. The church of Jesus Christ, united together and dreaming the desires of King Jesus, is an amazing thought to behold. The transformative power of that dream will be documented in a history not yet written, but nonetheless real.

Planting a new church for the Kingdom of God will always be reminiscent of a heroic rescue mission for one loved and lost lamb.

It is so much more dangerous than it sounds. And it is so much better.

Coaching Questions

1. What insecurities will be your biggest personal obstacle in church planting?

2. How can you address those insecurities?

3. What are your metrics for self-evaluation as a church planter?

Part 2: **Character**

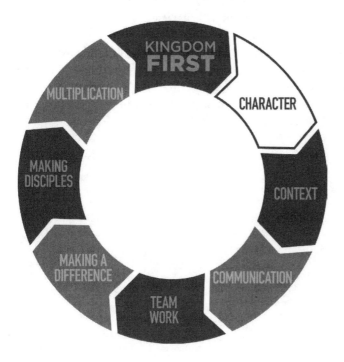

When it comes to leading a church, especially a new church, character trumps everything. A long-standing church can often survive the calamity of a disgraced leader, but a new church rarely can. There is much on the shoulders of a church planter.

A careful observation through the history of almost any city demonstrates that the single greatest source of a church plant's catastrophic implosion (and the further emanations of spiritual darkness over the landscape) comes not from imperfect theology but from deficient character. To be sure, there is a connection between the two, but aspiring to right ideals is not enough. Our character must be transformed by good theology.

Our most lofty public preaching does not have sufficient long-term lift to overcome the enormous gravitational pull found in our personal brokenness. Our sin, however carefully concealed, will more accurately describe the dark nature of our real theology over our well-rehearsed creeds and confessions. And worse, the swath of casualties hemorrhaging from our leaking character broadens as our leadership's influence grows.

When it comes to leading a church, character trumps everything.

It should be instructive to realize that in the New Testament *belief* is not a noun but a verb. We can never own a belief; we can only live a belief. Our best theology is never truly believed until it is first integrated into our daily lifestyle.

So however we slice it, our character reveals the true nature of our theology.

Chapter 5

The Character of Christ

Implicit in Jesus' call to discipleship was a call to personally take on the radical character of Christ. When Jesus ushered a fresh charge to His predisciples with these celebrated words, "Follow me, and I will make you become fishers of men" (Mark 1:17), He was with one breath describing both His Kingdom assignment and the only process that makes that assignment possible. "Follow me" always precedes "fishers of men." Taking on the responsibility of leading the charge for disciple making without first allowing the character of Christ to transform our personal brokenness can only lead to an unhappy ending. Conversely, the character necessary for multiplying true disciples of Jesus grows directly in proportion to our personal followship of Jesus.

This pattern of "following me" and newly derived "character" is clearly revealed when Jesus declared: "I am the light of the world. Whoever follows me will not walk in darkness, but will have the light of life" (John 8:12). This "light of life" is the authentication of our character as we follow and therefore resemble our King. The process of following Jesus is the only spiritual discipline that can transform the darkness of our broken character into the image of Christ Himself.

What Does the Character of Christ Actually Look Like?

Reflecting on Jesus' Sermon on the Mount, one sees a three-dimensional picture of Kingdom character that warrants a lifetime of study and personal application. John observed firsthand that Kingdom character and the glory of God were displayed in Jesus through the perfect blending of two spiritual realities, "grace" and "truth." "And the Word became flesh and dwelt among us, and we have seen his glory, glory as of the only Son from the Father, full of grace and truth" (John 1:14).

Grace and truth are eternally and inextricably fused together. In Jesus grace and truth were not a balanced duo or one moderated by the other but both dished out lavishly and unreservedly toward an undeserving humanity. It was as extraordinary of a sight in the first century as it is in the twenty-first. The character of our eternal Father fleshed out before us in the person of Jesus Christ. All grace. All truth.

It stands to reason that the process of following Jesus should build a life branded by the character of Christ. So, why is our character often so different?

Enter Sin

Sin, by definition, is missing God's intended mark.[5] What is His mark? Grace and truth.[6] Our deviation from God's mark causes us to embrace one and reject the other. Our damaged character finds appeal in one of two insidious and character-distorting forms of sin:

1. The Sin of Sensuality (License)

Sensuality is seeing ourselves small and therefore living in a way that is less than God created us to be. This is deviant grace without truth. A life of sensuality leads to a character damaged and enslaved by obsessive addictions of every shape. In Jesus' parable of the Lost Son (see Luke 15:11–31), this is the younger brother.

2. The Sin of Pride (Legalism)

Pride is seeing ourselves large and therefore living in a way that is greater than God created us to be. This is smug truth without grace. A life character-ized by pride leads to a character deformed by an arrogant self-righteousness and pseudo-spiritual superiority. In Jesus' parable of the Lost Son, this is the older and equally lost brother.

Oversteer

Growing up and learning to navigate the icy winter roads of Canada, one of the first things my father taught me was the danger of oversteering.

Oversteering is the tendency to overcompensate when starting to lose traction and beginning to spin. It seems at first like a natural response but soon leaves the inexperienced driver completely out of control. Instead of correcting a slight skid, he finds himself spinning much faster in the opposite direction. The proper correction is a minor change back toward the center of the road.

We can readily see spiritual oversteer at the heart of our discussion of the Kingdom character of grace and truth. It may come from an attachment to a historical movement ("This is truth"), following a personality ("This is who I want to be"), spiritual lethargy ("This is who I am"), from the need to overdefine mystery ("This is who God is"), or from the desire to make personal applications universal ("This is how you should be"). Attempting to correct without the character of Christ as our guide usually leaves us in worse shape than when we started.

What Are the Symptoms of Spiritual Oversteer?

When we singularly accentuate and consequently reduce one of the hallmarks of God's glory (grace and truth), we find certain symptoms that indicate we are now on a road to damaged character. Often our attachment to ideologies leads us to embrace extreme and rigid positions. This fanaticism drives us to a heretical understanding of truth devoid of the grace of Christ. Conversely our escape into a twisted understanding of grace sends us down a destructive path of self-fulfillment through sensual gratification. The end is always the same: selfish grace without truth leads to bankrupt character.

Oversteer can be seen in our contemporary theological trends. What undoubtedly started out by a godly propulsion to bring balance to a heretical overemphasis soon becomes dramatic oversteer by the ensuing followers who jump wholeheartedly on the speeding bandwagon. Back and forth we have swerved past the character of Christ in our attempts to self-correct. From liberalism (grace in isolation), to fundamentalism (truth in isolation), to the emerging church (grace in isolation), to the new orthodoxy (truth in isolation). From ditch to ditch we travel on our ineffective mission to be the church of Jesus Christ, all the while wondering why we rarely see the glory of God.

How Can I Lead with the Character of Christ?

It seems intuitive to our logic that when we are out of balance, we moderate and find some kind of healthy equilibrium. However, seeking an artificial balance by reducing a fact will never shape our character into that of our King's. It is impossible to reduce one part of Him in an attempt to become more like Him. We simply create another spiritual Frankenstein and tag it Christlikeness. We are no farther ahead.

The good news is that the gospel is actually great news to our sad theology. In Christ we have two spiritual realities that can assist us when we oversteer, either personally or corporately, that guide us to experience the mystery of grace and truth.

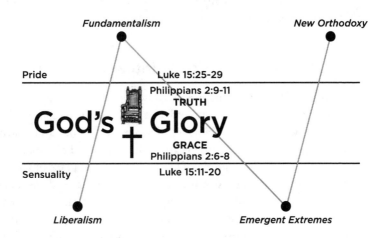

Model of **Oversteer**

The Cross of Christ

If the sin of sensuality is seeing ourselves as smaller and therefore living in a way that is *less* than God created us to be, then what higher expression of grace could there be than the cross of Jesus Christ. With His sacrifice He has once and for all demonstrated the eternal value we have to the Father. Unworthy though we may be, we are not worthless. Whenever we are tempted to revel in grace by excluding truth, we need only to gaze at the cross to remind ourselves of the high price paid for our position of holiness. "For our sake he made him to be sin who knew no sin, so that in him we might become the righteousness of God" (2 Cor. 5:21). The cross is history's best picture of absolute grace.

The Throne of Christ

If the sin of pride is seeing ourselves as larger and therefore living in a way that is *greater* than God created us to be, then what more humbling reflection could there be than the throne of Christ. Spiritual arrogance becomes difficult to maintain when we compare our sullied morality to the holiness of our sovereign King who sits without blemish on an eternal throne. Whenever we are tempted to swagger in our distorted version of truth without grace, remember that only One sits in perfection. "We have all become like one who is unclean, and all our righteous deeds are like a polluted garment. We all fade like a leaf, and our iniquities, like the wind, take us away" (Isa. 64:6).

Spiritual pride cannot strut before the throne of Christ.

And so the riverbanks of spiritual protection that keep us flowing in the character of Christ are His grace and His truth. By daily embracing both, we find ourselves walking closely behind the King.

And the world takes note.

Coaching Questions

1. Where do you struggle with living in a "way less than God created"?

2. Where do you struggle most with spiritual pride?

3. Whom can you talk to about these struggles?

Chapter 6

Leading Myself

The most difficult person you will ever have to lead is yourself. That person is a package of impressive strengths mingled with equally great insecurities, wounds, and inconsistencies, all judiciously wrapped as best as we know how to project the best possible public face. We are fully aware of the concealed brokenness inside the box, and that brokenness, if not restored, will be our undoing.

We have all watched the lives of public figures unravel as their weaknesses are exhibited in real time across every media outlet that has access to a news truck. Sports figures, television personalities, movie stars, politicians, and, the most salacious of all, religious celebrities are caught on countless cameras doing the "perp walk" while futilely attempting to shield their disgraced faces. There is a beguiling yet tragic patheticness to the whole thing.

Do you suppose any of them envisioned this degrading ending in the promising, beginning days of their careers? Not likely. A finale like this would be far from the thoughts of most. Yet week by week another icon's collapse is paraded in high definition into the sanctuary of our living rooms.

But what is more tragic and unquestionably far more detrimental to the Kingdom than the collapse of distant celebrities is the frequency with which trusted spiritual leaders are forced to abandon their Father's call due to a heartbreaking moral failure. The ripples of resentment, disbelief, and skepticism radiate from this broken trust for years and, in many cases, for generations. The gift of a promising ministry ends in a jaded legacy of scorched earth.

Surely no one starts out in ministry with this kind of ending in mind. Yet it materializes with such regularity that the spiritual skeptics seem to have a ready-built case personally supplied by the disgraced Kingdom servants. Money, sex, and power are darkness's simple tools to entice our gaps and fractures of character into disastrous choices with eternal consequences.

So, how can we protect ourselves from this kind of ending? How can we ready ourselves for a Kingdom ministry that flourishes for a lifetime? With all of our leadership responsibilities, how can we most conscientiously lead ourselves?

Over the next three chapters we will look together at foundational character and how it works itself out over our increasing levels of leadership responsibility. If we fail to master this at a foundational level, the inevitable, tragic results become increasingly far-reaching as our ministry broadens.

In this chapter we will discover three key factors that should inspire us to deeply desire to personally take on the character of Christ. These are: (1) My lowest point of character is my highest point of capacity. (2) The way that I do one thing is the way that I do everything. (3) Personal transformation only grows from intimate transparency.

My Lowest Point of Character Is My Highest Point of Capacity

This might strike some as unkind or unfair, but a close look through Scripture or current events leads us to the same inevitable conclusion: my leadership, especially spiritual leadership, cannot grow beyond my weakest point of character.

Picture an antique wooden water bucket made from vertical boards (staves) fashioned together into a cylinder. If those boards were of different lengths, the shortest board would logically dictate the limits of water the bucket could contain. If fifteen boards were twelve inches long, and one board was six inches, the defining limit of that container is determined by the shorter six-inch stave. Our weakest character point always determines our capacity.

Let's use Peter's life to illustrate this truth.

When we think of Peter's most tragic of moments, our minds index quickly to his public and profane denial of his dearest friend and rabbi, instantly punctuated by the crow of a rooster. To conceive that this sentence would ever pass through his own lips would be to Peter unthinkable: "After a little while the bystanders came up and said to Peter, 'Certainly you too are one of them, for your accent betrays you.' Then he began to invoke a curse on himself and to swear, 'I do not know the man.' And immediately the rooster crowed" (Matt. 26:73–74).

This uncharacteristically spineless scene seems to be an aberration to the typically masculine persona of this virile fisherman turned disciple. If it weren't for Jesus' prior prediction of the event, we would be left awestruck, for Peter wasn't one to cower.

Certainly there were no hints to foreshadow this breakdown.

Or were there?

Much earlier Jesus gathered His disciples for another opportunity to explain His Kingdom. But on this occasion the tenor of Jesus' teaching seemed more subdued. He began to explain the necessity of His upcoming crucifixion and resurrection. This was indeed a twist. Listening to colorful parables and watching jousts with Pharisees were much preferred by his closest of friends. "From that time Jesus began to show his disciples that he must go to Jerusalem and suffer many things from the elders and chief priests and scribes, and be killed, and on the third day be raised" (Matt. 16:21).

This really wasn't the news any of Jesus' friends wanted to hear. It really wasn't right. Jesus was a peaceful Teacher. His claims of Messiahship come prevalidated with numerous, unmistakable signs and wonders. He hurt no one and helped so many. The righteous indignation began to boil in Peter's blood until he could hold it in no longer. He must teach the ways of Palestine. Was Jesus going to take this lying down? Surely not. Stand up, Jesus. Fight like a man. "And Peter took him aside and began to rebuke him, saying, 'Far be it from you, Lord! This shall never happen to you'" (Matt. 16:22).

It wasn't that Peter disagreed with his rabbi on the premise that the religious machine would soon be coming after Jesus, looking to silence him once and for all. There were plenty of indications to see this inevitability. What Peter disagreed with was whether or not the pious bullies would triumph. Jesus had the crowds and the momentum. From where Peter stood, this "victim thinking" would and should never happen, not as long as his strong arms could wield a broadsword.

To most this declaration of solidarity would be both bolstering and reassuring. But not to Jesus. In Peter's words Jesus perceived an enormous character flaw. The Teacher had just finished explaining the "why" and the "what" of His Father's plan. It wasn't something from which He was trying to escape. It was something He must do. Peter was blind to the fact that his self-assured protection was neither wanted nor possible. "But he turned and said to Peter, 'Get behind me, Satan! You are a hindrance to me. For you are not setting your mind on the things of God, but on the things of man'" (Matt. 16:23).

With stout words Jesus corrects His friend. Peter was thinking from a fleshly perspective planning to use fleshly power. Jesus well knew this was a character pattern with Peter, one that, if not corrected, would devastate his discipleship.

Fast-forward Peter's story all the way to the upper room.

Jesus had just publicly called out Judas as a budding traitor (his character issues were about to be on display in full bloom), and then the teacher dramatically foretold, yet again, of His death and resurrection. This first Lord's Supper must have been a sobering experience for Peter. "And when they had sung a hymn, they went out to the Mount of Olives" (Matt. 26:30).

Gethsemane—and an excruciating appointment of emotional, physical, and spiritual abandonment—was next on the agenda for Jesus. History's greatest achievement would soon happen quietly and solitarily in a common garden. Ironically the lesson Peter needed most to learn was being lived out in front of his unseeing eyes. The King's strength was not found in His frame or his will, but in His complete surrender.

On His way to Gethsemane, Jesus prophesies about how His comrades would fare through the strain of the upcoming storm. It wasn't good news. "Then Jesus said to them, 'You will all fall away because of me this night. For it is written, "I will strike the shepherd, and the sheep of the flock will be scattered." But after I am raised up, I will go before you to Galilee'" (Matt. 26:31–32).

Peter's pulse began to pick up speed. He wasn't a quitter. He wasn't a fair-weather friend. Maybe Judas and some of the others but certainly not him! Jesus needed to know the depths of his devotion. "Peter answered him, 'Though they all fall away because of you, I will never fall away'" (Matt. 26:33).

I imagine Peter felt much better after his declaration. How could Jesus get this so wrong? This fisherman is made from much stronger stuff than that.

I imagine Jesus felt so much sadder after Peter's sanctimonious pronouncement. How could Peter continually get this so wrong? With a breaking heart Jesus shrugged, "Truly, I tell you, this very night, before the rooster crows, you will deny me three times" (Matt. 26:34)

Jesus knew the strength Peter needed did not come from sinew or resolve. This lesson had been repeatedly heard but never learned. It was Peter's most limiting character deficiency.

Ironically, with everything Peter had witnessed from Jesus over the last three years, he still felt the need to have the last word. Looking at Jesus with his chest puffed out and a furrow in his forehead, he brazenly corrected Jesus one final time.

These would be his last words to his soon to be crucified rabbi and friend. "Peter said to him, 'Even if I must die with you, I will not deny you!'" (Matt. 26:35).

Jesus had great plans for Peter. He handpicked him from the teeming crowds to be His own disciple, one whom He would send as an apostle of good news. He walked with him and taught him and brought him into His closest circles. There was no greater outlay of energy to a single individual than Jesus' investment in Peter.

Yet Peter's lowest point of character was his highest point of capacity. As long as Peter saw himself as his source of strength, there was no Kingdom future for this apostle. This "weakness of strength" was at the heart of Jesus' distress for His friend. In the midst of his own imminent execution, Jesus spent precious time and emotional energy preparing His companion for the most important lesson of his life.

Imagine how Peter's last words would have haunted his soul. He was so sure he would be the most faithful, but in the end he was the greatest coward. Where could he go from here?

The low point of Peter's character had been laid open and exposed to the bone. There was no strength Peter could point to. He had aborted his haughty vows to the farthest extent imaginable. He was alone and empty and uncovered.

Our lowest point of character is always our highest point of capacity. But how fortunate we are that we have a gracious God who "sets us up" so that we can see our weakness, and in that epiphany we can discover His strength.

For Peter, this transfer took place after breakfast:

> When they had finished breakfast, Jesus said to Simon Peter, "Simon, son of John, do you love me more than these?" He said to him, "Yes, Lord; you know that I love you." He said to him, "Feed

my lambs." He said to him a second time, "Simon, son of John, do you love me?" He said to him, "Yes, Lord; you know that I love you." He said to him, "Tend my sheep." He said to him the third time, "Simon, son of John, do you love me?" Peter was grieved because he said to him the third time, "Do you love me?" and he said to him, "Lord, you know everything; you know that I love you." Jesus said to him, "Feed my sheep. Truly, truly, I say to you, when you were young, you used to dress yourself and walk wherever you wanted, but when you are old, you will stretch out your hands, and another will dress you and carry you where you do not want to go." (This he said to show by what kind of death he was to glorify God.) And after saying this he said to him, "Follow me." (John 21:15–19)

Since Peter had no record of strength that he could appeal to in order to declare his devotion, he simply and humbly appealed to the omniscience of his King. He trusted that Christ knew his heart deeply loved him. And that was all he had.

With that low stave of character growing, Jesus reinstates Peter with his Kingdom assignment. He prophesies that Peter would indeed make good on his vow to die for Him. But first things first. Jesus reminded His friend about the simple keys to Kingdom character, just as He did when they first met.

"Follow me."

The Way I Do One Thing Is the Way I Do Everything

A common sentiment in contemporary thought is a compartmentalized approach toward character. A political figure badly misbehaves in office, and his supporters sing in unison the much too familiar song that a leader's private life has nothing to do with his job performance. It seems to be agreed by the majority of our culture that the two are separate and unlinked. Private lives and public functioning are entirely unrelated.

But as in the case of most moral opinions that have not been carefully scrutinized, this societal creed has not been consistently applied. Few would propose that a child molester or corporate embezzler should be given public office. Why? Because their offenses are acts that disqualify them as individuals who deserve public trust. So, in the sentiment of popular opinion, there is an unwritten list of character issues that will negatively affect public performance. It is simply an issue of agreeing on the list.

For the Christ follower this separation of private and public lives seems perfectly absurd. We understand that we are one person, and there are no artificial divisions separating the various areas of our lives. If I steal through my tax forms, I will steal anywhere. If I lie to my wife, I will lie to anyone. If I procrastinate doing a function at work that I don't particularly enjoy, I will procrastinate anytime. If I hold back from God the finances that are correctly His, I will pilfer from anyone. The moment I rationalize disobedience, that decision becomes a darkness that pervades the entirety of my character. There is no way to segregate that darkness to a private ghetto. I am one person.

The way I do one thing is the way I do everything.

As we have already observed through the example of Peter, Jesus noticed the disciple's issue of character and called it out. For Peter his private issue of self-reliance became a spiritually damaging point of character that publicly hemorrhaged throughout his relationships at the worst moments.

The potential church planter needs to come face-to-face with this reality. Not one of us is unflawed and walks with impeccable character. We all walk with a limp. But what should be more alarming to us than our character faults is our attitude toward our character faults. If our brokenness is no longer a source of personal heartache but instead is permanently nailed down as part of the package we self-describe as our "charm," we have no business leading God's people. There is far too much at stake.

All Kingdom leaders do walk with a limp, but in their uncertain steps Kingdom leaders walk with great humility. In their weakness God's strength can be found, and the Kingdom results flowing from that dependent limp are both redemptive and eternal.

Personal Transformation Only Flows from Intimate Transparency

On this journey of leading ourselves, we have discussed two Kingdom realities that should create a great sense of spiritual apprehension in the heart of any potential leader. The troubling fact that my lowest point of character is my highest point of capacity should drive us to a place of analysis and deep introspection. Knowing that the way I do one thing is the way I do everything should eradicate any semblance of self-reliance and move us to a place of desperate dependence.

But where do we bring the fruit of this authentic introspection?

Evangelical Christianity in the Western world has become a largely individualistic pursuit. We make much of a personal relationship with God, the priesthood of the believer, and discovering God's will for our lives. We worship corporately; yet often it is little more than group isolation as we listen to one speaker, make individualistic applications in our study Bibles, and take our leave until next week.

In this contemporary understanding of the body of Christ, it is left to the individual believer to get his house in order through sheer intrinsic motivation. There is no place for accountability and support because there is no place for self-revelation. We are all on our own. As a result, those in the church of Jesus Christ experience about the same level of social dysfunction as those outside its community. The salt, light, and yeast we are commissioned to be are impossible because our character reflects no radical differences that are captivating to the lost. Practicing this over time, our differences are now only distinguished by our political preferences. Probably not what Jesus had in mind.

So how does a Kingdom citizen break away from this culture of isolationism and experience something more transformative?

The humility of community becomes the key. It is imperative that a church planter experience and model a different type of faith, one far less individualistic and far more transparent. When James said, "Therefore, confess your sins to one another and pray for one another, that you may be healed" (James 5:16), he was taking for granted that his audience understood the concepts found in humility of community. The notion of corporate isolationism was foreign to them. His call was to go deeper in community and to honestly admit sins of character in an environment of support and accountability. Transformation. "Whoever conceals his transgressions will not prosper, but he who confesses and forsakes them will obtain mercy" (Prov. 28:13).

Because of the ecclesiological culture we have inherited, most potential church planters have rarely experienced this kind of spiritual community and therefore would have little idea how to reproduce it. If that is the case, let me suggest three ideas.

1. Make It Personal

Considering much of this church plant will reflect your strengths and weaknesses, it becomes essential that you begin the assignment of enlarging your character capacity. Gather into a peer-mentoring group with other planters/pastors that are geographically close and make a priority of meeting weekly. Read together, learn together, pray together, and grow together.

Don't let this become exclusively a "shop talk" gathering, but instead its purpose is to grow together as Kingdom servants. Allow the Holy Spirit to work powerfully through others as a part of your transformation.

2. Model It Publicly

Let your people know that you are a part of such a community. Share openly about the ways you have changed and what you have learned. It is probably not wise to publicly share struggles you are currently working through, but it is a powerful testimony to honestly share victories that God has given you through community. Model transparency.

3. Mark a Path

The Kingdom power you have experienced through the honesty and humility of community needs to be made available to all in the body of Christ. Carefully think through how you will introduce this principle as a central platform in your strategy for church planting. Imagine the transformational power this new church will have in your city because it is composed of a membership that itself is experiencing personal transformation. An unstoppable force.

When it comes to character transformation, leading myself is the first and foundational step to becoming a Kingdom leader of great capacity.

Coaching Questions

1. What is your lowest point of character?

2. What is your greatest inconsistency?

3. What is your plan for living in community?

Chapter 7

Leading My Family

If you're pondering through the idea of becoming a church planter, one of the considerations you are likely weighing is the effect that it might have on the health of your family. You have probably observed many discouraging examples of "pastor's kids" and wouldn't wish that outcome on your own flesh and blood. Perhaps part of your struggle in deciding whether or not to plant is related directly to its impact on your family. If that is so, the following chapter, although counterconventional, may be helpful to your soul.

The Heresy of the Evangelical Order

A divine order has become almost sacrosanct in the evangelical subculture that has preprescribed a pseudo-theological ordering of a believer's priorities. There are slight variations to the sterile formula, but generally they are outlined as follows:

> God First
> Family Second
> Career Third
> Church Fourth

At first glance this seems like a worthy ordering of priorities for the faithful Christ follower. It starts with God. Career is well behind family. It sounds so spiritual on every level. With the categories clearly in our minds, we are free to categorize, shift, and order appropriate time allocations as they befittingly rate on our precalibrated grid. It requires personal discipline, but that's about all. All the prayerful thinking has been done for us.

But if this ordering of priorities is canonical, then it poses a bit of a logistical and theological conundrum for the average church planter. First, the logistics of it. Since one's "career" is actually starting a church, are third and fourth commanded priorities covered in a single category? That hardly makes sense since the church planter's connection to "church" and the average layman's are entirely on a different scale. The whole thing starts to smell a bit arbitrary.

As we press into the theology of our codified divine order, we find an uncomfortable conflict with a truly divine rendering of priorities:

> But when the Pharisees heard that he had silenced the Sadducees, they gathered together. And one of them, a lawyer, asked him a question to test him. "Teacher, which is the great commandment in the Law?" And he said to him, "You shall love the Lord your God with all your heart and with all your soul and with all your mind. This is the great and first commandment. And a second is like it: You shall love your neighbor as yourself. On these two commandments depend all the Law and the Prophets." (Matt. 22:34–40)

The Pharisees liked prescriptions too. Their lives and careers were built around constructing and propagating protective lists of rules and schedules. Perhaps they would have been big fans of our new evangelical creed. Nevertheless, as always, they had a devious test in mind for Jesus. "Jesus, what's the most important priority in life?"

Reading the passage, you don't imagine a breath of hesitation before Jesus straightens up, looks them in the eyes, and replies, "The most important thing in life is that you love God above all else and with every ounce of your soul."

Okay, so the two lists seem to be in sync so far. God. God. Check.

Before the Pharisees could redirect or ask a single follow-up question, Jesus decides to finish the conversation by declaring the second priority of life. "You are to love others." "You are to love others to the same degree that you would love yourselves." "This simple declaration is in fact a summary of all Scripture."

Implied by Jesus, there is no third on the list.

Probably not a fourth either.

It seems that to the Author of creation, when a person keeps God as his first priority, he begins to see others as equal to himself. This then becomes the supernatural filter for every other decision in his life. With God first, and all others loved dearly, how do I spend my time, energies, and resources? The "evangelical divine order" muddies up the process by forcing a legalistic order over the fruit of a spiritual relationship. When God is first, I will see others as first, not my own selfish ambitions. When God is first, there are seasons that my family is first. When God is first, there will be times when my career must have priority. When God is first, there are times when my church family takes sacrificial priority over my physical family and my career. When God is first, He gets to make the call—Kingdom first.

How can God ever be first without the consequences of that "firstness" being worked out in the ordinary details of life? Certainly there is no way for God to be first apart from the ordering of my daily life as He directs, day by day, moment by moment. The heresy of a preordered list of priorities is that it superimposes a man-made legal code over the simple and quiet obedience of a sensitive heart bent toward the voice of God.

So the character of a godly leader as he leads his family is marked by a quiet submission. He pays close attention to his walk with the Father as he navigates the rhythms of life and spends energy differently in different seasons. His children watch and learn as to what it means to be a man of God. The math works out that by not prioritizing my family but prioritizing my relationship with God, the blessing that flows down from that proper ordering is an enormous grace gift that would have never been realized through idolatrous family worship.

When I insist that my family stays atop of my priority pile, what have I actually done?

The Idol of Family

What is an idol? Usually it is something that starts out as a worthy thing, until we make it a worshipped thing, and then it ends up becoming a worthless thing. Idols were never meant to stand up to the pressure of being God. They are temporal by nature and inevitably a whole disappointment to their worshippers.

In our clamoring to assemble our priorities according to evangelical code, we may unintentionally turn our families into idols. In ranking our dedication to our family above all else, we have actually elevated its place to unhealthy heights. Its number-one status can be easily seen in the price we are willing to pay in our allegiance. Apparently no price is too high. Whether motivated for personal feelings of neglect as a child, or just keeping up with the Joneses, we have bought into a manic culture of endless SUV marathons from cultural experiences to sporting events—all in the vain hope of assembling the perfect family.

In the end, the whole of family life revolves around our children and their endless schedule. They become the nonnegotiable dots in the calendar when there's a clash on the agenda. They become the reason we can't see people: we have no slack in the system. They become the reason we can't make the time for serving others. Everything else plays second fiddle to the interminable social nurturing of our children. And when we do that, we are actually not serving them; we are worshipping them.

It goes with the territory. Every idol requires sacrificial devotion.

One does not have to look hard to see that this cultural imbalance exists regularly in church-planting families. Perhaps it is motivated by the fear that our children might spiritually rebel because they missed out on some good thing. Maybe it originates from a sense of misplaced guilt by parents for leaving the familiar in order to fulfill their divine calling. For whatever reason it would seem that too often church-planting families seem to be caught in the same idolatrous trap as their secular cousins.

Protect or Share My Family?

In an age of bubble-wrapped children and ghettoized Christianity, the notion of our intact families being "shared" with the broken that exist around us seems radical at best but more likely unwise. After all, that is why we insulate and isolate: we have a household to protect. So downstairs they trot to their homeschools, or across town they carpool to their private schools, while we attend our prayer breakfasts and Bible studies. The imagery of salt, light, and yeast are far from our imaginations. "The Son of Man came eating and drinking, and they say, 'Look at him! A glutton and a drunkard, a friend of tax collectors and sinners!'" (Matt. 11:19).

Have you ever considered the implications of Jesus' contemptuous title, "friend of sinners?" Others observed His life and noticed that His choice of friendships was inappropriate for a sacred leader. Public opinion seemed to nudge Jesus toward a more wholesome crowd of friends. It wasn't that Jesus had a few unsavory acquaintances that was so troubling. It was that Jesus didn't give the time of day to the socially upstanding. His friends, His closest and best friends were . . . well, sinners.

I wonder if being a follower of Jesus might mean our family has close friendships with sinners? By involving your whole family in significant friendships with those far outside the family of faith, a marvelous discipling process happens in the most natural way. Children can see both the painful consequences of sin as well as the redemptive mission of Christ. Step-by-step as your friendship leaks the light of Christ, spiritual transformation takes place. These are miracles never witnessed when ensconced in the sterile safety of our sacred bubble wrap.

A decision to share your family with those around you who have never witnessed a healthy, Christ-centered relationship is a grace gift to both your community and your family. Both will be forever changed.

A Transparent Journey

A word of encouragement I often share when speaking to a gathering of church planters relates to the spiritual trajectory of their children. Having spent almost all of my adult life hanging around church planters, I have noticed a trend that is both emboldening and somewhat logical.

Somewhere in the pit of many church-planting parents' stomachs is a nagging fear that their children might grow up and want nothing to do with Jesus and His church. The fear may come from watching pastors' kids rebel so repeatedly. Perhaps all the spiritual advantages you have had as a young person with large youth ministries are not available to your children as they serve with you in this new plant. Maybe they will grow weary of helping and serving and helping and serving and finally say, "That's enough!"

What is different about the journey you are on compared to the journey of the average pastor is that you get to do this as a family. Once a church is long established, the role of the pastor is much more defined, and in many cases his family sees pastoring as "dad's job." For the church-planting family, the scenario is much different.

For most planting families, from the time they surrender to their call, to the time the plant is both self-sustaining and multiplying, planting entails dozens and dozens of miracles. To develop from nothing to a movement is impossible without the gracious hand of God. As you move from obstacle to obstacle, it is imperative that you include your family in the journey. Let them hear you pray and ask your Father for His provision. Let them hear you pray prayers of thanksgiving when He supplies your need. Let them experience and see the "befores" and "afters" of lives that have been changed. Interpret the miracles to them in ways they can understand and appreciate. Remind them over and over of the specific God stories you have experienced together as a family. These will stay deeply etched in their memories for their lifetime and will serve as grand monuments that will inform their life's spiritual journey.

Based on years of personal observation, the encouraging news is that children who grow up participating in a church-planting environment seem to end up following the Lord in similar ways at astonishing ratios. The faith seeds you are planting in your family will leave a legacy that will bless generations to come.

So relax. Your children are about to be really blessed as they walk with you in this faith-expanding, Kingdom-expanding journey of a lifetime.

But the question remains: how do you faithfully protect the health and vitality of your marriage.

Marriage and the Art of Husbandry

For children to grow and thrive in a healthy spiritual environment, they must be assured that their dad loves their mom more than his work. This life lesson extends beyond the immediate family and will influence marriages of new disciples who watch their shepherd and ask, "How does he love his wife?"

Scripture is clear on the role of a husband. That role is self-sacrificial and always looks to the well-being of his bride before his own. "Husbands, love your wives, as Christ loved the church and gave himself up for her" (Eph. 5:25). His is a servant's role.

The English word *husband* comes from an old fourteenth-century English term, *husbandman*,[7] which means "farmer." It was a husbandman's livelihood to ensure that his fields were thriving, healthy, and producing appropriate fruit. To neglect his husbandry would be visible by all through the quality of his gardens and detrimental to his future occupation.

The assignment of "husbandry" is given to all who have pledged themselves to a bride. My job as a husband is to know my wife. To care for her, as she needs, so that she thrives as a woman of God. God has given me the assignment to provide the right environment and conditions at home for my wife to *flourish*[8] in every way God intends. If I see that she is withering, it is my responsibility to self-sacrificially attend to what is lacking. When she is blooming, it is a testimony to a watching world what a Christ-centered, healthy marriage looks like.

So, how can a church planter provide the right conditions for his wife to thrive? I have a longtime friend named Brian Bloye. He and his wife Amy have planted a great church and from it created a prolific church-planting incubator. That incubator, in collaboration with Mac Lake's vision, morphed into a church planting system that has become known as, *"Launch."*[9] Brian and Amy, more than most, have witnessed the dark side of leadership as they have walked with numerous planting couples through difficult days. *It's Personal*[10] gives practical wisdom on how to thrive in marriage while being neck deep in church planting. Here is a taste:

1. Do what is important, not urgent.
2. Bring fun and adventure into your relationship.
3. Take time off every week.
4. Keep intimacy a priority.
5. Focus on being a team.
6. Find your significance and security in Christ.
7. Make time for meaningful communication.
8. Help your spouse go as far as he or she can go.
9. Share your spiritual lives with each other.
10. Make your spouse your project.
11. Set meaningful boundaries.

By loving your wife the way Christ loves the church (see Eph. 5:25), you will in fact give one of the greatest gifts possible to your new church plant, an example of a Kingdom home.

Coaching Questions

1. In what ways are you tempted to isolate your family from your church plant?

2. How can you share your whole family with people outside the family of faith?

3. How can you focus more on what is lacking in your spouse's life?

Chapter 8

Leading God's People

The apostle Paul, in his last words to a tearful Ephesian church, gave this spine-chilling charge to its leadership:

> Pay careful attention to yourselves and to all the flock, in which the Holy Spirit has made you overseers, to care for the church of God, which he obtained with his own blood. I know that after my departure fierce wolves will come in among you, not sparing the flock; and from among your own selves will arise men speaking twisted things, to draw away the disciples after them. Therefore be alert, remembering that for three years I did not cease night or day to admonish every one with tears. (Acts 20:28–31)

As I have mediated on this passage over the years, I have come to believe Paul's advice to these Ephesian elders succinctly encapsulates what every church planter needs to deeply internalize in his soul if he is ever to effectively lead God's people. As a seasoned church planter, Paul had seen it all. From the perspective of one who is winding down his ministry, and through the guiding brilliance of the Holy Spirit, Paul laid out the primacies of anyone who should dare to lead God's people.

After meditating on these instructive words and warnings, it might be proper to unequivocally ensure that the call we are following is that of the voice of our King. A call from anyplace else will be devastating.

1. Lead Yourself First

As we have discussed earlier in chapter 6, leading ourselves well today is the only way we can ensure leadership credibility for tomorrow. Paul says, "Pay careful attention to yourselves." Before he charges these elders with an outward responsibility, he directs their attention squarely inward. Here's the point. Any outward leadership that doesn't flow from a well-examined heart is suspect as to its validity. Any counsel, persuasion, rhetoric, or strategic advance that flows from the lips of a wandering undershepherd estranged for an interval from his own Shepherd is, at best, questionable.

Lead yourself first. With great reverence and humility, declare to those you are discipling, "Follow every part of my life, the way I want every part of my life to follow Christ."

2. Own Your Responsibility

With a well-examined heart, the leader of God's people becomes ready to lead God's people. Paul continues, "And to all the flock in which the Holy Spirit has made you overseers, to care for the church of God." In one brief breath Paul describes the breadth of the responsibility of any who would lead God's people. With quill in hand, Dr. Luke transcribed four key aspects of our accountability:

My Leadership Is Large

From Paul's perspective, "all the flock" requires leadership. Not just the ones who willingly submit. Not just the compliant, the low-maintenance, the no-extra-grace-required sheep but the flock in its entirety. Including the hard to love. (Yes, the church of Jesus Christ contains difficult people. New churches tend to gather a disproportionate share of the overcompensating, emotionally broken.) This should be enough to cause any swaggering would-be planter to take a long, sober second thought.

My leadership is large, but I am one man. How can I effectively shepherd "all the flock"? Obviously my leadership needs to include a road map for discipleship that includes all the sheep. We'll look at this in chapters 28 and 29.

My Leadership Is Sovereignly Appointed

Had Paul only mentioned the breadth of our responsibility, any lucid leader would head for the exit door. But he quickly follows up the *scope* of our charge with the *source* of our charge: "The Holy Spirit has made you." Stuttering shepherds are well aware of their infirmities and shortcomings. Fortunately, a sovereign God sees through and past our limitations to the seed of Kingdom potential that he himself had sovereignly planted. A faithful shepherd will regularly see himself as too deficient and lacking. But in that same sense of deficiency, draw deep into the Author of his calling and find a humble and quiet strength that is both unexplainable and undeniable. God's anointed equipping.

As a divinely called one to this divine assignment, take a deep breath. A sovereign God has put *in* you and *around* you everything you will need to shepherd all the sheep. Breathe.

My Leadership Is High

The calling of a church planter is a calling to become an "overseer." This will never be truer or heavier than in the early years of the plant. You will often feel very much alone. Over time you will spiritually scrutinize potential leaders and, through your discipleship process, begin to appoint the anointed to serve with you. But this may well be a few years down the road. In this example of Paul in Ephesus, we see it was sometime within the three years he was in that city (see Acts 20:31).[11] His charge now formalized the high leadership they had been given.

As we will discuss later in chapter 11: "Knowing Myself," the fact that a sovereign God is calling a specific leader to a particular context means this same God has a specific assignment in mind. Your leadership as an "overseer" in these early years is to firmly establish, redundantly cast, fearlessly execute, and tenaciously protect the vision God has indelibly written on your heart. It is a high calling indeed.

My Leadership Is Gentle

Determined apostle, meet the gentle Shepherd, "to care for the church of God." God's assignment for you as a church planter includes the full range of "truth" and "grace." The truth of God's vision is executed with the gracious gentleness of a caring shepherd. It seems that a biblical prerequisite to lead God's people is that you care for God's people.

The more apostolic your calling is as a church planter, the more you will need to find shepherding leaders to surround you and, at times, temper you. The sheep need to be cared for. A constant drone of "mission, mission, and mission" will grow wearisome to limping sheep that are daily beaten down by the world. Nurture gentleness.

3. Remember Whose Church It Is

When God gives you a vision, and you know within every corpuscle of your soul that God gave it to you, it can become a dangerous thing. Sometimes in the giving we become owners of the vision instead of simply stewards. In that exchange from steward to owner, the breath of God leaves. Our vision has mutated into idolatry. We grip it so tightly that we altogether forget the Source who first whispered it. It's now ours. And so it is.

God will have no part of glory sharing.

And it happens so easily.

Paul reminds the Ephesian elders that the church they are to care for was never theirs but was always Christ's. It is a spiritual community, "which he obtained with his own blood." Therefore it cannot be possessed by its overseers. Jesus alone paid the high price through His atoning sacrifice.

The greatest gift you can give your new church is a constant awareness that they are the King's people. This is King Jesus' church. We decide nothing; instead we seek our King's wisdom. We are His.

4. Be Prepared for Satan's Outsiders

You will never experience the full reality of this, and the subsequent point, until you plant a church. Paul warned the Ephesian plant, "I know that after my departure fierce wolves will come in among you, not sparing the flock." How did he know this? Was this a mystical prophecy? Was Paul exercising some supernatural gift that comes with being an apostle? Not likely. What is more probable is that he is simply recalling the trend that had repeated itself in every church he had started. It is a trend that happens every time you plant a church. Satan is anything but original. He knows what works and he sticks with it.

Darkness will always summon its minions to infiltrate a church but never so pervasively as when a delicate shoot begins to emerge in the Kingdom of God. If he can uproot it early and keep it from becoming a substantial

Kingdom force to have to reckon with, he will throw everything he can at it. Strategy number one in church killing is always infiltration from the outside.

I can give you a long list of names and faces of these outsiders that marched into our new assemblies and looked for acceptance and position but who were in fact "fierce wolves." Curiously few were from our target audience of "lostness." The vast majority came equipped with long and impressive evangelical pedigrees. But if you inspected closely enough, you could smell sulfur singes. They wanted "in" too much. They "loved you" too much. "You and your perfect church" was emphasized too much. And if you ever bothered to check them out, train wrecks piled in their wake.

Be prepared for Satan's outsiders. They are on their way. If you don't have a discerning spirit, find someone who does. This is war, and the prince of darkness does not play fairly.

5. Be Prepared for Satan's Insiders

Darkness's outsiders usually come hot and heavy to snuff the life out of a new Kingdom-expanding church as a phase-one attack. In phase two the evil one is a little subtler. Paul goes on to once again experientially predict, "And from among your own selves will arise men speaking twisted things, to draw away the disciples after them."

Next darkness's sleeper cells emerge. These too are usually the pre-churched, ones who made it through the sulfur sniff test and found their way into leadership. They were much less obvious—biding their time, gaining your confidence, and worse, the confidence of wide-eyed new believers. You don't know when, but at some point Satan will blow his whistle, and his sleeper cells show their colors. From the perspective of hindsight, you can see the whole thing unroll clearly, but unless your spiritual discernment is highly tuned, you will miss some.

Biblical church discipline (see Matt. 18:15–20) is now your only course of action. Church discipline is always done with a redemptive intent, but do not err on the side of being too gracious. There is a high probability that these insiders were never "of" or "for" you (see 1 John 2:19). Test their repentance carefully.

Damage control is now your priority. Just as you trusted this person, so too have new believers attached their new faith to the personalities of these false teachers. Tremendous damage is often inflicted on the new faith of many innocent Christ followers. In full shepherd mode, with as many trusted leaders as possible, interpret this situation from a heavenly perspective. Allow these new believers to fully understand that this is not a conflict of personalities but a conflict of spiritual kingdoms. Some will be hurt beyond short-term repair. Others will mature because of this.

6. Do Not Be Casual

I imagine that, as Paul was saying his good-byes when he gave this charge, many of these leaders pictured names and faces of the outsiders and insiders whom they were forced to reckon with. This was not at all an abstract concept for them but a painful reality. But there is one big difference. Their memories of war all included an old apostle clearly calling out the battle orders. Now he is saying good-bye.

Paul continues, "Therefore be alert, remembering that for three years I did not cease night or day to admonish every one with tears" (Acts 20:31). Paul was saying that these Ephesian leaders had heard the theory from Paul, and together they participated in living out that theory. They know it. They know it well. Now the same sovereign Holy Spirit that called them to the station of overseer will continue to guide them with His indwelling self. What was Paul's sole ending admonition?

7. Be Alert

Leading the people of God requires a shepherd who is wide awake. This is not a calling for a laid-back, casual, "let's be friends" leader. It is a calling for a vigilant man of God who understands clearly what exactly is at stake. This is war. And in this war darkness's only goal is the total destruction of the leader and the vision God spoke to him.

Therefore, be alert.

Coaching Questions

1. What key aspect of your accountability will you struggle with most?

2. What steps can you take to mature in that aspect?

3. What can help you stay alert for satanic opposition?

Part 3: **Context**

I recall a time as a church planter when a denominational leader came to lead a required church-planting workshop in our city. As statements were made, some of us would ask questions as to how "X" would work because of "Y" and "Z" being a cultural reality in our city. This repeated itself several times during the week. It was obvious that there were blanks to be filled in our notebooks, and any deviation from this blank filling was an unwelcomed distraction to our purpose of gathering.

At some point a planter asked one question too many. The denominational leader, with great emotion, passionately unloaded his frustration with us, "Everywhere I go, planters say, 'But it's different here.' But it's not. Lost people are lost everywhere. They're not more lost in Canada than they are in Georgia. They're lost. So if you work the program, the program will work. So get over yourselves and stop bellyaching about how different it is where you are!"

I closed my notebook at that point. This was one program I would never adopt. Why? Because I knew both intuitively and through experience that context changes everything. What is deemed as a good and worthy thing in one context becomes a despised and worthless thing in another. There are few universally reproducible methodologies. Those who promote theirs as an exception to the rule should be viewed skeptically and cautiously adopted.

Five contextual church-planting considerations worth spending some time in reflection are: (1) How will my efforts become contextually sustainable? (2) What church-planting models seem appropriate to my context? (3) How does my unique makeup play into developing a contextual strategy? (4) What process can I use to truly understand the heartbeat of my context? (5) What is the Father saying to us as a Kingdom way forward in church planting?

Chapter 9

Contextual Sustainability

Often an early question asked by a potential church planter is, "How much money will I need to raise in order to plant a church?" Understandably, it is top of mind because in many ways it may seem the first big hurdle.

The question might have been easy to toss out in a singular breath, but unfortunately it is impossible to answer as quickly. Many variables must be taken into account before any helpful numbers can be discovered. Each of these variables must be carefully accounted for in order to arrive safely at a destination of planting a self-sustaining new church.

Unfortunately, a one-size-fits-all approach has too often dominated the church-planting landscape. A standard financial package is frequently pre-scribed for all church planters, despite their widely varying personal capacities, differing planting models, and drastically deviating settings. "Here it is. Best of luck. We will see you in three years."

Three years hence, the funding stops. Success is gauged by the singular metric of cash flow. If the planter was successful, he keeps moving forward with the resources found locally. If not, he is forced to hang his head, take a part-time job, and try to keep a stiff upper lip.

Let's look at a better way.

Projecting Strategically

The problem with generic funding packages is that there seem to be few generic planters and even fewer generic contexts. What looks like a self-sustaining church of 250 strong in one location might be only half-funded. What appears to be a struggling plant of forty in another location might actually be flush with cash. The planter that has reached 250 first-generation immigrants is unsuccessful because he is forced to paint houses to survive. The planter that reached nine businessmen and gathered forty is successful because his salary is locally covered. Obviously there is a fundamental problem when cash flow is our sole metric to measure success.

So, how do we go about determining appropriate funding levels for a church planter? If there is value to a projection of self-sustainability, how do we fund in such a way that, at the end of the funding, there is no cataclysmic disaster but a smooth and natural transition?

The team I work with (North American Mission Board) has concluded that appropriate levels of funding come down to an accurate accounting of four significant variables: (1) assessed capacity, (2) contextual history, (3) contextual giving patterns, and (4) runway. Despite the sources of funding (self-funded/bivocational, denominational assistance, partnerships with churches or networks), the fitting level of funding is ultimately determined by the planter's projected trajectory in context. To that end we have developed an online tool called the Church Planting Growth Projector[12] to assist a planter in setting realistic expectations for a potential plant within a specific context.

1. Assessed Capacity

Just as there are no generic contexts, there are no generic planters. God has uniquely gifted each of us. As in Jesus' parable of the talents (see Matt. 25:14–30), we are all accountable for faithfully investing into His Kingdom the gifts He has entrusted within us. Although we may not be a "five talent" planter, we learn from Jesus that we are still eternally accountable for an appropriate Kingdom return on investment.

Church-planting assessments come in various forms, but we are learning that the best performance predictors include a careful look at church planting competencies, personal character, marital health (if married), financial maturity, as well as innumerable other considerations relating to leadership capacity, communication skill, social agility, and likeability quotient.[13] Some of these can be discovered through objective online tools; others are uncovered through personal interaction.

If every planter is assessed as a "10," then all we have discovered is that the assessment process needs to be seriously reassessed. Like Jesus' parable we all have different capacities, and we are not all five-talent leaders. This can present a problem for overly optimistic potential planters.

2. Contextual History

If I am assessed, in context, by a series of experienced leaders from that context as a solid 7.0 out of 10, then my growth expectations should be aligned with that assessment. If, as a 7.0 planter, I am financially banking on growing a church to five hundred people in five years, I may have a few important things to consider. I will need to study the track records of others who have planted in this context. If Planter Steve, who assessed as a "9.5," has grown the largest church in the area, which is 275 after five years, my projection, if realistic, might need a downward adjustment.

So by comparing my probable capacity to the contextual history of an area, I can begin to establish an appropriate trajectory for the end of my funding runway. It is recommended that a potential planter not undergo this exercise in a vacuum but include a church planting catalyst or a seasoned coach from that context to assist in this process of analysis.

3. Contextual Giving Patterns

The next step in determining appropriate funding levels for self-sustainability is gaining the awareness of the normative giving patterns of that context.

Let's assume, based on contrasting my capacity with Planter Steve, that my trajectory after five years would be around 150 people. The next piece of knowledge I need to gain is, "What is the average weekly per capita giving for this context?" This is where you again need local expertise to help make informed determinations. By understanding your strategy, which includes a target audience, you can start to project a realistic financial picture.

Let's also assume my target will be a mixture of university students and health-care workers that concentrate around the university. By visiting churches in similar areas reaching a similar demographic, you might discover that weekly giving averages out to eighteen dollars per person attending.

By projecting five years into the future, when 150 people call this new plant their spiritual home, you can likely project an annual local income of $140,400.[14] What happens if I have ministry vision that calls for an annual income of $300,000? In five years when the funding runway ends, I will likely be in a draconian cost-slashing mode. This painful story has repeated itself too many times.

4. Runway

Traditional wisdom has deemed that funding runways should be three years. The thinking has been, "If you can't get a self-sustaining church up and going in three years, you likely are not a church planter." That probably was a valid line of reasoning when we were evangelizing in a far less secular culture. Today a three-year runway seems appropriate only when you are planting in an exposed Christian environment.

The problem of a three-year funding window in contexts that have little gospel access is that extra time is required for the cultivation and sowing activities (which are assumed to be present in more Christianized cultures). If time is not allowed for these activities, planters are tempted to take survival shortcuts by gathering the already well churched. This shortcut is usually a prescription for long-term evangelistic sterility. At this point in history, an assessed, equipped, and effectively coached church planter will likely need a five-year runway to plant an evangelistically effective, self-sustaining church in a highly secular context.

As you begin to think through the possibility of planting a new church, and the question runs through your mind, "How much money will I need to raise in order to plant a church?" remember that the answer, if it is a good answer, is going to take some homework.

Intentionally Bivocational Team

Imagine a different scenario. You have a big heart for some neighborhoods within the downtown core of your city. The demographics are a fusion of 1.5 and second-generation immigrants from Southeast Asia, Mexico, South America, Korea, and China. Being a typical urban core, it is block after block of high-density housing, interspersed with some mid- to low-density areas. The area is young, with an enormous eighteen- to thirty-year-old clustering. Being several miles away from the financial district or any university, this is a thoroughly blue-collar neighborhood.

As you begin to strategize how to effectively gain a hearing with this neighborhood, you realize a few things. First, the average weekly per capita giving is going to be low. Second, due to the population density, there are scant possibilities for a large assembly. Many of the buildings have community rooms in them designed for twenty to thirty, but that is just about it.

And then the penny drops. What if I recruited a small team to join with me in moving into that neighborhood, get jobs, and begin to start missional communities within the community rooms in the buildings? What if we began to disciple a generation of young urban leaders to follow our example and start a missional community within every building in this neighborhood? What might happen!

And then you did the math.[15] In five years perhaps we could have eight missional communities going, maybe more. With an average of fifteen people involved in each, that's 120 people. If they gave an average of nine dollars per week, we would have over $50,000 to invest in the missional engagement of our neighborhood. With careful discipleship and strong leadership, this thing could become an indigenous movement. A completely reproducible movement.

As we begin to strategize on how to effectively plant within densely populated and highly secular contexts, the idea of *intentionally bivocational planting teams* begins to make enormous sense. The normal barriers that stop movements (money and qualified leaders in which to invest that money) are leveled, and the harvest itself becomes both the leadership pool and the financial backers of the mission.

Keep the thinking of this chapter in mind as you think through our next subject of context—church-planting models.

Coaching Questions

1. What have you learned about your church planting competencies?

2. What plans have you made for growth as a result of your learnings?

3. What are the unique challenges to reaching people in your context?

Chapter 10

Exploring Models

I hesitate to even use the term *models* as it can bring into the minds of many an adverse reaction linking back to the overindulgent era of age of church growth. Models are seen by some as merely formulaic methodology, devoid of any guiding spiritual impulse, that lead a planter to a "just add water" approach to his assignment. For many the term connotes an image of a conference, a significant fee, a hefty notebook, a series of similar testimonies from satisfied customers, and a significant disclaimer that was rarely believed or applied: "The ideas presented in this conference are from this pastor's experiences. Future results cannot be guaranteed and will vary. Adaptation to your environment is recommended." With minimal reflection and maximum zeal, scores of inspired church planters marched out of the megachurch, highlighted binders tucked under their arms, confidently prepared to take on their challenge. This scene has been repeated so often that to many the term "model" telegraphs an image of a franchised missiology that is neither desired nor honest.

At its base a church-planting model is simply an image of a concept that is used to help a church planter know, understand, and simulate a contextual application of that concept. What many have reacted against is not the concept of a model but the lack of contextual application of the model. We have watched the fiasco of full-scale, big-budget, attractional launches held in neighborhoods that look with a jaundiced eye at slick and rehearsed. We have also seen valiant attempts at organic, house-church movements that never got off the ground in communities skeptical of cultish religious expressions.

Obviously somewhere in our selection of models, a proper understanding and appreciation for our context needs to be gained. The purpose of this discussion on models is not to survey the numerous models that have emerged in recent history but to limit our discussion to current expressions that have the potential to be evangelistically potent. Absent from this discussion are models that prey on existing churches and church plants to establish its audience or any variation that requires the already evangelized to build its base.

As we have previously discussed, the planter that strip-mines his community of the well-churched normally finds that he has built a team that has no relational lines of connection or credibility with those who should be his target. It might be true, however, that if there is no missional expression of church nearby, Kingdom-hearted believers may be drawn to an evangelistically focused church.

It is also significant to note that the days of closely following a model's directions are well behind us. With the confluence of urbanization and immigration, a static and homogenous population has been reduced to a nostalgic memory of another era. Worldviews between adjacent neighborhoods can be universes apart. Choosing a model because your context is urban or suburban is like choosing shingles because your house is one story or two: the guiding wisdom becomes nonsensical. Worldviews in rural Vermont might have more ethical linkages to urban Montreal than to suburban Maryland. While some models have a better reception in some contexts than others, the contexts are defined by their spiritual experience and religious bias more than our classical environments of development.

Models generally originate from the heart of a planter by the guidance of the Holy Spirit for a specific context. Usually, by the time the model receives some notoriety, it is already several years old and wouldn't currently work as well as it did, even for the original planter and context. Skilled church planters will learn to hold their models loosely and have the leadership agility to adjust and adapt their strategies as the context requires. Early evangelistic fruit may give important clues for adapting a model to reach the networks where the gospel is bearing fruit. This early fruit may even be corrective from one model to another.

Each of these we will discuss is actually a missional variant from its predecessor that has been updated in response to decreasing effectiveness. Older forms have been morphed into expressions that have a greater Kingdom impact.

Missional Attractional

The missional-attractional approach to church planting seems to represent a merger of several older streams, most notably observed in the Purpose-Driven movement (Rick Warren) and movements within the Willow Creek Association (Bill Hybels). These "fathers of attractional" church planting were motivated to design their models from the evangelistic ineffectiveness they found in older, traditional, program-based methodologies. Their books and conferences influenced thousands of church planters to rethink their approach to evangelism.

The attractional model has undergone a series of incremental alterations over the past decades to reflect a much more missional impulse. Leaders who grew unsettled with a large crowd but little or no community impact began to rethink their mission and soon strategized to engage their congregations with the assignment of community transformation. Soon other planters began to plant new congregations with this "both/and" thinking to great effectiveness.

On the continuum between "attractional" and "missional," leaders often find it difficult to balance these two conflicting spends of energy. It is easily observed that often the "missional" half of the assignment becomes little more than fawning market positioning designed to increase the affectivity of "attractional" among the religiously predisposed. However, several skilled leaders have managed to emphasize both sides with great effectiveness.

Because of the attractional component of this model, it tends to find its greatest success in geographies where there is a Christian memory resident. Those in a community who sense a need for "church" will find this church both attractive and helpful. Areas that have a comparatively insignificant churchgoing population will be difficult soil to employ this model with any level of effectiveness. A "launch large" strategy in a mostly empty high school gymnasium usually signals a long and discouraging road ahead.

Typically this model builds momentum through a large launch and strong central communicator in a dynamic and well-honed worship service. It often has core values of (1) a mobilized membership, (2) projecting community ministry through small groups in order to, (3) multiply everything (disciples, groups, and congregations). Multisiting is often the expression of reproduction by those employing this model, although there are currently some strong examples of incubated church planting.

Possible Strengths

- Community transformation "wins" are associated explicitly with that Christian organization—builds credibility, trust, and leads to "asks" from community influencers for mutual partnership.
- It becomes a preferred choice for most people with a Christian memory.
- It provides a less relationally intense setting for Christians to bring their friends than missional cell or missional house-church models.
- Organization provides a platform from which to "speak to power" and push back on questionable ethical positions taken by community leaders. This is true even if the organization is relatively small.

Possible Weaknesses

- It is difficult to hit critical mass for the attraction component. Without a crowd in the room, the advantage of anonymity for seekers can't be realized. For success one of the following usually must be true: you are a brilliant marketer; you are skilled at starting multiple groups simultaneously to build a crowd; you came with a significant launch team; or you are planting in a highly Christian context.
- It seems to decreasingly be able to reach planters' growth expectations (without redistributing the saints of existing churches) in highly secular environments.
- It is heavily reliant on leadership to keep both attraction to services and projection of ministry through groups. It must develop a leadership incubator early on in church life or see initiatives choked out from lack of qualified leaders.
- It can easily slip into focusing only on attraction without honest missional effort.
- It requires the highest up-front cost of any model. Planters must be able to raise significant capital.

Characteristics of Probable Leader

- An extrovert or an introvert who has discovered their "actor" side. They must love to communicate up front and influence people through the spoken word.

- Visionary. Able to see where the church needs to go and how to shape a message to motivate people to join the journey.
- Comfortable with many varied, evangelistic approaches. This person can train leaders to share one-on-one, use evangelistic Bible studies, and communicate motivationally at evangelistic events for crowds.
- Loves to work in a team that he has recruited and trained.
- Persuasive fund-raiser. Able to effectively cast a vision to multiple partners to secure the required investment.

Missional Cell

The twenty-first century's version of the cell movement originated from Asia and was brought to the Western world more as a church-growth technique than a church-planting strategy. Proponents like Ralph Neighbor in his conferences and book, *Where Do We Go from Here*, influenced thousands of pastors in the 1990s to adopt a "cell, congregation, celebration" strategy. Pastors in the West watched with an envious eye at the spiritual explosion taking place in South Korea and began to adapt Korean principles to a Western church. While some churches were able to make the culture-shifting transition, most were not, and the concept began to loose steam in the West as a church-growth technique.

What failed to energize the West as a dominant church-growth tactic found limited traction among planters as a church-starting strategy. By stripping the prerequisite need for a colossal sacred-culture shift, the planter was free to create cultural expectations from the ground up (as long as he fished outside the evangelical subculture). Planters began to implement a cell-based strategy and found a new sense of intimacy within a discipling culture that became contagious.

A classic "cell" differed from a typical "small group" in the fact that it involved far more than a relational Bible study but in fact incorporated everything that was commissioned to the church. Cells often would fellowship, study, evangelize, worship, observe ordinances, and collect tithes and offerings. The physiological image of a cell was the metaphor for organic multiplication. Every cell had an apprentice leader in training, readying himself for the task of next-generational leadership.

Typically this church had some sort of organizational structure that tied numerous cells together for substantial corporate impact. A common mission, vision, and values were shared among an interdependent network of small groups that gathered formally in a weekly or monthly "celebration." The celebration was valued to leadership as "icing on the cake," where the "cake" itself was unquestionably the cell. Many cell-based church plants refused to publicly advertise their weekly/monthly celebrations, thereby forcing the issue that everything and everyone comes from the cell.

With the recent sensitivity of the Western church to engage societal problems (where the church's presence had been largely absent), the cell model was uniquely designed to engage and capitalize. Missional cells strategically placed throughout a city took ownership of brokenness in their communities. The process of missional engagement provides numerous opportunities to network with Kingdom seekers, and in community these seekers soon join their numbers as Kingdom expanders.

The missional-cell expression of church planting focuses on multiplication of biblical disciples that can organically lead to the multiplication of cells, celebrations, regional churches, and, in some cases, national movements. The movement always grows from the bottom up, but oversight is given top down. There is generally not "big launch" when it goes public because of the value as the cell being the front door. The larger celebration emerges as an organic outcome of clustering cells under apostolic leadership.

Possible Strengths

- More intentional focus on community impact through missional cells than through the small groups of missional-attractional.
- More strategic focus and guiding direction than with networks of missional-house church. An apostolic leader's influence can be felt through multiple layers of leadership.
- Better penetration of diverse communities with energy to multiply small units than either of the other two models.
- Able to better safeguard against doctrinal problems arising than missional house church.

Possible Weaknesses

- If the celebration level doesn't give strategic direction and inspiration, may flounder for purpose.
- Challenging to develop the layers of leaders needed to make this work well. Very leadership development intensive.
- Requires that individuals navigate a more relationally intense introduction to the group than missional-attractional. Difficult for some cultures/personalities.

Characteristics of Probable Leader

- Solid communicator, but major focus is training groups of rising leaders, so smaller communication context than with missional-attractional.
- Strong discerning gifts. Able to sift through groups to discover leaders of solid character.
- Loves working through teams, good delegator, natural inspirer, not a micromanager.
- Good strategic thinker. Must balance impact through groups working individually and clusters of groups working together.

Missional House Church

Describing the origin of the house church is not difficult, one can see that early on in our Christian roots, churches, all churches met in homes. The advent of churches meeting in their own dedicated sacred spaces came much later in church history in an era when the church looked far different from the church of Acts. Certainly there is little debate that in our history, as well as movements that can be observed currently, that churches that meet in homes find themselves in the center of the conversation.

Asking whether house churches are a healthy expression of the church of Jesus Christ, if one should endorse house churches as a preferred or at least acceptable expression of church? This is a completely different discussion. Personally, I couldn't support house churches any more than I could authorize nature. I enjoy soaking in a sunset from the safety of a folding chair firmly planted on the beach. At the same time I would be terrified to sit in a rowboat during a hurricane. I am experiencing nature in both; one is a good experience, and the other is not.

Like nature, house churches come in all shapes and sizes and have been formed from many different motivations. Many are incredibly healthy expressions of Kingdom living. Many others are unhelpful testimonies of the church of Jesus Christ. As a category their commonality is that their meetings take place in a house; yet their differences can be staggering. But once you get past the oft-attached stigma of a gathering of strongly anti-institutional and disenfranchised evangelicals kibitzing about their organic superiority, you will find numerous legitimate examples with a heartbeat of Jesus that would outstrip most churches.

House churches are not new, and they are here to stay. And that is a good thing.

Two leaders who have significantly advanced the contemporary discussion of a missional house church movement are Neil Cole and J. D. Payne—Neil as a practitioner/advocate and J. D. as a missiologist. Both are in agreement that the spiritual movement required to transform secular nations with the gospel is unlikely to emerge from complex structures that are usually associated with church. Something simpler, leaner, and far easier to reproduce is required to experience a gospel-saturating movement.

In J. D. Payne's book, *Missional House Churches*,[16] he contrasts five characteristics of missional house churches against more traditional models of church. He notes that they are:

1. More organic, less institutional
2. More simple, less structure
3. More participatory worship, less passivity
4. More community, less acquaintances
5. More ministers, less Ministers

Missional house churches, as a model, find both influence and impact when associated in a geographical network. This synergistic punch comes from lowering the walls of independence and autonomy and building collaboration through an interdependent missional cooperation. An overemphasis on autonomy and independence speaks more of our insecurities than our Kingdom priorities. The character of a founding planter waving the autonomy flag too hard should be looked at with suspicion. House churches that voluntarily link together, either through organic multiplication, or synergistic partnering, discovers an incredible Kingdom teamship that is strengthening both to the individual house church and to the mission.

The future of the missional house church in the West is bright. The continual secularization of society leaves fewer and fewer opportunities for more attractional models to find a ready audience. The persistent fragmentation of society increasingly neutralizes any approach that requires a large homogeneous base. Although these conditions are disastrous for traditional models of church, they are actually perfect for a missional house-church movement to network into high-density communities, unreached people groups, and systemic brokenness to present a clear and compelling gospel witness.

Possible Strengths

- Bivocationally friendly. The founding planter models in every way the expectations of every leader.
- High-density friendly. Able to penetrate buildings with the gospel like few other models.
- Most flexible and sensitive to new opportunities for planting a faith community. Quick turnaround from noticing the need to beginning ministry.
- Most appealing to anti-institutional people and others who reject the organized church.
- Doesn't have a public image, so mostly ignored by institutionalized anti-Christian groups. Able to continue a witness where other churches are banned.
- Able to customize discipleship to the individual.

Possible Weaknesses

- Often loses the missional impulse as soon as the apostolic leader moves on. The sacrifice required to multiply often fades away.
- Can't "speak to power" when encountering injustice, except indirectly. why?

- Can find it difficult to keep people when surrounded by churches offering compelling ministries (e.g., teenage son is spiritually drifting; parents are drawn to neighboring church with effective youth ministry).

Characteristics of Probable Leader

- Highly relational with an influencing personality
- Strong pastoral gifting
- ✓ Good small-group tuned communication skills
- Focused apostolic leader; can keep the Kingdom at the forefront

For many potential church planters, the "grassroots" nature of a missional house-church model is a compelling option to fulfill their "Kingdom first" aspirations for their city. By modeling every aspect of Christian discipleship, even the balance of secular employment with a missional calling, he embodies a redefinition and living standard of the normal Christian life. If his apostolic leadership gifts are strong enough, he can develop a network that penetrates into buildings and spaces few others would dare to attempt.

Legacy Church RePlanting

A fourth model that seems to be gaining momentum is a formalized approach to renewing plateaued and dying churches. Most evangelical denominations report that between 70 and 80 percent of their existing congregations are plateaued or declining. More mainline traditions have even more discouraging news to report. This unhappy intelligence combined with the fact that the majority of these congregations are located within metro/urban contexts (which also correlates with the geographies of highest spiritual need) leads many missional strategists to urge networks and denominations to develop approaches to engage these declining congregations before their key strategic assets are lost to nail salons, community theaters, and mosques.

For this writer no picture highlights a need for a comprehensive "full-court press" on this discouraging trend more than one that I can see in my own city of Toronto. Few would argue that one of the greatest theologians and preachers of the twentieth century was Aiden Wilson Tozer. His numerous writings such as *The Pursuit of God* have impacted thousands, including this author. As one of his generation's premier voices for the Kingdom of God, A. W. Tozer preached from the Toronto pulpit of the Avenue Road Church, an astounding stone cathedral located in the heart of the city.

After his passing, the historic Avenue Road Church plodded along for decades rehearsing the memories of the "glory days" when A. W. Tozer, their revered pastor, was at the helm. Attendance in this strategic church slowly declined year after year until they could no longer meet their financial obligations and were forced to sell their assets. Today the very place where A. W. Tozer faithfully preached the Kingdom of God now houses Canada's largest Hare Krishna temple.

This depressing story is being repeated every year in less dramatic fashion in metropolitan areas across North America. Churches that once had vibrant testimonies are reduced to monuments of past glory. Properties that sit strategically in the most spiritually needy neighborhoods are stripped of their sacred function and are often transformed into tools of further darkness. It rarely happens all at once, but as Mark Clifton described in a note to me, numerous indicators mark a church's path toward extinction.

The symptoms are many, and they include:

1. They value the process of decision more than the outcome of decision.
2. They value their preferences over the needs of the unreached.
3. They have an inability to pass leadership to the next generation.

4. They cease, often gradually, to be part of the fabric of their community.
5. They grow dependent on programs or personalities for growth or stability.
6. They tend to blame the community for a lack of response and in time grow resentful of the community for not responding as it once did.
7. They anesthetize the pain of death with overabundance of activity and maintaining outdated structure.
8. Confusion of caring for the "building" as caring for the church.

To date the primary way of addressing this growing problem has been a strategy that required members of the declining church to hand over the church keys and all governing autonomy to an outside guiding body who would redeem their asset by planting a fresh expression of the body of Christ within the forgotten walls of the former church. From time to time disbanding agreements like this would take place, often with remarkable results.

The problem with this strategy is that such a comparatively small percentage of declining churches is willing to face the truth of their own mortality. The majority will stubbornly resist any rescue attempts that involve co-opting their autonomy. Rarely it appears that a dying church will see their assets and their spiritually needy community through the lens of the Kingdom of God. As a result, not until most diminishing churches are financially unable to pay their "light bill" is there any openness for a more Kingdom conversation. But more often than not different decisions are made, and the strategic property is forever lost to the mission of God.

What Mark Clifton is pioneering is a model of rePlanting that is a little more emotionally acceptable to congregations traipsing down the path to extinction. It starts with a careful examination on the part of partnering denominations, associations, networks, or Kingdom-hearted local churches to discover the following:

1. Is it in a location where a new church is needed?
2. Is the building usable and worth saving? Will it be cost-effective?
3. Could the building be used as an incubator for multiple church plants and/or community ministry?

If a church agrees to rePlant itself upon the legacy of ministry and missions that once existed, an exchange takes place:

1. The church gives up command and control for a limited and prepre-scribed period of time to an outside leadership team.
2. The church receives an assessed and equipped Legacy rePlanter.

The Legacy rePlant strategy requires outside leadership to form the governing leadership team for the rebirth. This team consists of the rePlanter and five to seven people from the sending (or sponsoring) church and perhaps other interested entities. This team makes all strategic decisions short of closing the church or selling the building.

The Legacy rePlanter has three basic assignments:

First, he loves and cares for the remaining members. He seeks to again warm their hearts to the gospel that has likely been long neglected. He works hard to help the remaining members cast aside the idol of their past and cling only to Jesus through a fresh partnership in the gospel. He does this in several ways: Through Christ-centered preaching and teaching and spending quality time with the members, he begins to earn relational equity. By modeling a life of gospel-centered joy, instead of an obsession with performance, results, or control, he repositions a Kingdom ethic for the congregation. Likely for many generations the membership has seen leaders who seem to find joy in results or control and rarely in the gospel. It usually takes considerable time to deconstruct this in the members. But it is time well spent. It will be the foundation for trust and change required for a future movement.

Second, he does the work of a church planter in his community. He volunteers and imbeds himself in his community learning everything he can about his new environment. He understands his call is not exclusively to the expiring church but also for a major and sustained investment in the community. He prioritizes his evangelism and discipleship efforts among young men. Dying churches have largely been unable to connect to millennials and especially younger men; yet nothing can provide a more solid foundation for rePlanting than a core of young men who becoming disciple makers themselves.

Third, he serves his community with radical generosity. While the dying church likely no longer has many resources, the rePlanter is charged with the task of securing partnerships with other churches and networks in order to meet needs in the community. Serving the community brings a new market positioning to a dying church. It serves to engage Kingdom seekers in the community who are pursuing an innate Kingdom pulse. It also provides the long-term membership with a new and meaningful reason for the church to exist. In the area of radical service, the older members and the new people who are reached begin to work cooperatively together. Around mutual service a new Kingdom DNA is developed, and the trajectory for an entirely new future is fashioned.

This moderated process seems more palatable for churches not totally persuaded of their impending expiry than the radical surgery involved in former strategies.

Possible Strengths

- A more redemptive approach that seeks to heal a dying church rather than simply to euthanize it.
- The rePlanted church becomes a living sermon to the community. Something that was once near death has come back to life.
- Encourages a multigenerational church plant from the beginning as it includes members from the dying church.
- Redeems the building, which is the single greatest physical resource the dying church may have at this point in its life. Repurposes a sacred building for Kingdom purposes.
- Provides a church planting option for potential planters whose gifts may be more shepherding than apostolic.

Possible Weaknesses

- You have to spend time deconstructing a past before you can construct a future. It requires a longer on-ramp than church planting.
- The building can become a drain on resources and energy. It can consume a disproportionate amount of resources.
- If the church's reputation in the community is negative, the task of rePlanting can be much more difficult than starting from nothing.

Characteristics of Probable Leader

- An overwhelming passion for the local church, even a dysfunctional local church.

- An ability to work with older adults while still being able to lead and engage a younger generation. This leader must develop thick skin, not easily given over to fear of man.
- A proved ability to evangelize and make disciples who make disciples.

- The heart, hands, and eyes of a missionary who is called not only to the church but as a church planter is called to reach his community.

- One who is confident in his identity in Christ and is not driven by affirmation from the results of his work. This is key because in the initial stages the work may be slow.

Coaching Questions

1. What model best fits your church-planting context?

2. What adaptations would you need to make?

3. What unique strengths and gifts do you have to make your model "evangelistically potent"?

Chapter 11

Knowing Myself

We all have spiritual heroes. Leaders who are currently walking this planet have been used by God in powerful and history-altering ways. There are prophetic voices who were courageous enough to declare truths few wanted to hear. Strategic voices who audaciously carved clear Kingdom footpaths for many others to follow. Shepherding voices that summoned actions of deep courage and conviction from the demurest of sheep. We profoundly admire these leaders God has placed in our path, even if only virtually, because they have shaped us into the people we are.

It's not a bad thing to have a spiritual hero; admiring heroes is wholesome. It demonstrates a heart of genuine gratitude to our God for the creative work He has done in the heart of a yielded and obedient servant. Admiration is healthy. Mimicking is something altogether different. When I impersonate an esteemed hero, I unwittingly say to myself and those who follow me that "God has spoken to others, but I doubt He will speak to me." We limit God, straight out of the gate, to a second-generational iteration of something that was once good. Off we trot, with well-worn blueprints tucked under our arm, ready to duplicate something already well done.

The problem with borrowing a successful blueprint from somewhere else is that it originated from the heart and life experiences of another leader. God spoke specifically to him or her. The design was devised precisely to the spiritual gifts, personality, and passions of that leader. The reason it might be "borrow worthy" is that it expressed the King's desires. But it was the King's desires for another time and place. The big hitch is that it was inspired for neither your time nor your place.

The good news is that our Father has perfect plans for each of His children. Not stale rehashed leftovers from one of your Father's "favorite" children but new words spoken with fresh life to a child He loves without limits. The design will start with an accurate accounting of our gifts, personalities, and divinely inspired passions.

As a church planter, or a potential church planter, this assignment is relatively simple. You will start by looking honestly at your past and, from that observation, perceiving the possible trajectory of your future. The future DNA of your new church will take its cues from the fact that you took the time to understand the King's unique calling on your life.

Spiritual Gifts

Before I launch into this discussion, I want to confess a personal point of exasperation when it comes to this subject of spiritual gifts. For whatever reason much of the evangelical church has desperately tried to keep step with the more charismatic side of our family. But from my seat it appears to have been a pathetic attempt at best. When the charismatic section began to emphasize their experiences, other evangelicals, not wanting to be left out, began to construct complex forms, computer programs, and worksheets in the vain attempt to compete with our neighbors. I think the experiment has failed. Let's look at why.

For a Christ follower the most significant level of self-discovery is getting a clear picture of how much we have changed since becoming a subject of the King. The day we submitted our lives to the lordship of Christ, we received His Spirit as an indwelling and ever-present guide. This indwelling Spirit sensitizes us to the King's desires. Through a relationship of humble submission guided by the authority of His living Word, we begin to sense God's sovereign plan. The whole thing is incredible. God begins to renovate us from the inside out while He prepares us for a Kingdom adventure that is way out of our depth. We begin to understand that His plan for our lives is unlike anything we have ever experienced. It is indeed new.

This plan will often involve two uncomfortable steps that force us to reflect on our insecurities and weigh them against the omnipotence of God. First, it will highlight areas of our personal weakness. We know those all too well. Yet we sense that God is leading us toward something that isn't requiring our greatest personal assets. Our standard *modus operandi* of leading with our strengths is asked to take a backseat along with its accompanying pride.

As unsettling as it may be, God begins to stir faith in our heart toward steps that are clearly well out of our core strengths.

This leads us to the second awkward step. Having a good grasp on our weaknesses, God often leads us to make faith steps that are at the heart of those vulnerabilities. In faith, with the full awareness of my shortcomings, I obediently take steps toward the impossible assignment of God. In this weakness we begin to discover our spiritual gifts. With them we discover the strength of our King. When I am forced out of the comfort of depending on my strengths and see God work in power, I at that point comprehend that I have experienced a gift that could only be described as spiritual. God's power working through weakness. It's part of the whole package that comes with the Kingdom of God.

Stuttering shepherds often become the greatest Kingdom leaders.

This understanding might sound radically different from the understanding you might have gained through previous exercises with spiritual gift inventories. Gift inventories most often focus on our aptitudes, abilities, and preferences. Questions like, "In situation 'A' would you most likely 1, 2, or 3?" Our answer more aptly describes the strength of our personality than an opportunity to see God's strength emerge through that personality. Thus, after completing our two hundred questions, we have taken a completely accurate, sacred personality test rather than discovering anything truly spiritual. The sacred personality test is not altogether unimportant, but equating its calculated deductions with a spiritual gift will rob us of the opportunity of discovering God's greatest blessing in our ministries. Too often schoolteachers' results show they have the gift of teaching. Accountants always seem to end up with the gift of administration. But hadn't they been teachers and accountants long before they entered into a relationship with Christ?

Suddenly the whole thing smells a bit off.

Instead of looking inward to our strengths in search for clues of a spiritual gift, it might be wiser to look backward to our past. Look at the sweeping themes of our personal histories; pay careful attention to the times where steps of faith have been taken and where God has shown up in remarkable ways. What was the greatest faith issue? What personal weakness caused the greatest internal struggle? What were the lessons learned from those experiences? The answers to questions like these may well lead to the identification of the Spirit's gifting of our lives. Our weakness, God's empowering strength—a truly spiritual gift.

The design of a Kingdom-expanding ministry will always account for the King's powerful presence working His will through our yielded weakness.

Personality

We have dismissed the sacred personality test as noninstructive to the discovery of spiritual gifts; however, this does not mean the Kingdom design of our ministries is unrelated to our unique personalities. God has given our personalities as a gift in which to glorify Him. These varied personalities reflect something of the nature of God as it is expressed through people.

Our personalities are the "hard wiring" of how we approach the world. This individual personality becomes the lens by which we take in information and formulate a response. Varied people will approach the same situation and deduce considerably different courses of action largely prejudiced by the filter of their personalities. The Kingdom design of any ministry will show God's fingerprints by accounting for the personality with which He has created in us.

Personalities are varied. Some of us are energized by being with people; others need to draw alone to recharge our batteries. Some of us are sensible, down-to-earth people who make practical choices for efficiency and effectiveness. Others of us are highly imaginative and creative with abilities to intuitively discover new paradigms and processes. Some of us are focused people; we know what we want to accomplish and cannot rest until the list has been completed. Others are much more free-flowing in accomplishing assignments; new information does not derail our plans but simply redirects them. Some of us are logical and systematic in how we approach a problem and are not deeply affected by the emotions around us. Others of us take our cues from the sentiment of the situation and respond as the circumstances dictate.

Varied personalities, each fashioned by God are a strategic part of His Kingdom's design. Knowing and appreciating the unique personality God has given us will serve us well in understanding our place in God's Kingdom-expanding plans. For church planters it becomes important to have an accurate understanding of their hard wiring and how their personality affects and influences others.

Passions

Passions are the deep places where God lights up His Kingdom priorities within our spirit. They are unique to us as individuals and often originate from past experiences in which we have been profoundly touched. These experiences compel us toward a particular problem or cause with little need for stimulus of an outside motivation. Passions often have a life of their own.

But passions by nature are not the exclusive territory of the Kingdom of God. Darker passions can often become self-serving obsessions, even when located squarely in the sacred space. For passions to be Kingdom-centric, they will direct the objects of that passion to the healing, comfort, and transforming authority found in our King and in turn be strategically released to guide others to their newfound Source of life.

Have you ever noticed that when you drive a certain brand of car, you tend to notice that car everywhere? Until you owned it, that model just blended unremarkably into the vast grey traffic patterns. Now that you have invested time and energy in choosing, purchasing, and maintaining that vehicle, it seems as if it pops out of the dull, nondescript lines of traffic in fluorescent 3-D. You now even notice subtle differences between model years and trim packages. Until you owned a Volvo, you had never noticed a Volvo. Now Volvos are everywhere. Why is that?

Passions are highly sensitized areas of our personal experience that arouse emotion, a sense of justice, or a spirit of great mercy, while often going unnoticed by the general population who have not personally interacted to that experience.

To identify your passions, here are a few questions to ask yourself. What situations deeply move you while most others around you seem nonplused? What hurts or needs seem to arouse a profound internal reaction that seems out of proportion to the general populace? What misinterpretations or misinformation elicits a reflexive response of correction or rectification? What causes or injustices ignite involuntary sentiments deep within your soul? These passions may be clues to part of the Kingdom agenda that God has in mind for your church plant. Your unique calling will always be influenced by the deep inward things of your past that are now redeemed and pointed outward for the glory of God.

Understanding our Kingdom passions becomes essential in planting a church for the Kingdom of God. Through an acute awareness of our Kingdom passions, our ministries gain focus and motivation that a mere reproduction of a church-planting model could never inspire. Passions guide and propel.

Knowing who I am is necessary to understanding how God might desire to use my life in His Kingdom-expanding plans. God's Kingdom design for a new church will account for my weakness and His strength (spiritual gifts), my unique hard wiring (personality), and the internal Kingdom motivators that direct my actions (passions). Understanding these three will be the first step in knowing my unique calling and planting a Kingdom church out of that calling.

Coaching Questions

1. What from your past gives clues to identifying your spiritual gifts?

2. How can God use your personality for His purposes?

3. What situations or causes deeply move you more than others?

Chapter 12

Knowing My Context

The process of gaining an accurate understanding of my context is critical for a planter to successfully be able to start a self-sustaining and reproducing new church. If the planter is indigenous to the specific place that he is planting, many findings from such a process will actually be intuitive knowledge. If the planter is indigenous to a nearby context but not the specific community in which he is considering planting, then working through a community exegesis process is helpful. If the planter is a cross-cultural church starter moving across significant geographical and cultural distance, then a contextual learning process is vital.

Community exegesis is the process of digging out the operational realities within a context that are not readily observable on the surface. By unearthing these realities, a church planter can proceed with a sense of confidence that his strategy is contextually appropriate to the mission field. By neglecting this process, a church planter will often initiate a culturally inappropriate strategy that will make his task of gospel penetration much more difficult than it needs to be.

When exegeting a community, you are observing people and places as well as having conversations within cultural context. You have two goals in this process: First is identifying whether or not this community is in priority need of a new multiplying church presence; and, second, identifying what models and strategies would likely be effective in that context. If you are exegeting an urban context, the answer to the former question is almost always "yes." In some suburban and many rural contexts, the question of church density is something to prayerfully consider. An accurate answer to the latter question is likely only obtainable through numerous conversations in the field.

There is no doubt that modern missiologists have significantly advanced this discussion among the church-planting world. Before their voices, church-planting models were often forcibly pressed over a context with predictably disappointing results. Discouraging statements like this could be heard from the mouths of church planters as their U-Hauls were packed, locked, and gassed for departure, "We are leaving because unfortunately God is not ripening the harvest here."

Too often a Sovereign God was blamed for not doing His part when actually it was the church planter who failed to do his own homework.

Unfortunately, much of the missiological dialogue has been slanted toward the academic community and has not been extremely approachable for the average church planter. Barry Whitworth,[17] a good friend and colleague, has led in creating a system and culture that has established more than thirty (and climbing) Multiplying Church Centers in Pennsylvania. In Barry's systems of multiplication, he has developed a simple methodology to assist a planter in accurately understanding the heartbeat of a potential planting site. Much of the following process has been adapted from Barry's thinking.

How to Exegete a Community

There are four primary areas of focus in the process of community exegesis; these are gaining an accurate understanding of the *social, economic, physical,* and *spiritual* climate resident in that context. By carefully examining and gaining a clear contextual picture of a community, the planter will discover the degree of need within that context, as well as models and strategies that likely would be appropriate.

There are a few places online where a planter can obtain information about a prospective community. Websites[18] for helpful statistical data for either the United States or in Canada are readily available for gathering broad demographic information. The data collected on these sites is valuable in giving a general understanding of the area. However, data collection, albeit easy, is never an equivalent substitute for spending significant time among the people of that community. Only when you are personally engaged and interactive with that community can you truly understand the real story and determine how best to cooperate with the sovereign activity of God.

Under each domain we will go through a similar process: (1) Observation: What am I seeing? Looking beyond the superficial to understand how the community interacts. (2) Conversation: What am I really hearing? Asking good questions followed by the discipline of unfiltered listening without prejudice or presumption. (3) Implementation: In light of our learning, what probable steps should a planter take? This is the task of making initial and nonbinding strategic recommendations. By carefully rolling out this investigative process through the spheres of the social, economic, physical, and spiritual domains of a community, the planter will be well armed to construct a contextually appropriate strategy.

1. Social

The social structures of a community have significant and vital information to instruct our thinking. Since our divine assignment is to introduce a relational gospel (relationship with Jesus), we need to accurately understand how relationships are understood by the culture we are trying to reach. We can try to gain greater understanding of this through:

OBSERVATION (WHAT DO I SEE?)

- What kind of interaction is happening between the different generations?
- What is the diversity (socioeconomic, ethnic) of the community, and is it interactive or isolated?
- What groups appear to be slipping between the social cracks?
- How do people connect with one another, their community, their state or province, and the world?
- Are they open or resistant to interaction with outsiders?
- If they have an outsider's mentality, who is seen as an outsider?
- Who are the influential people or organizations in business/ manufacturing, schools/colleges/universities, financial, government, health, and civic organizations?
- Gather the most recent data by visiting social organizations such as schools, police, hospitals, fire departments, and realtors.

CONVERSATION (WHAT DO I HEAR?)

- Talk with the noteworthy gatekeepers or power brokers. Ask them questions relating to the health of relationships in the community, as well as their perception of what is "going well" in the community and what could be "improved."

- Ask gatekeepers specific questions on social problems and how effectively they are being addressed.
- Ask people questions about their community:
  - Who lives in this community/neighborhood?
  - Are there pockets of people of an ethnic background in your community?
  - If so, where do they live?
  - Listen carefully to what is being said to clerks, waiters, and in general conversation in the community.
- Try to determine the lifestyles and worldviews people operate with. What significant cultures and institutions are part of the fabric of their lives?
- Are you noticing any new construction in the community? How do people view "new things" beginning in their area?

IMPLEMENTATION (WHAT SHOULD I DO?)

- Once you have a better understanding of people's attitudes toward the existing social structures of their community, you are positioned to give some early guidance for engagement.
- Of the gatekeepers, I found these people _____ to be open and willing to help us in building strategic relationships with the community.
- To reach a particular group of people, I would recommend contacting and building a relationship with _____.
- To become socially accepted into the community I believe a new person would be wise to _____ and to avoid doing _____.

2. Economic

Once we have gained an introductory understanding of the social climate of our community, we are ready to understand the financial environment that governs people's behavior. The economic structure of a community is significant because it can give the people either a sense of stability or instability, growth or decline. Understanding the economy of the area can also help you determine what the community generally values. People always invest their time and money in what they deem as important. Therefore, examining the economic implications of the context is far more involved than just demographic information on median incomes and education levels;

it needs to get to values. Here are a few ways you can discover the economic heartbeat of your community:

OBSERVATION (WHAT DO I SEE?)

- What evidence of struggle, despair, neglect, and alienation do you see?
- What evidence of wealth and prosperity do you see?
- Is the community growing, stable, slowly declining, or rapidly dying?
- Who determines public agendas—town council, churches, neighborhood associations, organizations?
- What are some noteworthy strengths or weaknesses in the following systems: public schools, housing, police services, health care, recreation?
- Does the community provide assistance for the needy?
- Is public transportation adequate?
- Are there service organizations for the children, elderly, singles?
- How well are homes in the community maintained?
- Are there "toys" in the driveway or yard? (boats, ATVs, RVs, pools, snowmobiles, large play yards, lavish landscaping)

CONVERSATION (WHAT DO I HEAR?)

- Ask questions of community leaders and residents like: "If your community had extra money, how would you like to see it be invested?" "If you had a week to put toward something you valued, what would that be?"
- What is the average time a person spends at work?
- What is the average commute to work for this community?
- Ask school personnel, "How actively do parents participate in the classroom, at events, in organizations?"
- When is the busiest time of day at the shopping center? Which day of the week is busiest?
- Ask local gyms how large their membership is and how full the gym is during the week, on the weekend?
- Investigate the types of entertainment venues in the area and what draws the largest crowds.

IMPLEMENTATION (WHAT SHOULD I DO?)

- Because the people of the area value _____, a way to reach and build relationships would be _____.
- A church planter who enjoys these activities—_____, _____, and _____—would be an asset to help build relational bridges.
- Because of the strength and stability (or instability and decline) of the economy, I recommend that we _____ and that we should never _____.

3. Physical

After we have scratched the surface of understanding the social and economic realities of our proposed context, it would be wise to next gain a deeper appreciation for the physical layout of the community. When trying to determine the location of where to start a new church, it becomes important to notice any geographic boundaries that may impede a new work. Also, what does the landscape tell you about the place and people? Emerging from your exegesis should be a determination on several crucial aspects: (1) how far people will travel to gather together; (2) if one church plant will have significant reach; (3) if you need to start multiple congregations to reach the breadth of the community; (4) whether any strategic ministry projects could help connect a new plant within the life of the community.

OBSERVATION (WHAT DO I SEE?)

- What are some of the public places provided?
  - Are they well kept?
  - Who are they provided for, and how well are they being used?
- Are some paths of travel avoided by some residents?
  - Does a railroad track, river, or mountain divert people's travel or separate communities?
- Are there duplicate businesses in a seemingly short distance?
- Where are the schools located?
- How far do people travel to get to the local health care?
- Where are local big-box stores located? (Walmart, Lowes, Home Depot, etc.)
  - Are smaller stores located between housing and big-box areas?
- How close in proximity are local grocery stores?

Conversation (What Do I Hear?)

- Ride public transportation, if available, and ask people why they choose to use it.
- Ask recreation facilities about the distance their members travel in order to participate.
- Ask people if they know of a place to eat on _____ (use a street across town that you know has restaurants) and see if they are familiar with the area.
- Ask if they know where there is _____ (a service provider) and take note of where they direct you.
- Another question may be, "Is there any place you would recommend I avoid while in your town? Why is that?"
- Ask, "What is the longest drive you would do weekly if it were something you wanted to attend?"
- Ask, "Is there a direction you don't want to drive to get somewhere? Why is that?"

Implementation (What Should I Do?)

- I believe a way to build a bridge into the community could be through a service project _____ (what, where, and why).
- It is most likely that a single church plant will reach a maximum radius of or geographic area of _____.
- I found that there are boundary lines of _____ (this could be geographic, transportation, or other) and cannot be crossed.
- Likely, we will need to be planning other plants in _____ and _____ because _____.

4. Spiritual

The fourth and final area of contextual investigation is that of the spiritual climate of the community. While all aspects of our exegetical process are designed to determine the activity of God, this one has a specific focus. We are now studying the community to learn how people have been spiritually engaged in the past and how that is affecting the current reality. When we speak of "spiritual," we are looking far beyond the bounds of evangelicalism to gain a sense of any forms of connection with a person's spiritual nature. Some communities have a palpable spiritual presence that is not divine in nature. What this often transports is a greater sense of darkness mixed with a frantic searching for God. Some communities have an indifferent spiritual worldview that allows for an easy acceptance of nontraditional and global religions. This indifference happens more frequently where populations are more diverse. All of the information you will gain in this learning process will be an incredible asset as you begin to pray through your gospel approach.

OBSERVATION (WHAT DO I SEE?)

- From the Christian churches you have discovered, are they growing, maintaining, or declining?
- How many churches are evangelistic in their purpose and plans? (Have programs/classes or events been intentionally designed to share the gospel?)
- What are the "spiritual" places in the community besides churches (mosques, temples, palm readers, Christian Science reading rooms, new-age shops)?
- Is the community giving to support causes (United Way, local needs)?
- Are there any Christian schools in the area?
- Are there any Christian nonprofit, parachurch, or social agencies in the area (halfway houses, single-parent homes, boys/girls clubs, support groups)?
    - Where are they located?
- Have I noticed any likely "people of peace" in the community?

CONVERSATION (WHAT DO I HEAR?)

- When visiting a Christian church ask:
    - "What significant spiritual markers in this community's history have affected the spiritual climate, either positively or negatively?"
    - "What demographics have churches in this community found difficult to reach?"
    - "What is their average age in attendance?"
    - "What types of outreach methods to the unchurched are they currently employing?"
    - "What is the most important lesson you have learned in serving your community?"
- Visit a local tattoo shop and ask them to tell you the most popular tattoo they do? Ask: "What themes seem to be the most popular to local customers?"
- Ask residents:

– "Where are the places of life, hope, and beauty in the community?"
– "If you were able to make one spiritual request, what would it be?"
– "In what ways do you sense God's presence where you live?"
– "What do you believe about God and Jesus Christ?"

IMPLEMENTATION (WHAT SHOULD I DO?)

- From my exploration I believe the spiritual climate for a new work is _____.
- There are deep spiritual wounds in this community from _____ and _____. Therefore I would recommend that we concentrate on _____ and avoid _____.
- Persons of peace I discovered were _____.
- From my observations the most underserved and spiritually hungry demographic in our community is _____.

Accurately understanding the context in which you will be planting will be the single most important learning you will ever tackle in the church-planting process. The church planter that approaches his community with no preset strategy, but instead with a humble and teachable spirit, will discover open avenues in which to effectively introduce the gospel of Jesus Christ. Labeling a community, as many have, as "a church-planting grave-yard" usually speaks more of the planters than the soil. By using your spiritual eyes, ears, and hands, the Holy Spirit will direct you in an intoxicating journey of redemption. God will ripen the harvest.

Coaching Questions

1. What have you learned through your initial community exegesis that surprised you?

2. What major learning from this chapter will you implement?

3. What adjustments will you make to your strategy based on what you are learning?

Chapter 13

Knowing My Father's Heart

How does a Kingdom leader accurately understand his Kingdom assignment? How does he know his Father's heart for a community? How can he design a strategy that is both contextually appropriate and that fits his unique call and personality? There are clues. Let me share a story and a little idea that came from that story.[19] Perhaps you will find it helpful.

I was asked to fly to Chile and share with a group of missionaries about what we had learned in our church-planting work in Toronto. Specifically I was asked to help this team gain a vision and strategy for their shared work.

The meeting was to be held in a retreat setting in an extremely isolated area high in the Andes Mountains. I had thought through some general ideas of what I would share but had nothing as solid as I would like. On the fourteen-hour plane ride, I asked God to give me something that would encourage these selfless leaders and perhaps help them discover His plan for their corner of the globe.

As I quieted my heart, God began to remind me of how He had directed my steps over the past years. With scratch pad and pen in hand, I began to jot down the process He brought to my mind. It became a simple algebraic formula. It expressed precisely the patterns I had seen and learned from many faithful leaders who have gone before me.

The time together seemed to encourage my missionary friends, and for that I was grateful. Over the years I have used this little idea numerous times to help church planters construct a strategy that could have a Kingdom punch. It is exciting to watch a leader replace a strategy pirated from another context with one spoken directly to his heart from the familiar voice of his King.

The effectiveness of this concept depends on an honest and accurate accounting of three critical pieces of information: (1) I must honestly understand *who* I am; (2) I must accurately understand *where* I am; and (3) I must decide *whose* I am. Let's look at the idea.

Who we are.   Where we are.   Whose we are.

God's Kingdom Vision = [(SG + Pa + Pe)   Context3*]   ASP
                                        Micro Intel.
                                        Macro Intel.
                                        Repro. Intel.

The first phase of discovery is an accurate understanding of who we are as leaders. This is the "SG + Pa + Pe" section of the formula. We have already discussed these ideas in chapter 11, "Knowing Myself," but to briefly refresh:

Spiritual gifts look backward to our past. We look at the sweeping themes of our personal histories, paying careful attention to the times where steps of faith have been taken and where God has shown up in remarkable ways. They most often correlate to our weaknesses, not our strengths.

Our *personalities* are the "hardwired" instincts that determine how we generally approach the world. It becomes the lens by which we take in information and formulate a reaction. Evolving over time but rarely drastically changing, they form the platform on which much of our ministry is built.

Passions are the deep places where God lights up His Kingdom priorities within our spirit. They are unique to us as individuals and often originate from past experiences in which we have been profoundly touched.

Together these three components form your spiritual, physical, and emotional makeup and should help you accurately answer the question of why God is calling you to a particular context.

The second phase of discovery is designed to correctly help us to know *where* we are. *Context³* speaks to three different forms of contextual reconnaissance that need to take place in order to discover helpful intelligence. What is necessary to be discovered in any context to effectively develop appropriate strategies is: (1) micro-intelligence, (2) macro-intelligence, and (3) reproduction intelligence. All of these will be discussed in much greater detail in subsequent chapters.

Micro-intelligence is discovering the normative way a Kingdom seeker in a particular context of culture finds his way to the King. In contexts that have had the benefit of much positive gospel seed sowing, it might be a fairly direct line between the pre-Christian and his or her confession of faith in Christ. Unfortunately, those areas seem to be increasingly rare.

If the context of culture has not had the advantage of soaking in a positive Christian environment, the Kingdom seeker's journey to Christ, most often, becomes a series of mini-decisions. These mini-decisions are the responses a pre-Christian makes in overcoming personal objections on the road to salvation. The typical hurdles this person encounters relate to his *heart*, his *mind*, and finally his *spirit*. Usually in that order. We will discuss this in much greater detail in chapter 15.

Macro-intelligence. If micro-intelligence aids us in understanding how an individual in a context of culture typically responds to Christ, macro-intelligence seeks to help us ascertain how groups of people may travel down that road. This reconnaissance becomes particularly strategic when planting an evangelistically effective church because it informs a planter where major portions of the population are "spiritually stuck."

Macro-intelligence gathers critical information to devise a tactical plan of operation. Again, the spiritual history of the landscape you are operating within will inform the new church plant on pressure points that will need extra spiritual attention. For instance:

If the culture of context has been burned over with negative exposure to Christianity, the *heart* objections are generally high. Strategies that aim at the mind or the spiritual resolve will usually be ineffective. The population's emotional barriers to the gospel need to be leveled first. Employing the ideas of micro-intelligence on a corporate scale will help a population group receive a different image of Christ and His followers.

In this stage a church plant can cultivate its field of context by addressing a generally understood *social fault line*[20] within its community. The self-less living out the implications of the gospel by lovingly addressing a broken point in a community will drastically reposition the future effectiveness of a new church. By engaging Kingdom seekers in the process, the evangelism process speeds up, and an emotionally healthy leadership base is developed for further ministry.

If macro-intelligence points to little negative exposure to Christianity but significant intellectual objections, our strategies need to adjust. The contexts of culture where *mind* barriers are highest are usually found in very secularized environments. Here there has been little contact with the gospel allowing multiple generations to ingrain and personalize the doctrines of secularization. They become culturally secularized.[21] Because this group is often incongruently both altruistically idealistic and sordidly practical, a two-pronged approach can be effective.

In their practical pursuits, standards have been lowered from the morality of "right and wrong" to a much shorter-term perspective of "what works." By alternating teaching themes between the practical benefits of living God's truth to straightforwardly addressing intellectual objections from a biblical worldview, many Kingdom seekers will find an appeal. In highly secularized environments people are not accustomed to authoritative teaching; when combined with a transparent humility, the Kingdom seeker often becomes spiritually intrigued. An open door for gospel sowing is swung wide.

To address altruistic idealism a church planter needs to create significant distance between his own positioning within the community and the notion that "church" brings to many Kingdom seekers. To many in this space, a self-serving collection of superficial saints is the disreputable image "church" connotes. By working hand in hand to address neglected social needs in a community, the Kingdom seeker not only gets to sense the repercussions of the gospel but also is placed in relationship with Christ followers to understand its Source. New ideas for "Christianity" and for "church" are formed in his mind—ideas that deeply impress him.

If macro-intelligence suggests that neither the barriers of the *heart* nor the *mind* exist, a straightforward harvesting approach would be appropriate. However, this context might be difficult to find.

Reproduction intelligence—and so a thorough reconnaissance of the context of culture has taken place with helpful discoveries for the best path that both individuals and groups travel toward the King. Now we are at the point of research to determine a multiplying plan with fewest cultural barriers for major Kingdom movement.

Reproductive intelligence considers the findings of both micro- and macro-intelligence and, within that framework, seeks to develop contextual systems of Kingdom-expanding reproduction as the primary outcome. In order to do this, a church planter will need to carefully build two strategies based on what he has learned: (1) a church-planting model, and (2) a church-planting multiplication system.

As we learned in chapter 10, "Exploring Models," there are church-planting models that better fit particular contexts and particular planters. By going through this process of knowing *who* I am and *where* I am, model selection becomes a much more intuitive process.

But how will that model best reproduce in your context? What is the best way to shape a new church culture for a Kingdom movement? As you will later discover in chapter 32, "Exploring Multiplication Systems," you have a few options to sort through.

Who are we? Where are we? Whose are we?

God's Kingdom Vision = [(SG + Pa + Pe) Context³*] ASP

ASP—Absolute Surrender in Prayer. And now the rubber hits the road. We have spent time in honest reflection discovering the uniqueness of our fascinating and complex selves. God's creative investment in each of us demands far more than a less-than-perfect reproduction of someone else's life mission. God has something to say about His desires through our weaknesses and His strength manifested through our lives in a truly spiritual gift. His fingerprints on our personality give hint to a Kingdom design. Couple these with a unique passion that we cannot shake off, and we begin to see a picture of the kind of Kingdom leader God is asking us to become.

There is no one quite like you.

And then we have thought carefully about what it might be like to be a Kingdom seeker in the contexts where we live. We have imagined the possible barriers that block him from gaining a clear view of Jesus. We have pulled the lens back from that tight focus and tried to imagine a ministry design that would become a clearly marked path for groups of Kingdom seekers in our varied contexts to travel to Jesus. More than likely our paradigms of church are being stretched.

Taking all this contextual information into account, we began to think about what a church that majored on the Kingdom idea of reproduction might look like—systems well designed to produce a steady flow of Kingdom-centric results measured in new believers, new disciple makers, new communities of faith, and a transforming effect on our communities. We begin to see that this will not be a church design copied from a conference.

Likely there will be no church plant quite like yours either.

And this takes us to our third and final exercise. Absolute surrender in prayer.

We lay down everything we know about ourselves and everything we know about our contexts and declare our exclusive allegiance to the King of the Kingdom. *"Your Kingdom come, Your will be done through me, and in me."*

To shape a new church that becomes a Kingdom movement, what you desire above all is to know your Father's heart.

Coaching Questions

1. What have you learned about God's "creative investment" in you?

2. How does this influence your unique approach to church planting?

3. What steps will you take over the next thirty days to increase your "ASP"?

Part 4: **Communication**

In the first year of marriage, most husbands and wives begin to understand that communication is an exceedingly complex process. In the ordinary process of choosing a restaurant, you are forced to reconcile with this ominous complexity. There is simple language of words and intended meanings, there are love languages,[22] there is body language, and there are code words that are like hidden fields filled with live land mines that you are in the painful process of discovering. One seemingly benign comment about dinner can elicit completely unexpected responses. A single year of marriage teaches most people that communication is not easy. It is definitely a two-way street.

So, if a year of marriage can be so instructive on the complexity of communication, shouldn't that complication be expected to grow exponentially as we scale up the involvement from two to many? Very likely.

So how should an effective church planter proceed?

First, we need to rid ourselves of the notion that there is a single preferred way to communicate to everyone. Just as married people learn the preferred communication patterns of their spouse, planters need to adapt their communication style to their context.

In this section we will discover: (1) the importance of communication and how to understand the process, (2) understanding my varied audiences and learning the communication needs they require, (3) church planting preaching and what distinguishes it from classic preaching, (4) how to effectively communicate vision so that people want to join the journey with you.

Chapter 14

The Importance of Communication

Our English word *communication* originally came from the Latin *commūnicāre*, which means "to share." This sharing is the process of conveying information through the exchange of ideas, feelings, intentions, attitudes, expectations, or perceptions. This complex process is simply transmitted through ordinary vehicles such as speech, writings, and nonverbal behavior. At its center, communication is the meaningful exchange of ideas in relationship.

For effective communication to take place, four distinct components are required: a *sender*, a *message*, a *medium*, and a *recipient*. A church planter will spend considerable time thinking through these four components and, subsequently, develop a communication strategy that productively appreciates the characteristics of each. The communication process is only successfully completed when the receiver understands the sender's intended message. This simple task is actually more multifaceted than often observed.

For the church planter, of the four components in communication, two are *static* and two are *dynamic*. The static components are the *message* and the *recipient*. The gospel message does not change, nor should the sender expect the receivers (a lost audience) to adapt in order to accommodate our sacred preferences. A gospel-centered planter will defer his own communication preferences for the sake of a spiritually uninitiated audience. As the planter Paul modeled for us, "To the weak I became weak, that I might win the weak. I have become all things to all people, that by all means I might save some. I do it all for the sake of the gospel, that I may share with them in its blessings" (1 Cor. 9:22–23).

The dynamic components of communication are the *sender* and the *medium*. Since the message is unchanging (namely the core gospel message), and the recipients, like the lost sheep in Jesus' parable (Luke 15:3–7) are stuck and worthy of heroic measures, what is left in the process to flex and adapt is the sender and his medium. Patterning ourselves after the humility of Christ should inspire any church planter to a radical condescension from his own sacred rights and preferences to a place where he truly *tabernacles* (see John 1:14) where lostness lives. Language, tone, style, garb, and venue partialities all bend their collective knees to the greater mission of effectively communicating good news.

Communicating with any audience involves three principle steps:

1. Concept

An idea exists in the mind of the church planter (sender) that may come in the form of weighty information, a strident passion, or a nagging feeling. The church planter spends time processing and organizing his concept into a logical argument (message).

2. Encoding

Next, a message is constructed and sent (medium) to a receiver in carefully selected words or other symbols. At this point the influence of the communicator is officially completed. He now takes the station of a passive observer watching with interest as the next step unfolds.

3. Decoding

Finally, the audience (receiver) translates the words, symbols, tone, and body language into a notion that makes the most sense to him. This decoding may or may not be the intended meaning of the sender, but this is what has been communicated. If the communication process is designed with some kind of feedback loop, a miscommunicated idea can be corrected.

A church planter will communicate in many ways: preaching, social media, teaching, written correspondence, edited video, group facilitation, counseling, printed media, and interviews—to name a few. In each he should carefully consider his audience and skillfully craft his message and presentation style in accordance with the emotional, intellectual, and spiritual needs of the recipients.

The process of communication is much more dynamic and fluid than those advocating for uniformity in a specific preaching style seem to appreciate. Honing some soft skills that move a communicator from far less "telling" to far more "relating" will quickly advance his believability and efficacy with those who have lived their entire lives outside the sacred subculture. Church planters that become successful communicators rehearse this process repeatedly until it becomes instinctive.

And so the task of the church planter is simple, yet requires the humility and tenacity of the most faithful of missionaries. He starts by getting into the skin of his audience to learn biases, longings, and areas of deep generational woundedness. He then goes to the timeless Word of God to discover unchangeable truths that speak to the yearnings of his audience. Next, he shapes a message that interests his audience and leads them to the Source of all. Finally, he genuinely relates to his audience as he captivatingly communicates God's powerful message characterized by an authentic spirit of grace and truth.

In this exchange communication goes much deeper than surface levels of intellectual truths and ideas but travels from the preacher deep into the souls of his hearers through the quiet work of the Holy Spirit.

It's much more than a sermon.[23]

Coaching Questions

1. How is your church-planting audience different from audiences of your past?

2. What adjustments are needed to move from a "telling" to a "relating" style?

3. What steps can you to take to "get into the skin" of your new audience?

Chapter 15

Understanding My Audiences

As we have already discussed, a "one size fits all" communication style is certain to alienate any audience that is not culturally connected to communication patterns that may be "comfortable" and "easy" for me. The assignment of the selfless church planter is to leave comfortable and easy behind and begin to look at his message through the lens of his audience.

In a colorful metaphor of athletics, Paul described his personal discipline in ministry. In his imagery he spoke of skill, self-control, targeting, and productive effort: "Do you not know that in a race all the runners run, but only one receives the prize? So run that you may obtain it. Every athlete exercises self-control in all things. They do it to receive a perishable wreath, but we an imperishable. So I do not run aimlessly; I do not box as one beating the air" (1 Cor. 9:24–26).

To Paul, his Kingdom ministry assignment from Christ was worthy of his best efforts. He was skillful in his work; he ran to win. He gave up easy and comfortable by exercising self-control over what was second nature. His efforts were focused and targeted and did not run without aim and direction. Finally Paul gave testimony to the fact that he tried not to waste time and energy as a boxer beating the air. He made his punches connect. What were all this effort, discipline, and focus for?

The context of this metaphor in athletics drops immediately after Paul's extensive description of his contextual agility. His communication style always adapted to his audience's needs: "I have become all things to all people, that by all means I might save some. I do it all for the sake of the gospel, that I may share with them in its blessings" (1 Cor. 9:22–23).

So, following in the example of Paul, we will take a brief look at how and why a church planter may desire to customize his communication style in accordance to the needs of four different strategic audiences: pre-Christians, community influencers, a core group and congregation, and lastly, potential and invested partnerships.

Pre-Christians

If the primary assignment of a church planter is evangelism (especially in the first stages of his plant), then it follows that he may want to become somewhat adept in communicating with a spiritually uninitiated audience.

It should be troubling to a potential gospel-centered church planter that far too often his colleagues, while claiming to be gospel centered, build their new churches on foundations of the already evangelized. Planters passionately claiming a "call to preach," assemble an audience of starving saints to whom they can weekly deliver their gospel-centered sermons. The rationalization goes like this: "There are no true Bible-believing, gospel-preaching churches in my community. Christ followers are hungry for the deep teaching of the Word of God. I need to rescue these disciples from their captivity in all these lesser churches, nourish them, and transform them into strong, healthy disciples." Our proud declarations sound much like a prophet of old.[24]

And so our selfless mission of multiplication is vulgarly mutated into a selfish process of division. Neglecting the lost sheep, we tirelessly work to gain our fair share of the prepenned ninety-nine. If our communication strategy is subtly nuanced to create a spirit of discontent in the sheep pen, we know our sights are squarely aimed on wooing previously found sheep to our better brand.

If my communication dollars are directed to the sacred media and my message is designed to elicit a response from the preevangelized, then I have positioned myself in the community as a church for the already churched. "Come with your well-marked Bible in hand and you'll fit in fine." I may convince myself that this audience can be transformed into a gospel-engaging movement, but it's unlikely that I will convince them. I have attracted consumers by the superior bait I have offered. I now face a lifetime of "deep" feeding with little hope of seeing any return on investment. I have planted a church, but my work has not expanded the Kingdom of God.

I chose the term *pre-Christian* to describe a Kingdom seeker for two reasons. First, it speaks of faith. An effective church planter will always see his city as "fields white and ready for a harvest" and not "a dark and difficult field, doubtful to produce a harvest." When I hear a planter speak habitually about the difficulty of his soil, I have found that it usually correlates with little evangelistic fruit. Conversely, when I hear a planter, who is working in the same context, speak frequently of the spiritual opportunities that surround him, it usually associates with an ongoing harvest. What makes this difference?

When we look at the lost through the eyes of the Holy Spirit, we tend to see potential more than depravity. When we see that same audience through the weakness of our flesh, a human-centered strategy, and an untested gospel, we tend to instinctively recoil and downgrade the object of Christ's supreme affections to a miserable category of the debauched and indifferent.

The soil wasn't different, just the farmers.

The second reason I use this term is that the description "pre-Christian" can help us accurately think of evangelism as more of a process than an isolated event. Seldom does a church planter find himself in a context where the lost are collectively prepared as a city spiritually saturated with low-hanging fruit. Usually the spiritual readiness of the harvest is wide and varied.

In most cases the lost have not had the advantage of soaking in a positive Christian environment; therefore, their journey to Christ most often becomes a series of mini-decisions. These mini-decisions are the responses a pre-Christian makes in overcoming personal objections on the road to salvation. The typical hurdles a person encounters relate to his heart, his mind, and finally his spirit. The task of the church planter is to communicate in a manner that recognizes these realities and fashions a message and a manner that assists the pre-Christian in overcoming each barrier.

First Barrier: The Heart

If a prebeliever has had a negative experience with a professing Christian, or from a church, there is generally an emotional roadblock that prevents him from being open to the gospel. This *emotional barrier,* from the perspective of the Kingdom seeker, is generally much taller and wider than any picture of Christ that can be painted with a harvesting-intended gospel presentation. If a lost person's negative experiences lead him to the sincere conclusion that Christians are hypocrites, then a hard-selling evangelism approach will often be found as offensive and counterproductive.

This is the stage where communication is designed as an implement for cultivation.

In this stage the church planter must be able to communicate several messages simultaneously to his pre-Christian audience. First, he must position himself, and the assembly he is gathering, as a leader and community that is imperfect but authentic. Admitting a weakness is often an effective means of opening a door for a greater strength. Second, he communicates that the mission he and this church are on is one designed to help restore the brokenness of their community. In communicating the redemptive mission of the church, you often capture the altruistic impulses found in Kingdom seekers. Third, communication focuses on the inclusion of a pre-Christian audience into the Kingdom assignment of the church. A permeable membrane on the outer edges of the spiritual community you are building will allow for pre-Christian participation. For most belonging precedes believing.

Second Barrier: The Mind

If the pre-Christian has intellectual difficulties with the tenets of the gospel, no slick preaching techniques can induce a genuine and wholehearted commitment to Christ. If a person believes Christianity is no better or worse than any other religion—if there is a God, then all roads must lead to Him—then communication that pressures for a decision is premature and probably unhelpful. Real questions require real answers. Fortunately for the church planter the Word of God is filled cover to cover with real answers.

This is the stage where communication is designed as a tool for sowing.

In this stage the pre-Christian must, in relationship, hear and understand an alternate reality to his long-held intellectual difficulties. A patient, gentle, and careful explanation of the gospel and its implications will chip away at this barrier until one day the Kingdom seeker realizes that he no longer holds his former ideas. The Word of God has transformed his long-held worldview, and he is moments away from losing the prefix on his title, pre-Christian.

Third Barrier: The Will

With the leveling of both *heart* and *mind* barriers, the pre-Christian is emotionally and intellectually prepared to genuinely respond to the gospel's invitation with a whole and sincere heart. The lone barrier that stands is one of volition. Communication designed for the art of reaping is now entirely appropriate.

This is the stage where communication is designed as an instrument for harvesting.

Here the church planter acts much like a midwife in this new birth of the Holy Spirit. The Kingdom seeker has been on a journey that has overcome objections that had distanced his heart from the message of Christ. In becoming open to the messenger, he has become open to the message. He has laid down intellectual challenges and instead picked up clear biblical teachings that have relieved his restless mind. For the first time in his life, because of patience and sensitive communication, the Kingdom seeker can see a true picture of Christ's love. He is ready to respond.

The communication rhythm of a church planter toward his pre-Christian audience needs to be one of patience, humility, and visible honesty. Dropping the old ecclesiological lingo and replacing it with a glossary jammed full of trendy and chic jargon might be attractive at first but will quickly wear thin if not backed up by the authentic substance the lost crave so deeply.

A great resource for approaching pre-Christians with the gospel is the 3 Circles Life Conversation Guide. A free app provides access to a gospel presentation via iPhones (Apple App Store), iPads, and Android (Google Play) devices.

The strength of this tool is that the gospel conversation centers on brokenness, a place where pre-Christians can connect (as well as Christians). With corresponding resources, using 3 Circles with small groups and on the Sunday morning platform is simple and technologically impressive.

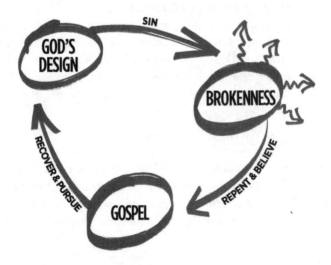

Using a tool like 3 Circles provides a common language for presenting the gospel everywhere, particularly to those with different worldviews. It is far beyond a memorized script; it becomes a discipling tool for people to hear, see, understand, and explain the gospel. The corresponding book *Life on Mission: Joining the Everyday Mission of God* by Dustin Willis and Aaron Coe helps disciples grow in their daily understanding of God's mission.

In the same way the first-century world was introduced to the glory of God in the incarnation, so the twenty-first century world needs desperately to hear the gospel communicated in both grace and truth. To a postmodern world that has grown contemptuous toward a mean-spirited faith and dismissive toward lukewarm spirituality, there lays a large and open door for a church planter to gently and sincerely communicate the greatest news of all.

Community Influencers

When one begins to dream about his future church plant, many thoughts and images come flashing to mind. Dreams of packed worship halls, brilliant music, baptisms, and living rooms filled with eager disciples easily spring to one's imagination.

But have you ever dreamed about your reputation?

Interesting question. The follow-up question should be, "Reputation among whom?" Normally, when a church thinks about its reputation, it thinks about its perceived standing among the Christian community in its local geography. Categories are subdivided so that more can claim victory in the high stakes competition, "Our church is known for its warm and welcoming community." Others boast, "Our church may not be that warm and fluffy, but it's the only place in town that delivers deep expository preaching." Still others brag, "Our church may not have long-winded sermons, but it is known everywhere for its passionate, Spirit-filled worship." And so it goes. Each sacred assembly staking out their "corner of the market" in accordance to their own highest ecclesiastical value.

But what if our reputation among the sacred crowd was not our supreme fascination? What if we were honestly more concerned with how the unchurched in our community saw us? How might a desire for an amazing reputation among the non-church-going crowd shape our communication plans?

In most every community there exists a substantial group of socially healthy leaders who rarely attend a Sunday service but who regularly invest their time, treasures, and talents in the dark and broken places of society (hidden places that often go unnoticed by the Sunday crowd). With a mixed bag of motives, these community leaders sacrificially mingle into their busy schedules a variety of altruistic activities designed to make their world a better place.

If you knew there was an untapped audience in your community that was emotionally warm to Kingdom activities, how might that affect your communication strategy? What reputation would you want to cultivate to elicit their interest?

My Core Team

Almost all would agree that the first stages of church planting involves a concentrated effort in assembling and developing a core team that will serve as the leadership and workforce for many operations within the new plant. It would seem logical to many that the way to proceed in assembling this team would be to stack the core with as many long-term stalwarts of the faith as we can muster. Intuitively we reverse-engineer our end game—that is, a self-sustaining congregation—and assemble the pieces that will take us to that high and lofty objective. We need a consistent cash flow, so we need tithers. The bigger, the better. Check. We need people who understand church, so we need churchmen. Check. We need people who understand Christ's mission, so we need mission-hearted believers. Check. And we need experienced leaders, so we need people who have held sacred leadership positions. Check. We sell hard for several months in an attempt to accumulate as large a core as possible. Of course we screen for caustic character issues, but our leading objectives are mass and innate proficiency.

By gathering the sacred pieces that will take us on the shortest route to self-sustainability, we may simultaneously be gathering the pieces that will lead us to evangelistic sterility. What does this impeccably pedigreed core team have in common? They likely have few deep relationships outside the community of faith, and they likely have numerous religious preferences that will erect high and insurmountable social barriers to the gospel.

From day one the church planter will be struggling to communicate two opposite messages to his core team: The first being, "You'll have to sacrifice for a while, but we will eventually build a church you will love." The second being, "This mission is not about worship services and brilliant religious experiences; it is about the healing of people, families, our city, and our world." These are two divergent messages that are impossible to balance to anyone's satisfaction.

Often the well-churched come preloaded with an unwritten contract, "We'll put up with many strange things as long as it leads to something we are familiar with." Even a signed statement of core values that intricately describes the mission and means of the new church rarely trumps the unwritten contract initiated members have tucked away in the small print of their study Bibles. Eventually the discontented will gather together and demand that their prophet lead them back to Egypt (see Exod. 14:11–12).

Communication within an ecclesiastically seasoned core team presents another fatal difficulty. If the *raison d'etre*[25] of the church is to be an evangelistically effective community of faith, this can become a problematic assignment for two reasons. First, as we have already mentioned, usually the well-churched have few meaningful relationships outside their subculture. It's not that they are philosophically against including the unchurched in this new network of friendships; it's just that long ago they have emotionally distanced themselves from these friendships. All their free time has been spent at church. A percentage of the core team might rise to the challenge and begin to reestablish significant relationships outside of church, but the majority will not rewrite their long-term habits of preference.

The second communication problem implicit in evangelistic engagement among a long-evangelized core is an issue of biblical and theological mastery. If the vast majority of the core team is somewhat familiar with the Scriptures, they unintentionally send an unhelpful signal to those who are not. For example, in a small-group study, the team is careful to drop the hallowed jargon and speak normally as they delve into the Word. If one of the group innocently comments, "That reminds me of another time in the Bible when Jesus met the woman at the well" (see John 4:1–26), instinctively the rest of the group nod their heads in agreement and begin to further elaborate on this insightful discovery. Well, almost all. If there was an unchurched person in that group, he immediately discovered that he did not fit in. He was a spiritual first-grader who mistakenly stuck his head into a university class. He had no idea who the "woman at the well" was and how these two biblical ideas meshed. What was unintentionally communicated was that, although he was warmly welcomed, he just didn't fit in. Consequently, unless he is extroverted, emotionally self-secure, and deeply spiritually hungry, he is unlikely to stick with the group.

Getting inside the skin of those who we are trying to reach should help inform the makeup of our core team. If the core group ratio of the "well-seasoned veterans of the faith" to "spiritual newbies" is heavily tipped toward the veterans, the uninitiated will tend to bounce off in high percentages. The "stickiness" of the unchurched to the group will be directly correlated to the degree to which they see themselves in the composition of the team. The more the team reflects the community they are trying to reach, the more effective the team will be in reaching it.

So the church planter's communication strategy in assembling a core team needs to accommodate the spiritual, emotional, and experiential needs that exist within his audience. A group of Kingdom seekers who have not yet pledged allegiance to King Jesus will find tremendous value in participating in the Kingdom mission. Of course there is a need for an "informal inner core" of deeply spiritual Kingdom expanders to help the planter navigate the road ahead, but this informal core should not long outnumber those who are beginning their Kingdom journey. Core-group ratios tilted toward pre-Christians will serve the planter well in getting traction within his city.

My Partners

For many church planters, gathering a team of supporting allies around the vision is not a luxury but an unqualified necessity. These partners may be individual believers, local congregations, denominational structures, or church-planting networks. This auxiliary network often includes prayer support, financial support, and human resources support. A network such as this, along with an emotionally invested and engaged "sending church," often spells the difference between success and failure for a church planter.

Effective communication skills become essential for both enlisting and maintaining helpful partnerships for the mission. Since the majority of these partnerships, quite likely, will not be confined to the local geography where you are planting, a communication strategy becomes helpful. Although not comprehensive, the following is a list of communication hints, as well as land mines to avoid, all designed to preserve the integrity of your partnerships.

Communicate Simply

Speak the language of your partners. As a planter you likely have read more on missiology in the last twelve months than many of your partners have in a lifetime. Avoid "trade-speak." If your strategy is designed around "missional communities," refer to them as "small groups" or "Bible studies." For most, large-group gatherings can be more easily understood as "worship services" than as "community celebrations." Skip cool when communicating to your partners.

Communicate Regularly

Believe it or not, most of your partners deeply desire to hear from you. Your communication with them is a source of joy and satisfaction. Although you may be miles away, when they hear from you, they gain a renewed sense of bonding and investment. At the same time do not overcommunicate. A weekly plea shrouded as an "update" will soon lose its influence with your partners. As graphic artists know, if everything is in bold, nothing is in bold. Strike a happy medium in the frequency of your communications.

Communicate Briefly

Long, elaborate communications usually send no message or, worse, the wrong message. Most will simply not read a protracted description of all the events happening in the life of your plant. Get to the point quickly. Lengthy and overdone communication sends the message. Two well-written paragraphs are far more valuable than two pages of information.

Communicate Honestly

As a church planter, you probably tend to be optimistic. This can be both a blessing and a curse. If your optimism leads you to "round up" with your figures, it will be inspiring for others at first but will eventually be the end of your credibility. Be honest. When you are facing a big spiritual battle, lead others to pray with you through it. In your honesty they will truly become partners with you in the gospel.

Communicate Spiritually

Help your partners visibly see the spiritual battle you are engaged in. Speak with faith. Sometimes in the process of communicating faith to others, God renews our own faith. Don't let your communication degenerate into dollars and cents, programs and strategies; let your partners sense the activity of God.

Communicate Unselfishly

This Kingdom vision really isn't about you. It's actually not really about the church that you are starting. It is about the Kingdom assignment of unleashing a wave of God's reign across the community that you are starting in—and way beyond. Advocate for the planter across town that has few supporting partners. Advocate for the young leader that is joining you to apprentice as another planter in your city. Let your partners see that your heart is way bigger than your church plant—it is for the Kingdom of God.

Communicate Inspiringly

You may not know it yet, but God is setting you up for some of the greatest "God stories" you will ever experience. The two things most potential church planters do not have are the two things that are critical for success; people and resources. Few Christian leaders ever go on the journey you are about to go on. To get from "nothing" to a "Kingdom movement" requires innumerable faith steps and the most stirring miracles of God. As you share these stories, you inspire faith in your partners, and you validate the spiritual credibility of your Kingdom vision.

Communicate Gratefully

One of the most observable signs of an emotionally healthy leader is gratitude. It simultaneously demonstrates humility, interdependence, and wholesome indebtedness. When communicated honestly, heartfelt gratitude actually inspires more generosity while a spirit of entitlement inspires detachment. Communicate in such a way that your partners not only see the words of gratitude but actually feel your thankful spirit every time they are in your presence, either physically or through your correspondence.

Coaching Questions

1. Which audience are you most comfortable communicating with?

2. Which audience are you the least comfortable communicating with?

3. How can you improve your communication with the least comfortable audience?

Chapter 16

Church Planting Preaching

The title of this chapter might have piqued the interest of some and the skeptical eye of others. "Church planting preaching?" some are quietly asking, "How can the sacred process of proclaiming the timeless and infallible Word of God to His people be different in a church plant than in a well-established church?"

As I have had the privilege of spending much time with church planters across North America, I have seen some who have intuitively grasped that there is indeed a difference and communicate directly to the hearts of their audience with candor and precision. I have also seen many who could not. I have heard eloquent messages that sounded eerily familiar to what John Piper or Henry Blackaby might have effectively preached but to an audience that seemed inattentive and uninspired. What accounts for the difference? John Piper and Henry Blackaby had their audiences leaning forward, engaged, busy taking notes on a weekly basis, and deeply spiritually moved. So, why does it feel so bizarre and ill fitting in a church plant? Is it the gymnasium? Maybe it's the music stand? Would a proper pulpit normalize the strangeness?

The fact that this discussion has been largely neglected leaves most church planters with little more than their personal experience to navigate an approach to preaching. If a planter has had the privilege of soaking in a church plant under a skillful communicator, he has numerous advantages as he approaches his own craft. Intuitively he sees his audience differently from the average preacher. He sees his biblical applications differently. And because of this learned sensitivity, his approach to preaching is radically different.

Let's start with our audience.

Most sermons experienced by a potential church planter were presented in the context of an established church. That means that most of the messages we have experienced were delivered to an audience with a thoroughly Christian worldview with all of the implicit assumptions therein. There is often an evangelistic appeal somewhere in the message, but it's presented with the assured confidence that the vast majority of the hearers are well experienced with the main themes of faith and culture of that assembly. Prayerfully, this is not the context you will be experiencing as a church planter.

For most planters, if they are engaging the constituency of their context, the audience they will assemble will look, think, and behave much differently from the long-standing crowd attending church across the street. Their operating system filters information much differently from those who have made Sunday worship part of their routine. Statements that would inspire comfort, nodding heads, and muffled "amens" to churchmen rouse irritation and disengagement to their less religious neighbors.

Not many ethical futurists saw this coming, but the defining cultural issue of this generation that separates the secular populace from their sacred neighbors is human sexuality. Convictional Christians and cultural secularists have deepened the divide of communication and understanding through the radically divergent ways each group approaches this subject.

Convictional Christians see this issue as a biblical issue. The Bible has clear and unmistakable teachings on homosexuality, and part of the package of being a Christ follower is to resist the impulse of aligning with the changing tides of culture and remain faithful to the Word of God. To Christians the issue is not easy, but it is simple.

Nominal Christians (men and women who associate with the Christian label but whose lives do not pattern the teachings of Scripture) and cultural secularists (irreligious men and women who have not thought deeply about the sources of their ideas but their opinions are informed by the culture that surrounds them) approach this issue entirely different. To Christians this is an issue of Scripture. To the nominal and secular, this is an issue of justice. Their worldview elevates the equality of all as the highest good and observes the Christian position on homosexuality as an unjust relic from a much darker era of human history.

If this is true, how should our proclamation methodology adjust for the sake of an audience who desperately needs to experience the gospel of Christ? How should we adapt for the sake of the gospel? Somehow the preacher needs to get into the skin of his audience and hear his message from their spot on the pew. As he invests the time and energy, not simply associating with the unchurched but building deep friendships with the unchurched, he will gain a far better understanding and sensitivity on how to approach the preaching process with a congregation that includes large groups of secular Kingdom seekers. This again will look, sound, and feel much differently from the long-established church across the street. It has to.

So church-planting preaching is different from other sorts of preaching in that the preacher is keenly aware that his audience is not conditioned with a Christian worldview, and therefore his cultural sensitivity needs to be dialed up significantly. He deeply desires to get a proper hearing for the gospel from his audience before they emotionally and intellectually "check out" from a loaded assumption casually lobbed in their direction. For an effective communicator this is an opportunity for a graceful explanation of how a Kingdom culture builds a better society. Instead of seeking the kneejerk "amens" from the religiously predisposed by railing against the darkness, he instead paints a far more enticing picture of Light. Everything in the universe was designed for the Kingdom of God, and as the preacher speaks of an alternate reality to the brokenness that is commonly experienced, the Spirit bears witness with the grace and truth of the message spoken. Old lies are abandoned. New truths are obeyed. Lives are transformed.

With sensitivity deeply imbedded in the heart of the preacher, his approach to constructing a message often differs significantly. He will come at it from varying approaches, styles, and methods, but you often see five similar ingredients weaving through effective church planters' patterns of preaching. These five ingredients are: framing the issue, giving a biblical answer, making two types of applications, introducing a bigger problem, and finally, providing an opportunity for resolution. Let's take a closer look at each.

Frame the Issue

This first step is universal with effective communicators. In some way the audience needs to understand that what is about to be communicated is not only spiritually substantial but has direct relevance to their lives. By diving in prematurely with an introduction like, "Today we will be continuing our series through Romans by picking up in chapter 2 with a message called, 'God's Righteous Judgment,'" he may be about to launch a thoroughly biblically accurate message, but he unintentionally prioritized his sermon above his audience. His audience is not spiritually, emotionally, or biblically prepared to process what is about to emanate from the platform.

What if, instead of starting with the sermon, the preacher started with his audience? From that same passage he introduces his message with a thoughtful question, like, "Have you ever felt like your prayers never made it past the ceiling?" He spends a few precious moments personally relating to thoughts and emotions that all in the room have experienced. After he has identified with his audience, he has an auditorium full of people spiritually and emotionally ready to go on a journey with him. From that point, from the same passage in Romans, he preached a message that contrasts the emptiness and devastation of man-made religion against the life-giving reality of a relationship with God. He ends by powerfully describing the marks of a true relationship with God.

When we start with the audience instead of the sermon, we will find ourselves naturally thinking of ways to help them see and feel their need for the answer Scripture gives. Once they have been personally reminded of that need, their hearts and minds are far more open and ready to receive the answer. Effective church-planting preachers normally begin by framing the issue in the souls of their audience before ever rolling up their sleeves to explain the answer.

Give a Biblical Answer

At this point, church-planting preaching parallels classic expository preaching in numerous ways. With the firm conviction that the unchanging Word of God speaks powerfully to the lives of twenty-first century issues, the preacher approaches his craft with the care and precision of a surgeon as he carefully exposes the eternal Words of God to the temporal situations of man. With the confidence that the Holy Spirit is guiding and empowering the entire experience, the preacher feels released to freely share deep and troubling concepts knowing that his words are being propelled by far more than skillful communication techniques.

If the audience of the church planter reflects the constituency of his local community more than the constituency of those who generally attend religious assemblies, the spirit of how the biblical answer is communicated is highly significant. Taking a lesson from our earlier discussion on the character of Christ, the preacher will want to, as closely as possible, emulate his King as one who is full of grace and truth.

The unchurched are familiar with the polar extremes. When they think of "preaching," images of isolated grace (which is not grace), or isolated truth (which is not truth) often spring to their minds. They think of angry preachers wagging their fingers and frothing at the mouth while they righteously declare "truth." Or they have images of Oprah-esque "grace" preachers softly saying sweet nothings as they dish out their weekly diet of lump-free pabulum. What they rarely see is a man of God, kindly and intelligently sharing the Word of God through a gentle and believable manner. When they see in the eyes of the preacher that this is not a sermon being preached but a message being lived and passed on, the audience's skepticism evaporates, and the Holy Spirit has much to work with.

It also may be noteworthy in this discussion of "giving a biblical answer" that we learn from Jesus and His disciples in "how" they communicated eternal truths. When you look at the teaching ministry of Jesus and the example of preaching in the book of Acts, you see messages that are generously illustrated with stories, validating testimonies, and contemporary parables. What should we learn from them about biblical preaching? By carefully and creatively constructing stories and images that further reinforce the deep biblical truths in memorable ways, we might more closely find ourselves preaching like Jesus. Stories and illustrations are not doctrinal "fluff" but are powerful tools in gaining understanding and acceptance of life-and-death concepts. Failing to follow in Jesus' teaching example will leave much of our audience uninformed, uninspired, and unengaged.

Make Double Applications

Perhaps this point is the single greatest distinguishing factor between church-planting preaching and the preaching with which we are most familiar.

We have been long conversant with the necessity of helping our audience navigate the path toward personal application. There is a familiar Christian saying, "The Bible was not given to increase our knowledge but to change our lives." This quote, often attributed to the evangelist D. L. Moody, captures an important truth about our relationship with God's Word. The Bible was never given to us for our information but for our transformation. There must be an application of spiritual truths in order to see a transformation in our spiritual lives. In other words sacred knowledge not personally applied is sacred only to darkness. Light demands a much more honest application. So biblical application to the lives of his audience becomes a priority for the preacher. Many help reinforce this practice by refusing to ever entitle a sermon point as a "fact" but only as an application. Imagine that you were going to teach from Philippians 1:

> I want you to know, brothers, that what has happened to me has really served to advance the gospel, so that it has become known throughout the whole imperial guard and to all the rest that my imprisonment is for Christ. And most of the brothers, having become confident in the Lord by my imprisonment, are much more bold to speak the word without fear. (vv. 12–14)

Traditionally an approach to outlining a passage like this would look something like this:

Three things we can learn about Paul's problems:

1. Paul's problems advanced the gospel (v. 12).
2. Important leaders heard the gospel because of Paul's problems (v. 13).
3. Paul's problems inspired courage (v. 14).

This would be a biblically accurate, factually based approach to teaching the passage. What is missing? The applications, if present at all, would be hidden several layers deep within the sermon. Another way to approach this passage would be to lead the hearer to make personal applications—front and center:

Three questions that will change my perspective on my problems:

1. How does God want to use my problems? (v. 12)
2. Who might be blessed through my problems? (v. 13)
3. What major breakthrough can come from my problems? (v. 14)

With personal application as the centerpiece of the message, what the audience takes home is a plan for transformation, not simply another set of biblical facts. Effective church-planting preachers, by intuitively knowing the needs of their audience, drive hard toward transformation by zeroing in on personal application.

A *second application* is almost unique to effective church-planting preachers—corporate application. When a major theme is conveyed, the personal application comes first, followed by a corporate application. Church-planting preaching is laced with vision. The corporate application is how your vision for the church is seen in Scripture. Often all a church planter has is vision. The substance of that vision is not yet constructed, so a vivid description of that vision regularly articulated is absolutely essential. Point by point, the preacher states, "That is why we . . ." "That is why we never . . ." "We live out this principle through . . ."

Examples of corporate applications (CA) to the message in Philippians 1 could be:

Three questions that will change my perspective on my problems:

1. How does God want to use my problems? (v. 12)

   CA: Our church plant wanted to rent Holy Trinity Church but ended up in this community center. We found ourselves extremely integrated into our community. This was always our greatest value.

2. Who might be blessed through my problems? (v. 13)

   CA: We were asked to start an "after-school program." It has grown incredibly. Parents who aren't from our church are now volunteering to help.

3. What major breakthrough can come from my problems? (v. 14)

   CA: We see a new missional community starting from this. We need a few leaders to help. We'll have a quick information meeting in the foyer after worship.

With every biblical concept an application to reinforce another facet of the church's vision is made available. A skillful communicator will work hard to never miss the opportunity.

Introduce a Bigger Problem

So let's quickly restate. After we frame the issue in the minds of our audience, we present a biblical answer that has both corporate and personal applications. The audience sympathizes with the need, understands the solution, and is grateful for the applications. But there is one big problem. For many in the room, the answer is impossible.

In the example given from Philippians 1, my perspective on my problems can only be changed when I have the ability to see my life from God's perspective. I need a new set of eyes. I need spiritual eyes. I need the presence of Christ in my life. For the church planter almost every principle he will teach will be spiritually out of reach for many of his listeners. This provides a perfect opportunity to introduce his audience to faith in Jesus Christ.

Setting up a universal problem and applying a biblical answer always leads the hearer to the limits of his personal resources. This leads us to the final phase.

Allow for a Resolution

With the spiritual need carefully explained, the church planter has the perfect opportunity to guide Kingdom seekers into a saving relationship with their King. The methods for "drawing the net" are varied, but it is essential that the church-planting preacher give his audience an opportunity to respond to the gospel in a culturally appropriate way.

Effective church-planting preaching seems to involve these five essential ingredients. With practice, the art of framing the issue, giving a biblical answer, making two types of applications, introducing a bigger problem, and providing an opportunity for resolution become a second-nature skill set of a planter.

And with it his craft becomes increasingly powerful.

Coaching Questions

1. What are some healthy ways to assess your current communication approach?

2. Who can help you with your assessment?

3. How can you more intentionally include vision in your preaching over the next thirty days?

Chapter 17

Communicating Vision

"What do you want to be when you grow up?" We chuckle when we hear children give big answers like "an astronaut" or "a princess" or "a professional football player." They can't possibly understand what it would take to live out their really big, audacious dream.

One crucial message that impacts the life and health of a new church plant is about the future. The message needs to be shared consistently, clearly, and creatively. We call that vision. Volumes have been written on the topic, and yet such a simple concept can be neglected or misunderstood in the planting process.

So many questions are in the heads of a church planter and his spouse that the vision question can take a backseat. "Where will we plant?" "When will we plant?" "Where will we find people?" "How will we fund the plant?" All these questions are important. But the most important question is, "What does God want our church to be when we grow up?" A clear answer helps inform many of the other urgent questions.

The Vision Loop

Early in the planting process a new church planter must get a vision from God. But sometimes the clarity needed does not come fast enough. The city where he is planting may require a cross-country move. Then time among the people where God has called Him is needed.

Why is a new church needed in a city? A common answer is, "Because we are going to do church better." This isn't a vision. At best, he is describing an uninspiring mission. These are methods a church planter uses to carry out the day-to-day operations of a church (mission). Vision is something that happens over time—a result—when God does what He wants through His people. Then this message becomes important for everyone.

Communication of the vision doesn't happen organically. The multiple demands that face a church planter and his team can force everyone into a "now" mentality. Using communication basics as a template forces vision to the center of everything. Below is an example of a vision loop.

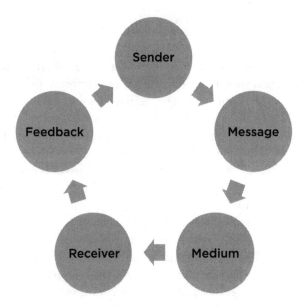

Sender

The sender is the word that becomes flesh to lead people to God's purposes. Moses is an example of vision made flesh. God's future for the Israelites in Egyptian slavery was freedom. Moses was to deliver the vision and lead people in that direction.

> Then the LORD said, "I have observed the misery of My people in Egypt, and have heard them crying out because of their oppressors, and I know about their sufferings. I have come down to rescue

them from the power of the Egyptians and to bring them from that land to a good and spacious land, a land flowing with milk and honey—the territory of the Canaanites, Hittites, Amorites, Perizzites, Hivites, and Jebusites. . . . Therefore I am sending you." (Exod. 3:7–8, 10 HCSB)

Moses embodied the vision of God to rescue His people. God planned a future for His glory and their deliverance. The "exodus" story becomes a template for what a visionary church planter does. He receives a vision from God and lives out that vision by leading people to God's purposes.

The visionary church planter is vitally important in the vision loop as was Moses. He communicates the message through various mediums, but the most significant medium is his life. His visionary leadership goes beyond his ability to communicate creatively to reflect who he is in the core of his being.

Jesus provides the ultimate example of visionary leadership. He was not sent merely to teach the message; Jesus was "the Message" that lived among the people so they could see, hear, and touch. "The Word became flesh and took up residence among us. We observed His glory, the glory as the One and Only Son from the Father, full of grace and truth" (John 1:14 HCSB).

The ultimate sender of the vision is God. But the vision rests first on the new church planter, who lives in neighborhoods across North America and the world. Then the vision can be seen, heard, touched, and owned by others.

Message

Most of us never lived in the world of television with black-and-white pictures. The US and Canada made the transition to television programming presented in "living color" in the 1950s and 60s. Color TV was an exciting technological advance. The world was a better place because of what we saw on our screens. Can you imagine the excitement when people saw images beaming into their homes in full color for the first time?

Vision is the full-color picture of what God has shown a church planter about the future. The planter must be cautious of making the vision so fact- and action-oriented that people miss the discovery of God's greatness along the way. Physical strength or numerical strength will not usher in God's future.

The vision message is the greatest asset of a new church. A new church planter cannot possibly offer the community an attractive menu of religious goods and services. The planter shifts his picture from what church has looked like in his past. He does not have the money, facilities, or volunteers to make church happen that way.

Ed Stetzer said, "Vision should cry out, 'This is something you long to be a part of, a purpose to which you want to make a major contribution.'"[26]

Vision is not exclusively what we are doing, but vision is what we are becoming. Vision is the future exactly the way God wants it. Paul burst into praise and describes God as the agent or "doer" of vision: "Now to Him who is able to *do* above and beyond all that we ask or think according to the power that works in us—to Him be glory in the church and in Christ Jesus to all generations, forever and ever. Amen" (Eph. 3:20–21 HCSB).

Communication is the process of presenting the vision in memorable ways. Vision is not what you are going to do today although it should influence what you do. It is what God has called you to be and where God wants you to join Him in the future.

Jesus taught the disciples about the Kingdom in His postresurrection appearances. At the end of the forty days of boot camp, He ended with vision. He looked in the future and saw a colorful picture that was critical for an overwhelmed group of disciples to see: "But you will receive power when the Holy Spirit has come on you, and you will be My witnesses in Jerusalem, in all Judea and Samaria, and to the ends of the earth" (Acts 1:8 HCSB).

Jesus' command to make disciples of all people groups was given in Matthew 28:19–20. Although an implied command or "do" is imbedded in Acts 1:8, it wasn't something the disciples could accomplish in a day of giving away bottles of water in their city. Neither was it a place they could focus their energies and offerings during "missions" month.

Jesus made a prediction and an invitation. He cast a vision. The Holy Spirit was the implementer for those who would join what He already had planned to do. Not only did He present a vivid picture in living color, but the entire book of Acts becomes the amazing video clip of exactly how it looks when God's people join Him.

Medium

Consistent communication through various mediums is critical for creating a culture where everyone understands and owns the vision. Stetzer explained why repeating the vision is critical to the effectiveness of a new church: "Listeners and followers have incredibly short memories. The leaders must repeatedly and consistently recast the church's vision and values in order to cement members to the vision. Come up with new and creative ways to share this vision with the church. Telling it the same way repeatedly can get boring or dull; so look for different ways to do this to make it fun and keep your congregation more attentive."[27]

Stetzer further emphasized that importance goes beyond the positive culture vision builds. Communication of the vision helps guards a congregation from "vision hijacking." Vision hijacking is the inevitable challenge planters face when people, often with good intentions, want the church to focus on priorities for faster growth.[28] Examples might include the desire to own a building or create better programs to attract more people.

When you design your own simple plan, you are doing it in the context of looping the vision. The vision then becomes the "why" of all you value and do, and that is clearly explained. The grid becomes an easy-to-maintain level of intentionality.

Receiver

Communicating vision is an important part of gaining healthy ownership from multiple people. Your audiences are always talking back to you, but often their lips are not moving! So understanding what's in their hearts about you and what's in your heart about them is crucial in vision communication.

Pre-Christians

Pre-Christians have a picture of church that usually is negative or neutral. They connect with the new church planter, a small group, or even a Sunday service speculating what it is all about. Kingdom seekers have a divine impulse for something bigger than themselves. But these hardworking, highly committed people have chosen to create something that is not bigger than themselves. A compelling, God-sized vision to a pre-Christian may not immediately produce their "Damascus Road" experience. But it can produce a significant "mini-decision" to come closer to what God is doing.

Community Influencers

As with pre-Christians, community influencers are even more likely to have a picture of church. Christians are perceived by many in the community as those who are perpetually disturbed about something who think the only solutions to the community's problems are church attendance and financial donations. The sad reality is that community leaders actually care more about the good of every man, woman, and child in the community than many Christ followers. A strong vision for the good of the city radically lived out by a new church is compelling.

Core Team

Core teams have expectations, no matter how committed they seem to be. And even more dangerous, they have assumptions. If they really like the church-planting couple, there are times they will overlook their vision. So communication with a core team needs to go to a deeper level. Asking open-ended questions is crucial. A new church planter must self-assess how much of the core team meeting time is spent with him doing all the talking. He should never make the mistake of confusing head nods and eye contact with ownership of God's vision.

Follow the example of Jesus and ask questions to get to the heart of those closest to you. Ask questions like: "What is your biggest question about our vision?" "What part do you think will be the most difficult for us to live out?" "What strengths do you have that will help us create the culture to support our vision?"

Partners

Partners have expectations. They may love the new church planter, but for long-term support they must see an executable vision. Here is where church planters commonly make mistakes, particularly when they are in the early stages of getting vision clarity from God.

Restlessness and discontentment with the status quo often begin the quest of a prospective church planter. "There aren't many churches in the community, and the ones that are there just don't get it," the planter complains during his meeting with the potential sponsor. But what if some of your best partners are using the same methods of the churches who are in the new community?

Partners need to look at the city and see what God has shown you. A passion for new methodology cheapens the vision of God for people. Methods change. Vision doesn't. God has shown the future and given the planter the mission to implement to get there.

Feedback

Feedback is critical in communicating vision and the final element of the vision loop. Receiver(s) must see the vision God has given to the extent that he/she can own it completely and communicate it informally. What God has shown planters about our future will influence what we value and how we behave in the present. How important is that?

Assessing how much God's vision is taking root in the people is an ongoing, strategic process. Church planters should never avoid asking strong, open-ended questions to discover how people are processing what they are hearing. And like a good coach they never assume if the vision is not connecting that it is the receiver's fault. When it comes to vision, the church planter must ask of himself and his team: "How well are we communicating God's vision? How can we communicate the vision better?"

Here are four ways to get feedback from people about how well you are communicating vision.

Test Groups

A new church planter (or core team member) can change a small-group meeting into a vision feedback session. Plan in advance through your small-group leader so they can promote your visit to build anticipation. Real feedback enters the room as an "asker" not a "teller." Ask key questions like: "What does God want you to be for Him in a year? What does God want our church to be? What is your biggest question about our future? How can we teach and communicate what God wants us to be more effectively?" You can recreate this process for smaller groups of people like leadership teams or Sunday morning attenders. The more test groups you can create, the more feedback you can get. Ask the same questions to every group to collect data. Then compare responses with your core team to look for themes and to affirm what you are doing well. Then make adjustments.

Online Surveys

Survey Gizmo, Survey Monkey, and other online tools are free and easy to use. Promote a simple survey (three to five open-ended questions) through e-mail, social media, small groups, and Sunday mornings. Make sure everyone understands how important it is for them to respond. Collect the data and compare results following the above steps.

Community Leader Interview

Real feedback can come from community leaders. Church planters must decide what questions will be most valuable. Be organized in order to get the needed feedback you are looking for as well as respecting other people's time. Ask questions like: "How can we be a better partner for you? What is your biggest question about our church? How can we be a greater influence in our community?"

Vision Debrief

Consistently assess the effectiveness of a particular vision activity. Don't just plan and execute like a box checker. Plan, execute, and evaluate. How did the sermon on vision go? How can we improve in the future? How did the small-group vision focus go?

Meaningful feedback is a friend not an enemy. God will use it to keep new churches on the path to His future. Fear of a negative response or negative people make church planters afraid to ask the tough questions. Questions can be asked in a positive way. Don't ask, "What do we do really bad?" Ask, "How can we improve?" And then take that feedback to make appropriate adjustments for future effectiveness.

The single greatest asset that you, as a church planter, will have is the three-dimensional, full-color picture of the future God is birthing in your heart. The thing you cannot help but continually dream about—it's in your soul.

Keep dreaming. Let the picture roll around in your imagination until you have new and better images to help people understand. If it's real, they'll see it in your eyes and hear it in your voice. If it's understandable, they'll be intrigued. If you build connecting points to them, they'll join you for the journey.

Coaching Questions

1. What aspects of your vision lack clarity?

2. What steps can you take to get greater vision clarity?

3. How do you plan to get feedback on how well you are communicating your vision?

Part 5: **Teamwork**

Every time I hear a church planter cast a big Kingdom vision, it stirs an excitement in my heart. I love seeing young leaders lead with a bold faith that takes prayerful risk. But too often I'm quickly disappointed when I discover they have little to no leaders serving by their side.

It's rare to find a church planter who is short on vision, but too often they lack the leaders and team members necessary to turn vision into reality. I encourage you to dream big dreams, but realize that the bigger your vision, the bigger the team you're going to need to make it happen.

I've heard planters cast powerful vision for eradicating homelessness in their community, empowering missional communities to bring community transformation or to evangelize an unusually large number of lost people in a short time. These are great aspirations but impossible to do without a team.

In his book *Planting Fast-Growing Churches*,[29] author Stephen Gray identified twenty-one differences between fast-growing churches and struggling ones. Among these was the importance of healthy launch teams. Gray found that 88 percent of fast-growing churches had a launch team in place before launch compared with only 12 percent of struggling churches.

The point is not to have a fast-growing church; the point is to have a healthy church that is positioned to grow and eventually multiply. And regardless of the model of your church plant, if you want to have a healthy and growing church, you must first have a healthy and growing team.

Early in His ministry Jesus traveled through the villages of Galilee preaching the gospel; but while doing so, He was also identifying and developing a team that could be a part of the mission. Luke gives us a glimpse into Jesus' team-building process, "In these days he went out to the mountain to pray, and all night he continued in prayer to God. And when day came, he called his disciples and chose from them twelve, whom he named apostles" (Luke 6:12–13).

It's interesting that when Jesus came down from the mountain He called His disciples to Himself, but He didn't select all of them as apostles. Luke says He "chose from them twelve." It's apparent there were more than twelve disciples at that time, so why did Jesus chose only twelve? Mark's account gives us the answer, "Jesus went up on a mountainside and called to him those he wanted, and they came to him. He appointed twelve that they might be with him and that he might send them out to preach" (Mark 3:13–14 NIV).

Jesus chose these twelve as key leaders He could develop and send out as a part of this Kingdom movement.

Chapter 18

Why Build a Team?

In Ecclesiastes 4, after expounding on the challenge of working alone, Solomon highlights the value of working with a team. "Two are better than one, because they have a good return for their labor: If either of them falls down, one can help the other up. But pity anyone who falls and has no one to help them up. Also, if two lie down together, they will keep warm. But how can one keep warm alone? Though one may be overpowered, two can defend themselves. A cord of three strands is not quickly broken" (Eccl. 4:9–12 NIV).

Consider these four benefits of having a team.

1. A Team Helps You Move Further Faster

You're passionate about your church plant, and for that reason it can be difficult to allow others to "touch" the vision. You might be surrounded by a good group of people yet not function as a true team. If you're the one making all the decisions, providing all the leadership, and casting all the vision, then you don't have a true team. An unwillingness to empower others with authority could be the thing that slows you down.

Solomon says, "Two are better than one, because they have a good return for their labor." From the beginning of your church-planting journey, you must discipline yourself to empower others to lead aspects of the vision. Empower people not only to do tasks, but empower them to cast vision for their area of ministry responsibility. Creating other vision carriers is a primary factor that will help the vision move further faster.

One planter I've had the privilege of working with had a small team of seven families he began to gather and share a vision for planting a new church in their city. He spent several weeks walking with these families, teaching them to live on mission. He helped them identify their sphere of influence and led them to pray for their friends who didn't know Christ. Next he began to challenge them to engage these individuals in a deeper relationship and initiate spiritual conversations. Over the next year this small team of seven families surprisingly grew to a gathering of more than one hundred people. Because he developed and empowered a team, this planter was able to reach more people faster than he could've done on his own.

2. A Team Creates an Environment of Learning and Continual Improvement

No leader wants to make a multitude of mistakes or fail in the process of planting a church. But mistakes are inevitable. You and your team will make wrong decisions and mistakes along the way. But having a team around you helps you process the mistakes, learn from them, and get better because of them.

Solomon observes, "If either of them falls down, one can help the other up. But pity anyone who falls and has no one to help them up" (Eccl. 4:10 NIV). When you have a healthy team around you, it makes you all better.

In my church plant I would gather my key leaders every two weeks for a lead-team meeting. These meetings were invaluable learning times especially during our first year. The primary focus of these meetings was to ensure we were staying on mission and determining the next steps God was directing us to take. As we gathered, we would discuss questions such as:

- Are we accomplishing our stated mission?
- How well are we living out each of our values?
- What's going well?
- What could be improved?
- What obstacles are we facing?
- What are our biggest needs?
- What are our next steps?

These meetings allowed everyone to have input and created a learning environment that made us all better leaders.

3. A Team Keeps You Encouraged

Leading without a team of people you love and trust can be lonely. Solomon points out, "If two lie down together, they will keep warm. But how can one keep warm alone?" I've watched many church planters move forward fast with an inspiring vision but no team. As a result they find themselves overworked and burned out. The few faithful followers they do have wear multiple hats and are unable to give their best to any of the work.

It's extremely draining and discouraging when you have to operate out of your comfort zone over an extended period. But when we position people in areas of their strengths, they will find themselves more fruitful and fulfilled. Sometimes planters feel they have to pick up all the incomplete tasks and fill all the leadership gaps. Soon they find themselves operating out of their weaknesses rather than their strengths. And that never ends well.

I received a call one day from a high-charged, energetic church planter friend who had hit a wall of discouragement. His two-year-old church plant was small and not growing as he anticipated. After asking him a series of questions, I discovered he was preaching every Sunday, leading worship, leading the setup, and leading the greeting prior to the service. It became obvious he had a group of people but didn't have a true team. And the lack of team was eating away at his emotional, physical, and spiritual energy. We worked over the next ninety minutes helping him identify key leaders he could empower to lead some of these key ministry areas. As we began to identify names, I could feel the energy and encouragement begin to refuel his soul.

Being surrounded by a team frees you up to use the primary gifts and gives you the energy to continually cast a passionate vision for the church.

4. A Team Strengthens You in Times of Spiritual Warfare

There are many organizational and administrative aspects of planting a church, but at the core, church planting is first and foremost a spiritual process. And for that reason Satan will make his best attempt to abort your new church plant in its infancy stage. Church planting and spiritual warfare go hand in hand; just expect it. The question is not, "Will you encounter spiritual warfare?" The question is "Will your team be unified and ready when spiritual warfare comes?"

During the months leading up to our church plant, I suffered from an unexpected medical problem. A team member tried to undermine my leadership. A donor who committed $25,000 decided not to support us. And we almost lost the facility where our church was planning on doing worship services.

Fortunately, God had surrounded me with a group of godly leaders who prayed with me and kept me encouraged during these challenges. I experienced what Solomon described in Ecclesiastes 4:12, "Though one may be overpowered, two can defend themselves. A cord of three strands is not quickly broken" (NIV).

Surround yourself with a team of faith-filled people that can fight the good fight with you, and you will stand strong against the opposition. Team members ought also to be team builders. Often team members suffer—albeit to a lesser degree—similar burnout rates as leaders. If team members also build a team, they reap the same benefits the lead planter does from his team.

Coaching Questions

1. What tasks are you currently doing that need to be given to team members?

2. What is your current area of greatest spiritual attack?

3. How can your team help you in this situation?

Chapter 19

Characteristics of a Healthy Team

One of the first fears many church planters face when they accept the call to plant a new church is finding people for their team. Building a launch team isn't an easy task because not just anyone could or should be on your church plant team.

You will struggle with the temptation to include anyone and everyone. You know you need people, and people are expressing an interest, so why not let them join the team? But not everyone is suited for church planting. So what do you look for in team members?

Calling

God has been at work preparing the hearts of people to be on your team long before you may have even met some of them. As you build your team, pray for those who are called to be a part of the early foundational team. You may be surprised when you discover a local pastor who wants to send some of his best leaders to help you. Or amazed when you come across a spiritually mature family that recently moved into town, and they tell you they've been praying about joining a church plant.

But let me warn you, some people who will hear about what you're doing will see it as an opportunity to shape the church they've always wanted. As you cast a vision for the church plant, be honest about what the church will and will not be. Sometimes it's tempting to compromise the vision to keep people, but in the end you both will be unhappy unless they're truly called to your church.

In the formational stages of our church plant, I had a highly successful businessman and his family ask to meet with me to discuss the church. During the lunch it became evident they could have a huge impact in our ministry. But when they shared what they were looking for in a church, I realized we weren't going to be a good fit for what their family needed. I was tempted to compromise because I knew the financial value this family would bring to our church, but that would not be fair to them or to the vision God had called us too. So I was honest with them and then recommended a few local churches that would better fit the calling and vision for their family.

Character

You're certainly not going to screen people based on their character and only allow mature believers onto your launch team. One of the joys of the team-building season is watching God bring unchurched people to be a part of what you're doing.

But I've discovered over the years that church planting can attract some real characters. Something about a new church draws people who may have other motives than being a part of the mission. Here are a few characters you will need to deal with prayerfully and carefully.

The Significance Seeker

The significance seeker is someone who finds significance in relationship with someone they consider to be in a significant leadership position. This person is attracted to your church plant because of the opportunity to get close to you as the lead pastor. While relationships are certainly important in the foundational stages of the church plant, this person's motivation is not the mission of the church plant but rather the relationship with a key leader.

The Agenda Driver

Agenda drivers come into your church plant with a predetermined selfish agenda. While they may agree with 70 percent of your vision, they come in with the idea that they will be able to change your vision to fit theirs. This person's motivation is focused more on what they can gain from your church plant than what they can contribute.

The Reconciliation Avoider

The reconciliation avoider is a disgruntled, angry individual who left their previous church because of a fallout with key leaders. They tend to carry a sense of hurt and resentment from the experience.

While the conflict may not have been their fault, it's wise to see if they sought the proper pathway to reconciliation with their previous pastor. If they did not handle it in the proper way, then you can counsel them in the biblical steps they should take to seek reconciliation.

Character is an essential filter as you consider inviting people into your launch team. The character of the individuals on your team will have a big impact on the dynamics of your team. While you're certainly not looking for perfect people, you do want to find people who will be excited about and committed to the vision and values God has given you for your plant. If individuals act selfishly, are argumentative or divisive, they can damage the unity and trust among your team as a whole.

Commitment

The people you recruit to your team should have a high commitment level to the mission and vision.

Cindy and I had a couple that wanted to join our launch team in the early stages of our plant. As we met with them and shared the vision, it became obvious: they were not going to like what we were doing. But they kept coming to our gatherings. One weekend I took our small launch team to a church in another city that was similar to the model and style we felt called to do. After the service I asked everyone on the team what they thought of the experience. Everyone was overwhelmingly positive except this one couple. They hated it. So I scheduled a lunch with them the next week and encouraged them to find a different church that would fit their prefer-ences. It wasn't that they were bad people; I just knew it would be difficult for them to commit to something they hadn't bought into 100 percent.

It's hard to let people go, but not everyone could or should be on your launch team. If you find people who are called, have the right character, and are fully committed, then you will see God work in and through your team.

Coaching Questions

1. How will you measure the health of your team?

2. What evidence of poor health do you currently see?

3. How can you address calling, character, and commitment on your team in the next thirty days?

Chapter 20

How to Build a Team

So, how do you go about building the right team?

Ask God to Send You the Right People

While it seems obvious, it cannot go left unsaid: you must start the team-building process by asking God to send you the right people. On two different occasions Jesus sent His disciples out to preach the gospel throughout the villages of Galilee. The first time He sent out twelve, two by two. A second time He sent out seventy, two by two. On both occasions one of the first instructions He gave them was to pray for workers.

He told them, "The harvest is plentiful, but the workers are few. Ask the Lord of the harvest, therefore, to send out workers into his harvest field" (Matt. 9:37–38 NIV; Luke 10:2).

Jesus had already gone into these regions of Galilee preaching the gospel. So there were undoubtedly a handful of believers in some of those villages. Now as Jesus sends His disciples to do another round of evangelism, He tells them to pray for workers. Jesus is challenging them to be praying for those who could be spiritual leaders in those towns.

I think too many planters use a "hope strategy" in developing their team. They are just hoping team members and leaders show up. But if you're praying for leaders, you expect leaders to show up. And if you're expecting leaders to show up, then you will be looking for leaders. And if you're looking for leaders, then you will begin to prepare roles for those leaders.

As a planter you have to begin to pray early and often for God to help you identify, recruit, and develop team members.

Identify Potential Team Members

The question I get more than any other from new church planters is, where do I find people for my launch team? There are six key sources for finding new team members.

1. Your Parent Church

Your parent church is the one who has bought into you, supported you, prayed for you, and sent you. Ask your pastor if you can have time to share the vision from the platform and invite people to be a part of your church plant. You may be surprised at how willing some people will be to pick up and move across town or the country to be part of a church plant.

2. Your Friends and Family

You have friends and family who love you and believe in you. God may be working on their hearts and calling them to join you in this mission of planting a new church. So don't hesitate to ask. Sometimes we make the mistake of assuming people don't want to join us, and we end up making a decision for them without ever approaching them. Friends and family often end up being some of your most committed leaders.

3. New Residents

When Cindy and I moved to Myrtle Beach to plant Carolina Forest Community Church, we moved into an apartment complex where many new residents were moving while they were building a house in the community. Each evening when we went for a walk or sat by the pool, we would engage new people in conversation. I discovered that people who are in transition are open and happy about meeting new people. Meeting new residents had a big payoff for us. Three of the best couples on our launch team came from sitting by the pool on summer nights talking about life.

4. Pre-Christians

Your launch team members do not have to be believers. In fact, we encourage you to engage with the unchurched in your community and invite them into relationship and then invite them into your team. You will encounter spiritual seekers in your community who don't know Jesus, but they're in a place in life where they're open to learning more about God. It could be they've experienced a recent tragedy or transition, and the Spirit of God is moving in their lives. As you meet new people, be sensitive to what God is doing in their lives, and pray about your next step in engaging them in a spiritual conversation. We had unbelievers on our team that recruited more people to attend than some of our key leaders did.

5. Serve Events

One planter friend of mine moved to a city that is 97 percent unchurched. He knew it was going to be tough building a team large enough to start a new church. So he took his small team of people and began to prayer walk specific communities. After a few days of prayer, they would do a community block party in that area inviting all the families to join them to eat and play games. They did this repeatedly until people were asking them why they were serving in this way. It opened the door for them to share the love of Christ and give information about the new church that was forming in the area. Their team steadily expanded because the people in the area were so hungry for this type of community and authentic relationships.

6. Community Leaders

Getting to know the leaders of your community may be one of your biggest opportunities. Think about it. Even though you may not know them yet, you have a lot in common with the leaders of your community. You both love the community. You both want to see the community get better. You both have resources you can direct toward the needs of the community.

A church planter friend of mine in Tennessee moved into a new community in 2011 with three families to start a new church. This small band of believers said from the beginning they were going to move there and just get to know and love on the community for one year before even trying to plant a church. Once they made the move, they immediately went to work getting to know the leaders of the community. They invested time in building relationships and volunteering to help with what city officials designated as key needs of the city. One year later their little team had grown, but more impressively they won the award for the Best Volunteer Organization in the city, and they weren't even technically a church yet.

Start Discipling Your Team from Day One

You've asked God to "send" workers, and now you find yourself with a good number of people who are committing to the vision. So what do you do with them now? I think we can take a clue from Jesus' words as He was commissioning His disciples to carry on the mission and expand the reach of the gospel. He told them, "All authority in heaven and on earth has been given to me. Therefore go and make disciples of all nations, baptizing them in the name of the Father and of the Son and of the Holy Spirit, and teaching them to obey everything I have commanded you. And surely I am with you always, to the very end of the age" (Matt. 28:18–20 NIV).

Jesus made clear that their priority was to make disciples. Discipleship in your church begins from the first day the first person agrees to join your team. One of the biggest mistakes we see planters make is waiting until they've launched their church to begin the discipleship process.

We don't have the option or convenience of delaying discipleship until our church is up and running. The time is now. Discipleship will enable you to develop a healthy team that gives birth to a healthy church.

While there is a lot of work to plan for your church plant, don't let that work supersede the work of growing the people God has given you.

Decide What Your Team Target Should Be

Another common question I get from planters is, How many people do I need on my team when I start? That is tough for me to answer because your model and your vision will determine the number of people you need on your team.

Once you've determined the model and vision for your church plant, identify the key leadership roles it will require to execute that vision. Next think through the various ministries your church will have. Calculate how many people it will take to do those ministries effectively. Then begin to pray for the right people to serve in those roles. This process will give you a target number of people you can start praying for as you build your team. I always advise planters to think what size they envision their church being one year from now and build a team around that number.

Plan Your Team Development Process

Church planting is a process. Just as it takes nine months for a baby to grow and develop in the mother's womb, it takes time for a new church plant to develop its systems, structures, and DNA. I recommend you first decide when you would like to start having public worship services. Then work at least nine months back from that date and plan the specifics of how you will disciple and develop your team.

When we moved to Carolina Forest, our small team immediately began to engage in the community. We started attending high school football, basketball, and baseball games. We built relationships with school administrators in the three local schools. We started volunteering in the community. We knew it would take time to get to know the people of the community, understand them, and become a part of that community. At the same time we laid out four phases we knew we would have to go through in order for the church to develop in a healthy manner.

1. Vision Development Phase

We started with the Vision Development Phase where a small team prayed, discussed, and defined the vision for the church plant.

2. Strategy Phase

Next we moved into the Strategy Phase where we talked about how to turn the vision into reality. We planned logistical details and drew out a detailed picture of the key ministries of our church. We studied the community and tried to understand the spiritual, emotional, physical, and social needs.

3. Team Development Phase

Next we moved into the Team Development Phase. In this stage we took seven weeks to walk our team through a biblical definition of church. Through this study we discovered God's intent for the church, the purpose of church planting, and how God had uniquely designed each of us for Kingdom impact.

4. Expansion Phase

Then we moved into Expansion Phase. We challenged our team, which had grown to about forty adults, to reach out to their unchurched friends, engage them in a deeper relationship, and invite them to join our gathering.

Through these phases we saw God draw people who were called to church planting join our team. We saw unbelievers come to faith and get excited about being a part of taking the gospel to others. And we saw God build the systems and structure needed to start a new healthy church.

Recruit Your Key Leaders

Having a team of people around you is essential for planting a new church. But you have to go beyond that and identify those who can take key leadership roles within the church plant. Below are six key steps to successfully recruiting a committed leader and making it a positive experience for him or her:

1. Give Them Time to Pray

Never ask someone to make a decision on the spot. When we do "on the spot" recruiting, the individual feels the pressure to say "yes" to you rather than truly having the opportunity to say "yes" to God's calling for them. Once you make a proposal, tell the person you'd like for him or her to take three to four days to pray about the opportunity before giving you an answer.

2. Tell Them Why You Thought of Them for That Particular Role

Be specific. The initial recruitment moment is your first chance to cast a vision for the importance of that leadership role. Take the opportunity to develop a picture of how this person's gifts, passion, and personality match up with God's vision for the leadership position. Help them see the potential for having significant impact in this position. Remember, you're not just trying to fill a position; you're casting a vision that helps them see the potential of what could be.

3. Ensure the Individual's Gifts and Passions Fit the Position

Having the wrong person in a position is just as ineffective as having no one in the position. Be patient and let God lead you to the right person with the right gifts. When we recruit the wrong person to the wrong position, we not only do the ministry a disservice, but we also do that individual a disservice.

4. Give the Individual a Written Description of What You Expect

You know what you want from a leadership position. However, we often recruit someone and just assume the person knows what we want. It's a recipe for disaster when we don't put our basic expectations for the role in writing. Be as thorough as possible. People appreciate it when they commit to a position and there are no surprises.

5. Provide Adequate Training

We all know this is important, but few people do it. Some planters make the excuse that they don't have time to do the training. But when a new leader starts making mistakes, you will have to invest more time on the back end to correct what's wrong. Be wise and make the training investment on the front end.

6. Meet with Them Regularly

Within the first thirty to sixty days, your new leader will surely begin to experience some disappointments, defeats, or disillusionment that could dampen his or her enthusiasm. That's why it's essential that you communicate with them often by phone, text, and e-mail. But also schedule regular times where you meet one-on-one. One-on-one meetings allow you to connect relationally, open opportunities for you to coach them, and give you both time to celebrate what God is doing in and through their area of ministry.

When recruitment is done right, it makes people feel honored and enthusiastic about serving. More importantly, they will be more effective at helping accomplish the mission of their area of ministry.

Coaching Questions

1. Which of the "six key sources of finding new team members" have you not tried yet?

2. What steps will you take to connect with that source?

3. What is your discipleship process for team members?

Chapter 21

Leading Leaders

As a church planter, you must build a team in order to maximize the vision God has given you. But you must also surround yourself with a solid group of leaders in order to maximize the giftedness God has given you. Here are four essentials for leading your team.

1. Keep and Maintain a Consistent Team Meeting Schedule

No matter how competent, committed, and creative your leaders may be, if you are not consistently getting together to talk about key objectives, you're failing to synergize the power of your team.

Regular team meetings allow your leaders to communicate key priorities, check on the progress, talk through challenges, and celebrate wins. If your leaders aren't meeting together regularly, they will quickly begin to drift toward a silo mentality. When they develop a silo mentality, they lose sight of how their area of ministry fits the overall mission.

Put your team meetings on the calendar at least one-quarter in advance, and you will have a greater chance of being consistent.

2. Develop a Culture of Authenticity

As leader, you set the tone for the level of trust among your team. If you're guarded, reactionary, critical of others' ideas, or only looking for input to support your ideas, then you will quickly create a culture of distrust.

Teams operate best when they feel a freedom to share their best and worst ideas and know there will be a healthy spirit of dialogue and debate. When this level of sharing takes place, the team makes one another better and brings the best thinking to the church's mission.

3. Build Time into Your Schedule for One-on-Ones with Your Key Leaders

Meeting together as a team is crucial, but you will also want to meet with your key leaders one-on-one. One-on-one meetings give you the opportunity to check on the soul of your leaders, discuss key priorities in their areas of ministry leadership, troubleshoot problems, celebrate wins, make midcourse adjustments, and pray together.

4. Develop Your Team

I find that a lot of pastors expect their ministry team leaders to do leadership development with their team members. But they fail to do leadership development with their leadership team. You can't expect your leaders to develop leaders if you're not modeling it yourself.

There are five simple ways you can develop and add value to the leaders on your team.

1. Once a month use thirty minutes of your regular meeting for leadership development. Watch a leadership video, or discuss a leadership blog post together.
2. Read a book together. Break a leadership book up into five to six segments, which gives you five to six sessions.
3. Go to a leadership conference together. Conferences not only inspire your leaders but will challenge them to grow in their leadership as well.
4. Bring in a field expert for an interview. You can easily bring in business leaders from the community, ask them questions, and draw from their leadership wisdom and experience.

5. Once a quarter talk about each leader's personal leadership development plan during your one-on-one meeting.

You cannot forget that the leaders on your team will face discouragement and spiritual warfare on a regular basis. A team is not something you put in place and expect it to operate and function on its own. As you lead your leaders, you're developing them in their role as a leader and nurturing the health of their soul.

Coaching Questions

1. Which of the "four essentials of leading your team" do you need to develop further?

2. Which team member needs more individual attention from you now?

3. How can you "add value" to team members in the next thirty days?

Part 6: **Making a Difference**

In 2004, Eric Swanson and Rick Rusaw wrote a groundbreaking book that has had a piercing effect on our evangelical subculture's collective conscience. In their book *The Externally Focused Church*, they dared to ask an often disregarded yet fundamental question, "If your church vanished, would your community weep? Would anyone notice? Would anyone care?"[30]

For a church to carry the descriptor of "a church of Jesus Christ," it follows that it should emulate the life and values of its namesake. Remember when King Jesus, with full rabbi status, walked into His familiar hometown synagogue and was given the honor of leadership over the second part of the service. What did He do? With His assignment of leading in the *Haptarah*, the reading of the Prophets, came the obligation of a message to be delivered by the rabbi. Jesus carefully selected one of the Isaiah scrolls, unrolled it to the section we now call chapter 61 verses 1–2, stood and read: "The Spirit of the Lord is on me, because he has anointed me to preach good news to the poor. He has sent me to proclaim freedom for the prisoners and recovery of sight for the blind, to release the oppressed, to proclaim the year of the Lord's favor" (Luke 4:18–19 NIV).

Having finished reading, Jesus, with great care, rerolled the synagogue's precious scroll, handed it back to the attendant, and, as was the custom, sat down to preach. All eyes were upon Him. Expectations were exceedingly high, for the word on Jesus was out. Miracles just might happen. Who knows?

But what did happen next was unexpected. Instead of doing what rabbis do—explain the meaning of what was read—Jesus did something no one had ever seen. He didn't explain anything. Instead He made this astonishing claim, "Today this scripture is fulfilled in your hearing" (Luke 4:21 NIV).

Without qualifying His credentials, Jesus announced that He, Himself, embodied the complete fulfillment of all prophecy and that His Kingdom agenda on earth would have a transformational effect on the designs of society. He declared that His Kingdom gospel would be really bad news to any power structures that gained advantage from poverty, captivity, disability, or the oppressed. King Jesus, Himself, was the voice for the unrepresented and the advocate for the overlooked. His gospel was the supernatural transference of His omnipotent power to the defenseless and regal significance to the marginalized. In substance it was the reordering of creation back to the eternal Creator's intent. It was the Kingdom of God.

And this was Jesus' mission.

So when Swanson and Rusaw asked the contemporary evangelical church if the neighborhoods juxtaposed to the community of Christ would be adversely affected by their disappearance, they were simultaneously asking: "Does the modern evangelical church represent the mission of Christ? Are we about the King's agenda? Are we making a difference?"

Therefore, when planting a new church, it seems that it might be wise to plan with your end goal squarely in mind. Thirty years down the road, when you have long completed your ministry at this local church you're starting, what do you want to mark your leadership?

Will you be able to look back at your life's work and say that your church made a difference in your community? You may be able to point to numerous mission trips, local ministry projects, Bible studies taught, marriages performed, and other examples of ministry activity. While we shouldn't discount these evidences of God's blessing on our work, we still have to ask the hard questions: "So what? Did you start a church that affected your community at the root level?"

Here is the key thought for this section: only churches that seek the Kingdom of God first, which includes—at its core—extending that Kingdom to its community, will make a difference that lasts. If you want to start a church characterized as a transformational movement—one that really affects the foundations of your community—your congregation will assemble a reputation and a track record of addressing difficult issues in your city. This community standing surpasses a resume of thirty years of successful ministry activities. It exceeds plaques and peer accolades of decade after decade of organizing our internal ecclesiology rightly. It dwarfs our ecclesiastical reputation as a steadfast and constant zealous fighter for correct doctrine. The Kingdom of God includes, yet profoundly transcends these concerns.

As we will see in the chapters of this section, our reductionistic understanding of successful church planting can lead us, in the end, to an unfulfilling place. To get to the end of our own seasons of ministry without experiencing anything that felt like a movement might signal that we lived a life pursuing good things but missed the heart of the Kingdom of God.

Chapter 22

The Gospel: Good News Included

In Part 1 there was a key image that packs enormous implications for this chapter. We characterized the Kingdom of God as what the world looks like when King Jesus gets His way. The gospel of the Kingdom is the physical, emotional, and spiritual manifestation of good news on every strata of society. It is good news to those both inside and outside the family of faith. It is good news to all except to the reign and territory of the prince of darkness. To that shadowy knave it is bad news indeed.

So, why does the gospel so often sound like anything but good news? Sure, the word *gospel* means "good news" technically, but is the gospel we extend to others really good news? Simply by claiming to be doctrinally "gospel centered," are we in reality "gospel centered"? What does that actually mean? In some cases claiming to be gospel-centered refers to a ministry that is centered on a prescribed set of theological understandings. To these the *kerygma* is the beginning and ending of the gospel. Being "gospel centered" is nothing more than intellectual agreement with theological content; the gospel is reduced to a set of propositional claims. Many will assert their doctrinal superiority with every ounce of their beings. They will argue as a standard way of conversing. Some will marginalize for the slightest divergence from the truth claims in which they claim unique understanding. Ultimately the gospel they proclaim isn't very inviting. It is anything but good news to their theologically disinterested neighbors.

So, what is this good news?

The Gospel Is Jesus

The gospel is more than a set of propositional truths. It is a person. It is the person who was simultaneously God and man and lived within the constraints of human history. Do you worship a set of truths that make up what you consider to be the gospel, or do you worship Jesus, the person about whom those truths speak? It may appear to be splitting hairs at first, but it is a distinction you cannot miss. One is a journey to life; the other is a cold and ominous path to death. Bring people to Jesus, not precepts about Jesus. Communicate Jesus the person rather than a set of statements as if you are convincing people to change their views on politics. He is the Messiah whom the Old Testament anticipated and whom the New Testament celebrated. If we are going to offer good news, rather than simply winning sacred arguments or changing people's moral positions, we must bring people to the ultimate good news: the person of Jesus Christ.

The Gospel Includes a Message

The preceding thought does not, however, discount the content in Scripture that serves as the clear message from God to mankind. There can be no good news without biblical content. God revealed an objective standard in the Bible, a standard of perfection. Who can possibly uphold the standard of the Sermon on the Mount, which climaxes in the admonition to be perfect (Matt. 5:48)? No one measures up to this unattainable expectation. And therein lies the greatest human predicament.

As discussed earlier, you will often encounter the difficult task of convincing emotionally healthy people that something is deeply wrong with them. Too often people believe they have faults just like everyone else, but they are not as bad as most people. This is comparative righteousness: measuring oneself by the perceived faults one finds in other people. The gospel content however, hinges on the problem of God's required perfection and mankind's deep and irreparable imperfection. Our message—if it is truly good news—centers on Christ's fulfillment of the law, substitutionary atonement, and physical resurrection from the dead. Apart from this content we have nothing to say that people cannot find in any world religion. This content also sets us apart from secular humanism that relies on the frailty of human effort. The gospel message is good news to our irredeemable state but terrible news to our self-sufficient pride.

The Gospel Is the Kingdom of God

Although brokenness abounds within individuals, institutions, and structural systems, there is good news. Jesus, our triumphant King, wants things to be much different in our damaged world. He desires to bring the peace of His atonement and His eternal victory into all the manifestations of brokenness in our world (according to Col. 1:19–20). While we now live in the tension that we will not wholly see the fullness of Christ's peace until the new heaven and the new earth, there is a promise of peace where sorrow currently abounds. This is the gospel of the Kingdom. As we already looked at Jesus' fulfillment of Isaiah 61:1–2, we read about His self-proclaimed realization of this text in Luke 4:16–21. The Kingdom of God is being ushered by a King who Himself is exclusively and eternally prepared to cooperate with any of His subjects humble enough to cast aside their own kingly aspirations. "For the eyes of the LORD run to and fro throughout the whole earth, to give strong support to those whose heart is blameless toward him" (2 Chron. 16:9).

According to Jesus, who is the Gospel, He Himself proclaimed the good news, liberated captives, healed the sick, freed the oppressed, and brought the Lord's favor to the least. All of this was Jesus' activity on this earth and His fulfillment of Isaiah's prophesy. This work of our King is what brings the Kingdom of God to the dark and broken realities of a desperate world. Peace where there was chaos. Healing where there was pain. Comfort where there was deep sorrow. Wholeness where there was systemic fragmentation.

As the body of Christ, we are given the task of bringing the healing peace found only in Christ to our malfunctioning communities. We are to bring people from the dominion of darkness and brokenness to the Kingdom of Light and wholeness . . . to the Kingdom of God.

The Gospel Is Powerful

As people encounter the church, the prevailing cultural value that tests Christianity's veracity is the theme of authenticity. They want to observe the lives of Christ followers to verify that their sacred confession really does make a real-time difference. The objectivity of our message must lead to a subjective lifestyle of holiness (being "set apart"), marked by an indelible and indisputable distinction between prostrating bond servants and wobbling autonomous agents.

According to Romans 1:16, the church must be an example of the power of the gospel, showing that something fundamentally changes when a person or a family unit or an entire community comes into relationship with Christ. "For the kingdom of God does not consist in talk but in power" (1 Cor. 4:20).

Many issues that are hotly debated in our pluralistic society come down to the validation of authenticity. Does it really matter? Why should someone embrace your Christian beliefs rather than Islam, secularism, or any other widely held worldview? This issue is discussed in greater detail in the next section, Making Disciples, but do not miss the point here: a community of disciples will be a people marked by authentic faith that leads to deep personal and community transformation. It is marked as a community of faithful disciples who exhibit the fruits of the same triune God that is living in and among them (Gal. 5:16–25).

So, how does a Kingdom-centric church planter understand the application of the gospel?

First, Kingdom-centric church planters are convinced that good deeds and good news cannot and should not be separated from any orthodox understanding of the gospel. The good news always clarifies, and good deeds always verify. Separating the two is like flying a plane with one wing. The results are predictably discouraging.

Second, Kingdom-centric church planters believe ministering and serving are the natural expressions of everyday living out the gospel of Jesus Christ. They believe believers can gain knowledge through good teaching, but they are rarely spiritually transformed apart from personal involvement in gospel ministry and service.

Third, Kingdom-centric church planters see their gospel presence as vital to the health and well-being of their neighborhoods. Only when the church is unselfishly woven into the fabric of life and exchange of the city can it be an effectual gospel force for change. In connecting with the life and cadence of the city, Kingdom-centric church planters seek to serve and bless the city and never to monopolize it.

Fourth, Kingdom-centric church planters anticipate a positive reaction by Kingdom seekers to the living gospel being demonstrated through word and deed in a manner of grace and truth. These planters' spiritual antennae are not tuned into further validating the hardness of the soul but instead are seeking connection points with the Kingdom impulses they see surrounding them.

Fifth, Kingdom-centric church planters are evangelistically potent. The powerful punch of the gospel message validated by a community whose priorities are transformed by that same gospel has an irresistible gravitational pull on a skeptical world. These planters routinely find gospel fruit in places where those with a one-dimensional gospel understanding habitually blame the fields for their own lack of preparedness.

The gospel is formidable because it is the God-man Himself who has brought the message of peace. Wherever disciples take the gospel, we see the Kingdom of God take root and begin changing the mourning of Christless people.

So, how do you gain a hearing to introduce this gospel to the people of your targeted community? The next chapter will attempt to answer that question as we turn our attention to the issue of social fault lines.

Coaching Questions

1. What will your community look like five years from now if King Jesus gets His way?

2. How will you communicate the gospel to "emotionally healthy people"?

3. How will you communicate the gospel to people who are broken?

Chapter 23

Social Fault Lines

As we have discussed earlier, when we move past the threshold of our competency and comfort, we find ourselves in the spot where God can use us. That truth is never more relevant than when we talk about the broken places within our communities. When you are willing to move beyond the comfortable territory of internal ecclesiological or doctrinal matters and the programmatic approach to "doing church," you will find a whole world that is longing for a Redeemer. Typically, churches focused singularly on theology and programmatic ecclesiology are internally focused. They may have been charitably engaged in their communities at a former time, but now the primary concerns of the congregation revolve around club matters. How can you avoid this sad story line in the life of your own church?

Maybe start with a firm grip on what it means to be charitable? When we hear the word *charity*, it reminds us of an organization designed for the benefit of society. It is a group that makes a practical difference in difficult situations. If done well, it is an organization prized in society for both its effectiveness and its sacrificial devotion to an important issue. In Canada, for a church to gain legal charitable status, it must pass an altruistic litmus test; that is, it must prove it exists for the benefit of the general community, not for the benefit of its membership. How like God to take an irreligious institution and remind the church of her sacred mission and calling.

The place where you will be planting will be surrounded by an ever-present brokenness for which there is no sustainable or truly satisfactory answer apart from a redemptive gospel. Your sacred mission will include leading your people to engage biblically in the myriad expressions of brokenness. It is you and your new church that a sending God of grace guides into the heart of this brokenness to usher in His peace with the advent of His Kingdom.

Resident in every community are varying degrees of seismic social fault lines of pain, desperation, and hopelessness. Left ignored and "ungraced," the impending common upheaval affects all in the community, even the most well insulated. The gospel's implications brought to bear on these desperate points of hurt provide many eternal opportunities.

Social Fault Lines: Creating Interest

As we discussed earlier, one of the most intuitively difficult assignments a church planter has to accomplish is to convince an emotionally healthy, generationally unchurched person of his need to attend church. It is inherently difficult because we instinctively know that almost everything that happens on a Sunday morning would be of little interest to him. He doesn't sing, he doesn't understand religious speak, and he is likely very busy. The whole business of church seems entirely tedious to him. Establish and execute the evangelical world's best marketing campaign, and you're still unlikely to rouse his curiosity. His attentions are focused elsewhere.

What could awaken his curiosity? Is there anything that a new church could do that would secure the attention of Kingdom seekers?

There is a direct correlation between a church's gospel-centered engagement in social issues and a community's positive response to their existence and evangelistic efforts. In many cases new churches find that they win freedom from social marginalization and subtle or even overt persecution through building genuine ministries that demonstrate Christ's mercy to the broken places of the city. By mercifully touching widely acknowledged social fault lines in a community, Jesus and His bride are fittingly perceived as a common community blessing instead of an unconnected sectarian faction. You earn one of the most valuable commodities for spiritual influence within your community—good will.

In most cases your church's wider community will be shocked to learn that your church cares about social justice issues. They have been long taught that we are only interested in the sterile religious section of life, not the messiness of sin and brokenness. Curiosity regarding your interest and engagement in such matters builds relational capital that you would not have—or would take years to cultivate. Men and women—who have never considered church, Christ, or religious affiliation—find themselves drawn to a community of Christ that sacrificially loves the community's neglected. As they inspect more closely, they discover a deeper love than they knew existed as they serve beside men and woman who attend to the abandoned as if they were ministering to their Savior Himself. Compassion at this level can only inspire a deeper spiritual yearning within Kingdom seekers.

Compassion creates passion. The disinterested become fascinated. Skeptics become advocates. The spiritually disengaged become co-owners of a mission and celebrants of a sacred community they once believed existed only in tales that began with "once upon a time." Instead of a fragile and fickle audience gathered through superficial tickles and artificial punch lines, you have built a Kingdom corps that will stand with you through the life and death battle against darkness.

This should be compelling enough, but there is an even more appealing reason to engage in mercy ministry.

Social Fault Lines: A Biblical Mandate

Some might be wondering: "This is all fine and good, but is it really biblical? Or are we simply getting trapped in yet another cultural fad? Won't this distract us from our biblical responsibilities as a church? Aren't we called to focus on making disciples? Doesn't God's Word tell us to raise up deacons and elders, have strong Bible studies, gather together for earnest prayer?" Of course, but biblical ecclesiology leads to much more than an internally focused congregation. If we really desire to disciple our people, we will lead them to live out the *full* counsel of God.

Most evangelicals are people who believe the Bible and seek to be faithful to its teaching on all issues. It is, after all, the "rule" or the guide to living, as God would have us live. Caring for the neglected and needy people in our communities in the Spirit of Christ is no different. Almost all biblical scholars who have studied this subject agree that at least two thousand dedicated verses in Scripture speak of God's desire to care for the weak and vulnerable. Many of these verses are direct commands from God to His people to be His instruments of mercy and grace.

Passages such as Psalm 10; Jeremiah 22:1–3; Acts 4:34–35; 2 Corinthians 9:7–15; and James 1 are but a sampling of declarative messages that permeate all of Scripture: God deeply cares for the oppressed, for the widow, and for the orphan. We should consider that over one-third of Jesus' personal interactions were ones of His offering mercy to suffering people around Him. Thirty percent of the recorded ministry of our King Jesus revolved around healing the sick, defending the weak, and caring for His society's most undesirable inhabitants. This should be a deeply troubling realization to those of us insisting on fostering an internal dialogue largely limited to concerns of a preferred ecclesiology. All of these "Jesus examples" lucidly reveal to us the heart of God toward the everyday sorrows of the most marginalized among us. As the body of Christ, we are called to be concerned about the concerns of God and to be His hands of healing; it is our biblical mandate.

Social Fault Lines: Areas of Opportunity

When we begin to shift our theology from theoretical talking points to the tangible action plans (which is the evidence of true belief), we will begin to see our communities through the compassionate eyes of a loving King. Our LoveLoud team at the North American Mission Board has identified three primary categories to frame this discussion.[31] Obviously you will find various areas of overlap, but this framework can help guide a church planter to uncover the possible social fault lines that may lay unaddressed within his community.

1. Neglected Communities

Entire communities and population segments have been ignored and marginalized. Your new church can establish a faithful presence and begin to experience community transformation as you meet legitimate needs with the love of Jesus Christ. John Perkins, one of the sages of mercy ministry and community development, said in his book *Beyond Charity* that Christians must step into the vacuum of moral, spiritual, and economic leadership that is desperately lacking in broken communities. A new church has the historic opportunity to slowly and gently become the "stabilizing glue" that rebuilds the broken infrastructure of depressed communities. Your new church can become uniquely positioned by God to address substantive issues such as job creation, medical care, and literacy with the goal of relieving the suffering of people around you.

2. Neglected Neighbors

Our communities are filled with hurting people. Mercy ministry does not simply address broken structural and systemic issues but seeks to serve the precious individuals trying to survive within that fragmented system. We are in the people business. Ultimately we glorify God by addressing the temporal suffering of people in hopes of bringing people into an eternal peace. This goal is not an ulterior motive, as if we are pulling a bait and switch, but rather our ultimate goal. To bring people to God, we have to be in authentic relationship in the lives of people. What better way to gain a hearing from people than when they understand that we honestly care about their deepest concerns?

So, who are the people living in your communities? One growing segment of society living within urban North America is widows.[32] The average age of a first-time widow is a woman in her mid to late fifties.[33] Along with the emotional turmoil of losing one's spouse when they enter this period of life, widows experience tremendous financial hardships associated with this experience, living on $721 per month ($8,652 annually).[34] Yet they remain one of the most overlooked population groups in our society. Alone, vulnerable, and often neglected, this segment of society is often a prime target for unscrupulous scammers who prey on their trusting dispositions. A community of Christ actively embracing an overlooked widow with the full love of Christ will likely find an unloved heart open to Christ and a new network of lives suddenly interested in the gospel.

What about people emigrating from other countries? The world is coming to the cities of North America at an unprecedented rate. Communities that have been historically homogenous are now a mosaic of cultures and nationalities. But coming with this immigration is often a deep and overwhelming sense of disappointment. The dream of a new life is often replaced with the cold reality of repeating a similar life to the one they left, but this time they are living it all alone. Transplanted into a new context, often without any familial ties or cultural skill, immigrants are forced to navigate a plan of survival alone and unaided. Disappointed and lonely, hundreds of thousands of people are experiencing tremendous loss associated with relocating and would be extremely receptive to a relationship with you and your new church. By ministering to internationals, you fulfill a biblical mandate, you have the joy of meeting a great need, you discover an audience often ready for the gospel, you plant a church that reflects the multicultural reality of heaven, and you position your new church in a way that is attractive to other Kingdom seekers.

3. Neglected Children

Children are often collateral casualties innocently trapped in a web of pain and neglect. Your new church can have great impact by meeting specific needs of children while sharing the love of Christ through several established arenas of ministry: pregnancy care, adoption, foster care, tutoring, and mentoring. Study after study shows that generational poverty is determined by a child's third-grade experience. Efforts such as tutoring lead to mentoring, which opens the possibility to be in the lives of extended families, which can be a key to ending the cycle of poverty in a child. Also, you will win unimaginable favor among community leaders in your neighborhood. Schoolteachers and principals, city officials, parents and grandparents will look at your new church with genuine respect as you demonstrate the humility of unpretentious care for their children. By meeting the specific needs of children in your communities, you will find tremendous receptivity concerning your underlying message of grace, peace, and love through Christ. Do you really want to know the people of your communities and become the feet and hands of Jesus? Start with the children.

Social Fault Lines: A Dose of Reality

Before we prematurely run headlong into this assignment, our King once gave us an axiom of His Kingdom centered around counting the cost (Luke 14:28–31). Before we storm the gates of our evil enemy by ending human trafficking or global poverty, we must be wise about how we approach such issues. We need to consider our calling and our capacity as a new church—and if we are able to deliver what we promise. People who are hurting and filled with sorrow often have long lists of broken promises, including the good intentions of Christians that went unfulfilled.

Before overpromising and underdelivering on proposed solutions to the sorrows of people around you, take a realistic assessment concerning calling and capacity. I mean, a *real* assessment. Are your people willing to let prostitutes live with them? If not, maybe you shouldn't "tackle human trafficking" because there will come a point when a woman, who is selling her body, will trust in Christ and need a place to live for a season while she escapes the clutches of an angry pimp and qualifies herself for other employment. Can she crash in homes of your people for several months or even a few years? Think through those realities. There is no shame in small steps. There is tremendous shame, however, in just being another example on someone's list of grand but broken promises.

Be realistic in your social fault-line engagement. Make a commitment to a people and place and stay involved in their lives year after year. This is not social tourism. This is sleeves-rolled-up, long-term engagement with a community that you will grow to love in ways you perhaps cannot yet imagine. But before beginning, count the cost for a long-term engagement.

While meeting needs, two things will happen: first, your new church will gain tremendous relational capital within the community, and second, you will have an opportunity to give an account concerning your motives. Obviously this is a conversation where you can point to your role as an ambassador of Christ, simply carrying out the concerns of God.

Will you lead your new church to follow the Bible's teaching by caring for the weak and vulnerable? Will you lead your new church to be a gathering of compassionate people? Will you lead your church to be the hands, feet, and mouthpiece of Jesus, the caring and compassionate Christ? By doing so, you will lead your people to join the movement of churches demonstrating God's love by meeting significant human need through a holistic sharing of the gospel of Christ. This approach to offering mercy to your communities is the essence of God's heart and what He expects of His people in order to have a faithfully biblical ecclesiology.

Coaching Questions

1. Who can help you engage in mercy ministries in your community?

2. Where are the greatest areas of brokenness?

3. What small steps will you take to lead your new church to engage the broken in your city?

Chapter 24

Leadership:
Both For and From

Church planters are faced with numerous decisions that inform their trajectory but none more central or influential than the question of leadership. Although this topic will be addressed in greater detail in the next section, it's important to speak a word about leadership at this point as we think through the subject of social fault lines, your new church, and its leadership. To properly address this issue, we must think strategically about the leadership base that is necessary to effectively engage your community. An effective engagement of social fault lines usually requires a local mission strategy that is both *for* the mission and *from* the mission.

Leadership: FOR, Not From

Intuitive to most church planters is the need to form some kind of leadership base that will serve as an operational core. The decisive question is, Who will be on that team? Few decisions a church planter will ever make will more accurately telegraph his future success than how he answers this question.

Usually when Kingdom-centered leaders attempt to do missional mercy ministry with an eye to consolidate their evangelistic efforts through planting new churches, they face a series of predictable problems in their quest of finding qualified leaders. Although the old adage remains true that "the resources are in the harvest," in this situation there is often a twist. People experiencing crisis are not generally ready for significant leadership contributions. Whether their personal crisis originates from their own destructive choices or from other stumbling blocks imposed upon them, a church planter must be realistic about their potential leadership contribution according to a true-to-life timetable. Generational brokenness is rarely fixed overnight and often exacerbates the protracted nature of a normal discipleship process.

Often a big-hearted church planter, unaware of this dynamic, approaches his planting assignment with a sole concentration of evangelizing and discipling those in the most distress. With the purest of motives, he seeks to develop a leadership base from the broken, oppressed, or mentally unstable within his targeted community. He deeply desires to hold up indigenous trophies of God's grace and declare, "Follow them as they follow Christ," but this can often be a disappointing process. Once in a while it can be observed that God does perform a miraculously quick work of sanctification in the life of someone deeply broken, but generally it seems that God works through a more normative process of incremental transformation. As a church planter gathers his team around his God-called social fault line, he will often experience great frustration in his inability to gain leadership traction. Soon, overwhelmed by the endless need that surrounds him, the new church plant involuntarily inches into a grinding maintenance mode.

With every problem comes an opportunity.

For planters consumed with a holy passion for the gospel to be front and center in every aspect of their new church, this leadership problem of, "for, not from" presents a unique opportunity for them. As we discussed earlier, lying dormant and largely unmoved by any sacred messaging lies a vast and untouched audience of Kingdom seekers who share a similar empathy for what is broken in their city. Often these socially healthy men and women find that a new church's Kingdom heart and vision are both admirable and utterly compelling. By building lanes of connection and opportunity for Kingdom seekers to attach themselves to the mission, you have created a discipleship track that starts with prebeliever and ends with the kind of leadership that much can be built upon. These prebelievers also become community advocates opening many doors for ministry that would likely be unavailable without their personal involvement. One by one these men and women bend their knees to the King of the Kingdom and find themselves at the center of the spiritual heartbeat of a transforming community.

Leadership: FROM, Not For

In 1936, Robert King Merton, one of the most influential sociologists of the twentieth century, wrote a groundbreaking Harvard paper entitled "Unanticipated Consequences of Purposive Social Action," in which he introduced a sociological construct of analysis to perform before introducing any major social change. This work is generally credited for giving birth to the popular adage, "The Law of Unintended Consequences," which is simply an issued warning that an outside intervention into the fabric of a complex system tends to create unexpected and often unwelcomed outcomes. Looking back at some of history's most well-intended social programs, one can easily point out the devastating dark side that ushered from their implementations. In many cases the cure was much worse than the disease.

Learning the lessons of history, no church planter would want to further damage his community in his altruistic attempts to bring good news by creating systems of dependence characterized by a lack of indigenous ownership. Therefore, the last impression any planter would desire to leave his community with is as an outsider with a saccharin tone of superiority. In communities that have been ravaged by social injustices and personal oppression, planters must avoid ministry efforts that will further rob people of their God-given dignity and further perpetuate a flawed and distant gospel. Our sacred calling is to become agents of Christ, rightly restoring the inherent dignity of individuals and communities as image bearers of that same God.

A key area where church planters often misunderstand this concept (and unintentionally reinforce degrading messages that many people have heard all too often) is in the realm of leadership development. Every Kingdom-hearted church planter should regularly ask himself a few questions: "Have I thought about the people I am highlighting in visible positions? Do they reflect the demographics and socioeconomic makeup of our community? Or does their leadership proclaim a message that is contrary to the gospel I am sharing from that platform: 'that you, in the audience, are different (lesser) than those of us leading?'"

Perhaps one of the biggest reasons as to why a new church does not gain sufficient traction in a given community is because locals see it as a grand company of interlopers and outsiders. Great care and attention should be given to developing and highlighting leaders who are already indigenous to your community. The only church-planting path that is sustainable in the long term is the way of developing a local leadership base. Any shortcut to that goal usually yields an anemic and sterile assembly with little reproductive viability.

So the team members that weekly immigrate to a neighborhood from a distant community should see their public face as a short-term bridge. These early days are devoted to identifying and developing Kingdom-hearted leaders already long resident in the community. Generally an observant church planter will find key strategic men and women as he gracefully engages in social fault-line issues. As you work alongside these men and women, you have wondrous opportunities to gently and respectfully share the good news of Christ. Over time you will likely find that these leaders have become astoundingly strategic and unshakable trailblazers as your church marches forward.

Remember that when Jesus chose His disciples, He quickly skipped past the religious who seemingly "had it all together" and instead chose a squad that perfectly reflected the substance and vibe of Judea. Initially you may need to introduce leadership into a community by bringing some preevangelized team members with you from your sending church, but these leaders should be forewarned that success means they have indigenously replaced themselves. The humility expressed in this behavior demonstrates that you have selected the right team.

Prayerfully you will find Kingdom seekers who are willing to partner with you to bring relief and mercy to the deep sorrows of people around you. In such cases church planters find that Kingdom seekers are receptive to the gospel and relationally come to Christ as they mutually serve together. These men and women will catapult a church plant into great fruitfulness much more quickly than outsiders could ever manage. This synthesized approach to leadership development is one that is both *for* and *from* a great missional harvest.

Coaching Questions

1. How does your core team reflect the people you are trying to reach with the gospel?

2. What steps can you take to make better connections with indigenous people?

3. What steps can you take to avoid appearing as outsiders in your community?

Chapter 25

Going Glocal

In 2003, Roland Robertson, a Scottish sociologist, delivered a white paper at the International Forum on Cultural Diversity and Common Values called "The Conceptual Promise of Glocalization: Commonality and Diversity."[35] This was a capstone to his pioneering study of a new sociological phenomenon that identified how the world was becoming seamlessly integrated locally and globally. With this global/local "glocal" compression of nations, geographies, and culture into an almost continuous large-scale integration, few locales are isolated from the effects of another. Events that occur in one nation have effects that imposingly transmit far beyond their bordering nations. It is a glocal world.

Likewise, Thomas Friedman, in his book *The World Is Flat,* described the local consequences of globalization on communication, technology, travel, and business. To Friedman, the flattening of the world has resulted in common worldwide conversations from nations that were once either intentionally, politically sequestered or involuntarily, geographically insulated. Few islands of isolation remain untouched by the flattening effects of glocalization.[36]

Entering early into this conversation was a pastor from Keller, Texas, named Bob Roberts Jr. Roberts, with genius perception, saw before others the missional linkages that correlate with the sociological observations of academics like Robertson and Friedman. First, through years of personal implementation in Vietnam, and then through his lectures and writings, Roberts has done more to advance the discussion of glocalization and the mission of the church than any other contemporary evangelical leader. His book, *Glocalization,*[37] was the first expression of its kind on how current global impacts should affect the missionary strategy of a church. Having been personally impacted from a long friendship with Bob, my thinking has been affected in four key areas that change everything about what we traditionally understand as "church."

The Church as a Missionary

Unconsciously we often perceive missionaries as ecclesiastically disconnected individuals that serve semiautonomously in far and distant lands. These detached heroes of the faith pop into our churches with no great frequency in order to report on their progress and spiritual conquests. To the degree that we are spiritually and emotionally moved, we repledge our annual support to the great missionary endeavor. After all, we are a "missions-minded" people.

It would seem to the majority of churchgoers in the West that our divine missionary obligation is solved with an annual gift sent to an outside agency. A special envelope dropped in a special box and sent to a special address means that I, too, am on mission. While I do not wish to disparage either the incredible sacrificial work that is being done by missionaries throughout the world (my sister and her family being among them), nor do I wish to denigrate the sometimes enormously sacrificial giving by churches on behalf of these missionaries, I do wish to point out one incredibly important fact: the Great Commission was given to the entire church, not just a professional class of missionaries and pastors.

For a church to be truly "mission minded," it has to be missionary. The leader's goal is that everyone is involved in the mission. Every lead planter sees himself as the CMO (chief missionary officer). These are not "extra credit" activities for the spiritual leaders but are positioned within the church as a normal part of disciple making. The goal of the church isn't to gather people into the sacred assembly but to equip to release into the sacred Kingdom mission.

So, what does it mean for a new church to be a missionary? Much of this question has already been answered in previous chapters, but what is particularly germane to this discussion is a clear understanding of our divine global commission and the human resources God will make available for that assignment.

We will start with the people of God.

Domains

Often when we think of the vocational missional expression of the people that make up our churches, we think in terms of their evangelistic engagement at their workplace. We correctly teach that their "call" is to be an effective and faithful witness for Christ at work. A small percentage of the Sunday morning assembly takes the challenge seriously and sets out on a mission of an office Bible study or some type of evangelistic accountability with other believers in the workplace. But in the minds of the vast majority of people attending weekly church services, the "call of God" is something reserved for religious workers and a few fanatical outliers plucky enough to reserve the office conference room to hold a religious meeting. The call of God is definitely not for them.

Perhaps we should approach this "call" conversation with our people in a slightly different way. Instead of limiting the idea of "being called" to only what has an overt religious expression, consider the impact that could be gained by broadening our understanding of calling. This leads us to understanding the subject of domains.

The basic platform that society is built upon is a series of infrastructural categories often called domains. Although opinions vary on how thinly these categories are sliced, Roberts states that these can be boiled down to eight: education, health, agriculture, governance, civil society, communication, science, and technology. Every vocation in which every churchgoer earns a living operates within one of these eight domains.

When the church is the missionary, part of the leaders' responsibility is to teach the church that their domains are not simply places to earn salaries but are their primary platform for Kingdom advancement. The "calling" they sensed when they started their careers was far greater than a calling to a paycheck but was actually a way they could serve humanity. Teachers originally wanted more than union salary but cherished an opportunity to inform and inspire. Many mechanics, as adolescents, were the ones who took great joy in voluntarily fixing broken things that others could not. Accountants, because of their value of order, were organizers and coordinators long before their designation as CPAs.

The people of God have always had a calling.

The church of Jesus Christ has not always had a place for that calling. Why? Because we, in our spirit of isolationism, have mistakenly viewed ourselves as the ninth and most preferred domain. Instead of integrating Kingdom within the other eight, we have set up our own insular category and called disciples to leave their secular passions behind in order to serve a grand sacred domain.

And so teachers and mechanics and accountants count the church's offering, stack the church's chairs, and vacuum the church's carpets. It's church, but it might not be Kingdom.

Start a Church for Your City

We have already extensively explored the need to plant churches for lostness. Other than a couple of theological camps who feel their sacred assignment is to convert those who disagree with their theological constructs, it seems that most planters today are clearly after the lost sheep.

It is also encouraging to see that these same planters who are seeking to engage lostness have a different goal from many church planters of the past, Their aim is much truer than starting a worship service; they are about planting the gospel. And as often observed, the gospel planted in the heart of a believer bears the normal fruit of far-reaching transformation. The person becomes far more than a religious version of his previous self. He is new.

In the same way, the gospel planted in the heart of a city will bear the normal fruit of far-reaching transformation. Structures change, institutions change, prejudices change, neighborhoods change, and the socioeconomic landscape of the community changes. So how is the gospel planted in a city? This is where we return to our discussion of domains.

Imagine in your mind's eye a tale of two new church plants within the same city. Alpha Church skillfully exegetes its context and brings the full weight of the gospel to bear on its growing assembly. Week by week, men, women, and young people place saving faith in the lordship of Jesus Christ. A great path of discipleship is built, and these new believers quickly grow in their faith and take significant leadership roles within the new church. Great wisdom was shown in leadership placement, and this little plant soon grows to five hundred strong with a full complement of age-appropriate programs, each with an aggressively evangelistic bent. Space is soon an issue, and the excited and highly competent leaders begin to solve that issue with some plans that will further establish this new church as a healthy and vibrant option within the city. These are good days for Alpha Church.

Beta Church also successfully exegetes its context and winsomely introduces many to the gospel of Jesus. Week by week, men, women, and children respond to the good news. This is also an exciting new church to attend. A great path of discipleship is built, and these new believers quickly grow in their faith and are challenged to engage their vocational "domain" with the gospel. Teams, or "units," are formed and are dispersed throughout the city. Church members who work for Correctional Services find themselves serving at several "halfway houses." A group of teachers and drama students congregate in a subsidized neighborhood and host a "reader's theater" designed to increase reading skills to at-risk children. A group of store managers, accountants, and bookkeepers team together to offer support, budget training, resumé writing, and other business skills to an immigrant-rich area of the city. These and many others "units" imbed themselves in neighborhoods throughout the city and over time develop deep and trusting relationships. Soon small groups are gathering around the city, and people who had no bridges to Christ were also routinely placing saving faith in Jesus. Several of the people within these groups would migrate on Sundays to what they called "the big church," but most would not. For most their spiritual community was in their neighborhood. Beta Church had more modest growth and numbered fewer than two hundred. There were no immediate building plans either.

From this tale of two church plants, which one more efficiently planted the gospel in the city? Which one, over time, will have the greatest transformational affect? Which one had a membership engaged in their redeemed calling?

Which one sounds like more fun?

Start a Church for the World

Few would argue that implicit in our gospel commission is a commandment for global engagement. Although some would understand Jesus' words in Acts 1:8 as progressive (once Jerusalem is taken care of, head to Judea. Once Judea is thoroughly evangelized, head to Samaria), most would see such an interpretation as an aberration conveniently constructed to stay selfishly coasting in their own comfortable Jerusalem.

As a new church planter, you have a once-in-a-lifetime opportunity to encode some truly biblical DNA within the life of a new church. When your vision reaches beyond starting a church for a community to starting one for a city, your spiritual imagination is forced to stretch. You have no choice but to imagine a life of multiplication. You see disciples differently. No longer can your strongest leaders be held hostage for more mundane internal matters because you see the Kingdom potential in their eyes. Your discipleship of these leaders is designed with a movement contingent on their part well played.

What happens to your vision when you move beyond planting a church for your community, and beyond planting for your city, to taking up the mantle of planting a church for the world? How do you now look at the people God brings?

As you plant a church for the world, you prepare your future for an unexpected journey of faith. Through your understanding and engagement of another culture, your church will be far better prepared to understand and engage your own culture. Through deploying Kingdom leaders in the area of their domain expertise to another nation, those same leaders will be far more open and ready to roll up their sleeves in their own city.

In the first months of the life of your plant, prayerfully seek God's wisdom on the nation to dig deeply into and stay with it for life. Don't be guilty of missionary tourism, but instead leave indelible footprints in a nation your children will long to follow. Something intensely powerful happens when a leader humbly leads in a long obedience in the same direction. The congregation shifts and soon you have an army that is ready and willing to take whatever beachhead is necessary. Let the heart and soul of this effort come from the lead planter. Let your whole church understand that this endeavor is not an optional add-on for supersaints but is the normal pattern and rhythm of this church. It is a pattern lived by its leaders.

As you humbly and honestly engage another nation through a servant's posture, any provincial understanding of the church and Kingdom of God has no choice but to fade away. You are forced to come to grips with the fact that God is much bigger than my categories or spectrum of experience.

And in those humbling moments, you are being intimately fashioned into a Kingdom servant.

Coaching Questions

1. What domains are already represented in your new church?

2. What are your next steps to help people engage their domains for Kingdom influence?

3. What can you do to help your church to be planted "for the world"?

Part 7: **Making Disciples**

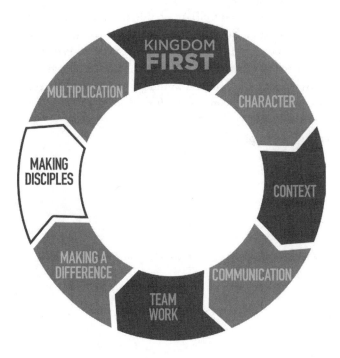

Discipleship happens to all of us, every hour of every day. We are all being daily formed into a likeness. The troubling question is whose? "I appeal to you therefore, brothers, by the mercies of God, to present your bodies as a living sacrifice, holy and acceptable to God, which is your spiritual worship. Do not be conformed to this world, but be transformed by the renewal of your mind, that by testing you may discern what is the will of God, what is good and acceptable and perfect" (Rom. 12:1–2).

Our culture has a definite vision for our lives. Daily we are bombarded with messages designed to "conform" our opinions, values, and worldview to an ever-evolving societal code of norms. The process moves us from love to insecurity, from trust to skepticism, from community to individualism, from contributor to consumer, from contentment to dissatisfaction, and from rest to utter exhaustion. Our discipleship leaves us hopeless, insecure, isolated, indebted and very tired. With little excess margin, we dutifully tack on our sacred obligations, muster a happy face, and try to convince a watching world that Jesus makes all the difference.

Society has discipled the church well. As a result one has to really squint to differentiate a Christian from his culturally secular first cousin. A plastic-chrome fish on the bumper is a likely tell. Perhaps pleated Dockers. Other than a few funny evangelical phylacteries, we seem to have become virtually indistinguishable. Apparently our one-hour Sunday spectacular, as prepped and polished as it may be, cannot compete with the endless grinding drone of our culture's indoctrination.

We may need a different plan.

Chapter 26

What Is Discipleship?

Christian discipleship is what happens when people live daily with Jesus. Before you too quickly dismiss this as a weak, feel-good definition, take a deep breath and then an even deeper look.

Jesus drew incredible, mammoth-church-sized crowds during His earthly ministry. People who were in those crowds, like most crowds, had multiple agendas. A quick reading of the Gospels reveals that Jesus discouraged and excused more people from those crowds than He kept. Only twelve people lived with Him every day.

His first disciples noticed a full-sized problem in Jesus' Kingdom-assimilation strategy. John's Gospel contained a series of spectacular miracles in chapter 6. From witnessing Jesus' feeding at least five thousand people with five loaves and two fish to walking on water, the crowds were in awe of Jesus' power. Who wouldn't be impressed?

As the crowds grew larger, the teaching went deeper, and the angst grew greater. Jesus' focus shifted from feeding the hungry crowds to teaching about eating His flesh and drinking His blood. The Jews grumbled and argued about what He was saying. Even the disciples complained about the difficulty of His teaching. Jesus obviously needed a good communications consultant.

Everyone in the mammoth church who heard the message didn't become fully devoted disciples. Half-devoted perhaps? The exit door to the Kingdom swung open wide as disappointed disciples trudged out en mass to become ex-disciples: "After this many of his disciples turned back and no longer walked with him" (John 6:66).

The same Jesus who wept over the city of Jerusalem and asked His Father to forgive His murderers responded in a most surprising way. He asked the twelve disciples who lived with Him, "Do you want to go away as well?" (John 6:67). Really? Was Jesus inviting His disciples to leave? Jesus loved them but wanted them to understand the cost of living with Him. Peter, as usual, was the one who responded: "Lord, to whom shall we go? You have the words of eternal life, and we have believed, and have come to know, that you are the Holy One of God" (John 6:68–69).

Somehow Peter comprehended the eternal importance of living with Jesus. He was more than a half-devoted groupie who was hanging around for the big show. Why did Peter refuse Jesus' invitation to the back door? Because something dramatic happened inside him.

Peter trusted Jesus with his life. And his heart and mind were transformed through the intimate experience of living with Jesus daily. He was further along the discipleship path than those whose backs were fading in the distance. The Kingdom exit door was nailed tightly shut in Peter's life. Even though there would be many mistakes yet to be made, for Peter there was no looking back. The "Holy One of God" had forever transformed him.

Peter had his moments; when we read his story in the Gospels, they are many. But this was not one of them. This was another defining moment in Peter's spiritual journey that would prepare him for an incredible Kingdom trajectory.

Most people move through distinct phases in their spiritual journeys. They move from not curious to curious, to disciple, and beyond. I will talk more about phases later. But moving from being curious about Jesus to becoming a fully devoted follower of Jesus is the most challenging step.

A rich young ruler was curious about Jesus but would not move beyond that stage. Jesus' teaching challenged him to live beyond moral compliance to absolute surrender. He chose instead to exit the back door of the Kingdom. Mark commented, "But he was stunned at this demand, and he went away grieving, because he had many possessions" (Mark 10:22 HCSB). Many who connect with you will struggle as well.

The Target on the Wall

"Someone who lives daily with Jesus" is our working definition of a disciple. But how does that look? What exactly are we making again? How do we know if we are succeeding? Assigning more concrete attitudes and behaviors to this "one who lives daily with Jesus" gives us a way to assess if they really are. Then you can create environments and conversations where God can inspire growth within these disciples.

Back in the day my tribe kept a discipleship scorecard through a weekly envelope submitted each Sunday. I wouldn't be surprised if some still continue this practice. At the beginning of the year, you would get a box of fifty-two envelopes dated for fifty-two weeks. Each week you were to check boxes based on the good things you did for God and the church. (You'll notice that we even got credit for being on time!) I have little idea what leaders did with these envelopes after the contents were emptied. Maybe nothing.

The way we used to do things is often a topic of laughter and ridicule. There is no question the envelope system felt a little like guerrilla accountability. But at least the system attempted to establish metrics that moved us beyond "saved" or "lost." In essence we were saying the "saved" or disciples should be accountable for maturity.

Another extreme is much more common now. There's only a single metric: be there! It's all about the weekend. "Do your part to make our parking lot, lobby, and auditorium exciting, welcoming, and full of smiling people. Expand the brand; we've worked hard on it. And please volunteer on Sunday morning. There is plenty to do. After all, we want more happy people to come, experience us, and then, of course, come back."

The single discipleship-accountability metric comes with a series of mushy middle-class talking points. "Don't give unless you want to, and then give only what you want to. You would love our groups, but only if you want to come. We don't mind if you connect with people outside your church friends, if you know any." No one is keeping score or trying to create environments where God develops disciples. No one is responsible for developing fruit-bearing disciples. Just come to church for heaven's sake!

And with our long established, well-oiled Sunday-centric emphasis, we often miss Jesus' original point of making disciples. A growing disciple is one whose life is producing the supernatural fruit of a Kingdom citizen. This moves far beyond metrics that are more focused on expanding the sacred brand through a well-orchestrated, consumer-driven Sunday experience.

The Fruit of a Disciple

Jesus addressed audiences who were familiar with farms, farming, trees, vines, and fruit. But no matter how little you know about the world of agriculture, Jesus' use of these pictures demystifies where to start the discipleship target discussion. Let's start with some definitions:

Fruit Is People

The mission a disciple is called to is to produce fruit. *Fruit* refers to different outcomes in the life of a disciple. One example is when fruit represents people. Fruit was one of the most valuable and attractive commodities in the biblical era. So to compare a person to harvested wheat or beautiful grapes was an indication of their inherent value. "Already the one who reaps is receiving wages and gathering fruit for eternal life, so that sower and reaper may rejoice together" (John 4:36).

Prosperity is redefined beyond the natural harvest to a supernatural harvest of people. Disciples are made to become fruit bearers. Jesus explained: "You did not choose me, but I chose you and appointed you that you should go and bear fruit and that your fruit should abide, so that whatever you ask the Father in my name, he may give it to you" (John 15:16–17).

Fruit Is Obedience

To live as a fruit-bearing disciple is an appointment from God. *Appointed* means to "put in place," a strong picture of God's strategic intent. As people are harvested, their value for His mission becomes increasingly exponential. *Fruit* is used to describe love that is demonstrated through obedience. Bearing fruit is one of the surest confirmations that we are His: "By this my Father is glorified, that you bear much fruit and so prove to be my disciples" (John 15:8).

Fruit Is Character

All the biblical references of fruit work together to describe a distinct quality of life that becomes a thing of beauty. God's glory is displayed through the extraordinary lives He creates. Our fruit is of such quality and consistency that it also validates that we are not self-made but are products of God Himself. Our fruit is observed externally by the people we have influenced toward the gospel. But our fruit is also seen internally from the character God has constructed inside of us. "But the fruit of the Spirit is love, joy, peace, patience, kindness, goodness, faithfulness, gentleness, self-control" (Gal. 5:22–23).

Fruit Summary

If you have ever talked to a successful farmer, you learned how focused and intentional he was about producing fruit-bearing plants and animals. Can you imagine a farmer whose mission in life was merely to work hard? What about a "relational" farmer who loved spending time with his cows and chickens? The sweat on his brow and his love for his animals may impress you, but he won't last long. He is likely to soon be out of the farming business. His profession requires intentional focus on producing high quantities of quality fruit.

Disciple makers focus their energy on seeing fruit. What kind of fruit are they looking for in the lives of the people they disciple? *People, obedience,* and *character.* Fruit is discovered and cultivated through being in community. People in a new church plant learn to disciple people from their leaders. The first step for a new church planter is to disciple people in the community. Here is a review of the basics:

Spend Time with Them

To be an effective disciple maker who makes disciple makers, start by spending *more* time with *fewer* people. See how they relate to their families, how they relate to work, what they talk about, and how they respond to adversity. Be an example of what it is like to follow Christ. One of the best ways to learn if disciples are growing is to take long walks with them. That is what Jesus did.

Ask People to Assess Themselves

God asked Adam, "Where are you?" (Gen. 3:9). God didn't need the answer, but Adam needed the question. If discipleship is living with Jesus daily, then you have helped them move closer to the target. Consider leading with your ears as opposed to your mouth. You will learn more about them, and they will learn more about you when you talk less.

Help Them Move One Step Further

Prayer and patience are critical. But remember the examples of those who have poured into you. Don't feel that as a disciple maker your role is to "fix" everything that is broken in people. You don't have to point out everything you see; God is more patient with us than that. Trust the quiet work of the Holy Spirit. Let Him disciple through you.

Our Hope Is the Good News

Normally we struggle with two extremes in our relationships with people who are not like our tribe. We become too pharisaical, pointing out a long list of shortcomings; or we feign "niceness" and let everything slide. Yet these "different" people are often the target for our disciple-making efforts and the gospel.

An example of this polarity is seen in the account of the woman caught in the act of adultery who was forcibly dragged to Jesus by her religious accusers (see John 8:1–11). The motivation of her accusers was to trap Jesus. She was simply bait, a prop to be further exploited in the unfolding drama.

Jesus seemed to have only two choices when they asked, "So what do you say?" (John 8:5). One choice was strict compliance to the law of Moses, which was death by stoning. The other was complicity with the morally depraved culture of Rome, which would argue to release her without consequence. This choice would put Jesus and His movement in the category of just another sexually immoral religious cult leader. The crowd was watching intently.

As disciple makers of broken and messy people, we always live in tension between the same two extremes Jesus faced. Jesus chose another path. First, He made her accusers take responsibility for their scheme, which publicly humiliated them and sent them, tails tucked between their legs, skulking away. He then created a "judgment-free zone" that focused on His compassion and the future of the broken woman who was, in fact, guilty as charged.

Jesus did something for the woman that only He could. What an awesome picture of the gospel. He removed the penalty for her sin that she fully deserved and, instead, showed her a future that she never dreamed possible. Jesus told her to "go, and from now on sin no more" (John 8:11). That is our story, too. He introduced her to the Light of life, and that Light was a person: "I am the light of the world. Anyone who follows Me will never walk in the darkness but will have the light of life" (John 8:12 HCSB).

Making disciples is not creating a grace environment that ignores our moral struggles and their natural consequences. Neither is making disciples taking on the hypocritical and rigid position of judging and sentencing people who are sinners just like us. Making disciples is living out the gospel without apology. We proclaim Jesus as the solution for sin by His act of taking the punishment that rightfully belonged to us. At the same time, we show people a "sin no more" future with Christ that they thought was not possible. "For our sake he made him to be sin who knew no sin, so that in him we might become the righteousness of God" (2 Cor. 5:21).

Coaching Questions

1. How are you measuring the maturity of the disciples you are making?

2. How do you communicate discipleship metrics to your church plant?

3. How do your systems provide personal coaching for disciples to take next steps?

Chapter 27

What Disciple Making Isn't

Discipleship is messy because our lives are messy. Deciding whose house our small group will meet in next week and if we will meet in the summer is minor league stuff. Figuring out how to have a difficult conversation with someone we love about his or her destructive choices is an altogether different story. Caring for a couple in our small group who has lost yet another pregnancy is not another Friday night fellowship at the bowling alley.

Discipleship is complicated. One size certainly doesn't fit all. People grow spiritually at different paces. Most are unpredictable—up and down as much as a puppy mastering stairs. They struggle with different addictions and respond to different spiritual disciplines. Some are extremely comfortable in the space of unbelievers and have strong influence with them. For others it's terrifying to acknowledge Christ around anyone but Christians.

Much of our disciple-making efforts do not result in disciples who live with Jesus. But to test the value of our efforts, we must agree on metrics. How can you tell if you are making disciples? Below are four poor examples of things we substitute for making disciples. All of these are valuable and can contribute to spiritual maturity, but standing alone from an intentional discipleship process, they are better identified as what discipleship isn't.

Small-Group Groupies

Depending on someone's personality or background, a small-group meeting in a home can be incredibly attractive. Really good small groups offer fun, food, and a needed break from the daily grind. Special outings and ministry projects can be a great connecting time. Open discussions and inspirational studies or sermon debriefs also add value. It's like a weekly Tupperware party without the hard close.

Small-group involvement as a single discipleship metric is a mistake. You are making a lot of assumptions when you say, "Sue is a growing disciple because she is going to Bob's small group." First, you are assuming the people in Bob's group are really good at making disciples. That can be addressed through strong internal processes like leader discovery, coaching, and training. However, the small group's discipleship environment is always a work in progress, as are the people who attend.

Second, you are assuming she is fully connected to the discipleship people in Bob's group are offering. Checking the discipleship box because Sue attends a group assumes Sue has compliant heart, ready and prepared to change. That's impossible.

In the early stages of discipleship, different things will drive Sue to a small group. That is not a bad thing, but once she gets there, hopefully others will pour into her. They will ask her questions and be mutually accountable. And most important, they will have transparent and direct conversations that go into the deep water of one another's lives.

The third faulty assumption about using small groups as a single discipleship metric is about those who do not attend. Bill doesn't want to attend Bob and Sue's group or any small group for that matter. Does that mean he is a bad disciple or that he has no interest in growing? Bill may have had a negative experience the last time he tried a group. He may work seventy hours a week or evenings when no group is offered. Don't read too much into his lack of engagement.

Bill may have never attended a small group before, or a church for that matter. For someone new to church or following Christ, going into someone's home can be terrifying and awkward. Will they be asked personal questions? How about Bible questions? The Bible is a strange and unfamiliar book to them. Will they be forced to talk or read in front of the group? And what if the people are weird? How does he kindly tell them he is not likely to come back?

God uses small groups in homes and public meeting places as well as traditional Sunday school classes to make disciples. Traditional and nontraditional groups have been a part of my spiritual journey since I was a child. But don't make the mistake of believing that if you have small groups you are making disciples. Strong group leaders, well-focused systems, and a healthy small-group culture are required. Alternatives to small groups for discipleship delivery are important too. Don't leave Bill out!

Class Envy

People like Beth Moore, Dave Ramsey, Henry Blackaby, and many more have produced material that is biblical, captivating, and practical. But a steady spiritual diet of these classes is as unhealthy as eating broccoli casserole three meals a day. Broccoli casserole has elements of healthy food as well as some tasty add-ons, but we need more.

Seminars and special classes consistently neglect to offer elements that are crucial to making healthy disciples. A curriculum-centered class is not designed to offer all the key elements necessary for growth. Like broccoli casserole, they can be incredibly delicious and uniquely nutritious but not at all life giving as the only item on the dietary menu. Here are five elements that limit the discipling potential of seminars.

1. Leadership Development

In most classes the option to "listen, learn, and leave" as a consumer is readily available. If a disciple is one who makes disciples, the listen, learn, and leave approach is the undoing of legitimate discipleship. A video-focused seminar can also send an unintended message of "you have to communicate like Beth Moore to lead a small group." True discipleship moves people from consumer to reproducer.

2. Year-round Accountability

Being more accountable for managing your money, reading the Bible, or finding God at work in your life in thirteen-week intervals is helpful but not nearly enough. I need disciples in my life who ask me questions no one else is asking all year long. To be in community with believers means "I know people are watching me." They are watching beyond my ability to complete this week's lesson and participate in the discussion. They are watching how I handle my kids, talk to my wife, and relate to unbelievers.

3. Strong Relationships

People can hide in the smallest of small groups. What makes life-on-life discipleship effective is that you spend significant time with a few people. You care for one another in crisis. You take care of one another's cars, houses, children, tools, and pets. You are happy and sad together: "So if one member suffers, all the members suffer with it; if one member is honored, all the members rejoice with it" (1 Cor. 12:26 HCSB). You become family. In a class or seminar meeting that need is impossible.

4. Opportunities to Serve

Anything learned or practiced with a group of people must be easily transferable to daily life with Jesus. We can't merely follow Jesus in groups. But one strength of group life is learning to serve others by serving together. The before-and-after conversations are incredible environments for growth. Classes and seminars seldom give space to serve together.

5. Deeper Conversations

Most seminars and classes are rushed. Time is limited to cover this week's lesson. The teaching time starts late, and some people have to leave early to care for children and prepare for the next day. The space to talk about life with Jesus is usually nonexistent. Jesus' disciples spent significant time in informal conversations with Jesus about life. Disciple making cannot be reduced to sixty or ninety minutes of structured time a week whether it's a living room or a classroom.

Doctrinal Fluency

A third defective metric of discipleship is measuring one's ability to fluently rehearse Bible-speak. Beliefs are important. The Bible has a distinct Jewish thread that involves knowing, understanding, reading, and reciting the truth. One of the most familiar examples is from the Old Testament:

> "Listen, Israel: The LORD our God, the LORD is One. Love the LORD your God with all your heart, with all your soul, and with all your strength. These words that I am giving you today are to be in your heart. Repeat them to your children. Talk about them when you sit in your house and when you walk along the road, when you lie down and when you get up. Bind them as a sign on your hand

and let them be a symbol on your forehead. Write them on the
doorposts of your house and on your gates." (Deut. 6:4–9 HCSB)

Jesus agreed about the importance of accurate beliefs and truth. "For if
you do not believe that I am He, you will die in your sins" (John 8:34 HCSB).
But what does belief look like when lived out on a daily basis? How is the
truth setting free the disciples you are making (see John 8:32)? Truth was
never meant to be an end in itself, but truth applied to the life of a disciple
has an amazing, transformational effect.

Ears are great discipleship tools, particularly if you know how to process
what you hear. But beware of assessing the heart of disciples based on their
ability to fluently speak the language of Bible doctrine. Some people love discussing theology and doctrine as much as others love talking about hockey
or football. Others are merely Bible fact-checkers who are the contemporary
equivalent to Pharisees. Jesus called them "whitewashed tombs . . . full of
dead men's bones" (Matt. 23:27 HCSB). Their exposure to right doctrine has
resulted in their becoming a strange aberration of being biblically erudite yet
spiritually illiterate. They have learned the language of the gospel without
experiencing its transforming effect.

A healthy diet of biblical preaching and Bible study is important to build
healthy believers. But strong interpersonal coaching and accountability are
also critical to help disciples hear God and live out what they are learning.
After all, discipleship is living daily with Jesus.

Good Deeds

Sometimes the opposite side of a one-dimensional fascination with
doctrinal fluency is an equally unhelpful enchantment with performing
good deeds. Many new church plants have a strong emphasis on serving
their communities, which, as preciously discussed, is incredibly wise. The
first church in history was a group that found special favor among people in
the community who were spiritual outsiders. People were being added every
day to this new church. Lives full of Christ were on display as they engaged
people and neighborhoods. Note that they gave from their common fund to
"all, as anyone had a need" (Acts 2:45 HCSB). Does that mean people outside
of their life group? More than likely.

In spite of their obvious limitations and inexperience, the first church
of the Christian movement was highly attractional. But there was no really

rockin' band, video clips, or children's ministry to grab the attention of those being added. What was attractional was radically changed lives.

One benefit of a good-deeds emphasis is that people far from Christ can find a significant place. No Christian language requirements exist. No belief · statements or giving records are needed to qualify them. "Leave your resumés at home and come love our city with us" is an open-ended invite.

New church plants need an engaged labor force to serve well. A good-deeds approach requires all hands on deck. So shepherds often default to separating the "sheep from the goats" by those who serve and those who don't. Mature disciples serve their city, right? Then good deeds provide more than simply a place to belong. They become a place of acceptance and affirmation. "The more I serve, the more they love me" can be the unintended message. Serving, as a single discipleship metric, is dangerous.

Right behavior is another aspect of the good-deeds conundrum. We can sometimes add "our transformation" to the long list of good deeds to be performed. Yet we know this is a short-term and ultimately disastrous mindset. Spiritual transformation is never a matter confined to one's will. As the spiritual transformation process happens through the Holy Spirit's influence, people naturally become increasingly uncomfortable with certain former attitudes and behaviors. Values are in process of being forever changed. But notice I said "in process." With most people this takes time and there are stages.

The first stage of the Holy Spirit's work can result in behavior modification. The attractiveness of a better way of life without the work of Holy Spirit in the heart leaves us no other option but to change by force of will. Paul Tripp called this "fruit stapling" or producing artificial fruit or behavior. In his book *Instruments in the Redeemer's Hands*,[38] he said: "Change that ignores the heart will seldom transform the life. For a while, it may seem like the real thing, but it will prove temporary and cosmetic."

Coaching Questions

1. What examples of "bad discipleship" have you tried in the past?

2. What alternatives to small groups do you have to make disciples?

3. What practices of your small groups contribute to disciple making?

Chapter 28

A Process
for Making Disciples

In the mid 1990s, Rick Warren's baseball diamond[39] reintroduced the evangelical world to a "process approach" to corporate discipleship. The bases represented different growth environments. The idea was that people were to run the baselines to new stages of maturity. To some, discipleship processes may feel too institutional—too "do" versus "be" oriented—but without some kind of process, people generally fall through the discipleship cracks. The elements involved in a discipleship process are actually a strategic attempt to create environments where God makes disciples who live daily with Jesus.

Intuitive to the design of a discipleship process is a proper understanding of the roles involved. What is our part in making disciples? What does our partnership with God look like? How organic is discipleship? How intentional? Do we simply preach, organize small groups or classes, and leave the results totally to God? Or do we use guilt, manipulation, and confrontation to make sure people do what we think is needed?

The obvious answers are somewhere in the middle of the previously mentioned extremes. Paul gives us a picture of how we work together with God to accomplish His mission.

The ancient city of Corinth was filled with spiritually bewildered and morally bankrupt people. Corinthian citizens came to Christ broken, struggling, and confused. Their discipleship process landed squarely in the "it's complicated" category. Putting them in a "new member" class would have left their needs completely unmet; they were "EGR" people (Extra Grace

Required). Extra grace was required to care for them and keep them moving forward toward spiritual maturity.

Apollos and Paul were weighty leaders in the lives of the Corinthian people. God assigned them completely different roles in the process of making disciples. Apollos's role as a discipler was different from Paul's yet equally important. Apollos had built quite a following. This is how Luke introduced him in Acts: "A Jew named Apollos, a native Alexandrian, an eloquent man who was powerful in the use of the Scriptures, arrived in Ephesus" (Acts 18:24 HCSB).

"Powerful in the use of the Scriptures" and "eloquent" are vivid descriptors of Apollos, the disciple maker. He had a "presence" that God used to capture and challenge people on their spiritual journey. There is no doubt that you knew when Apollos was in the room.

Part of his prowess was his uncommon moral strength, a refreshing example for a morally challenged Corinthian disciple. Apollos embodied the greatness of the gospel. He was a disciple-making disciple of Jesus Christ. He had an important role in the lives of many who attributed God's work in their lives to him.

Apollos, Paul, and no doubt others along the way had unintentionally built followings among the Corinthian disciples of Jesus Christ. When Paul learned of this, he desired to set the record straight. To Paul they were simply God's tools in a spiritually empowered process. Paul explained how a discipleship process worked:

What then is Apollos? And what is Paul? They are servants through whom you believed, and each has the role the Lord has given. I planted, Apollos watered, but God gave the growth. So then neither the one who plants nor the one who waters is anything, but only God who gives the growth. Now the one planting and the one watering are one in purpose, and each will receive his own reward according to his own labor. For we are God's coworkers. You are God's field, God's building. (1 Cor. 3:5–9 HCSB)

Paul was the missionary, apostle, and God-ordained entrepreneur for the gospel. Digging a hole in the soil, placing the seed in the ground, and covering up the hole are parts of the process Paul mastered. Apollos came along and nurtured the plant, another intentional and indispensable role in the process.

But God makes the plant grow.

You couldn't be more intentional than Paul and Apollos. They knew their roles. But when growth happened in the life of a Corinthian or Ephesian disciple, they both knew how that happened. Only God can make disciples. But He uses our intentionality as a platform to do what only He can do.

In my mind's eye I can go back to incredible stories of spiritual transformation in the lives of spiritually bewildered and morally bankrupt people in the churches I had the privilege to plant. The stories I see, hear, and experience firsthand are happening everyplace. God's new apostles are intentionally taking the gospel everywhere and making disciples. It's incredible to watch this happen at an unprecedented rate. Yet the fact remains, without God's work true spiritual transformation is not unlikely; it's impossible.

From Bases to Stages

Rick Warren created places for people to go with his baseball diamond. It was a welcome renaissance back to some attempt at corporate discipleship. As the idea gained momentum, a new question emerged: Does everybody start in the same place?

We knew that in baseball everybody doesn't stand in the batter's box in the same place: some stand on the left or right side; others switch at will. Many contracted players were not dressed for the game. Others were neither in the stadium nor in the same city. As the season wore on, the disabled lists tended to grow. Weary baseball players often sat at home watching the Golf Channel.

Many baseball players were a long way from first base.

If you have ever been lost in a local mall (or anywhere that requires a map), the first vital step to recovery is to actually find yourself on the map. The big red "You Are Here" dot on the map becomes the most significant marking for anyone who shares my limitation of being geographically challenged. From that all-important red dot, even the least navigationally inclined soul can intrepidly plot his way to Starbucks.

If disciple making is your destination, one path will not help them all. Why? Simply because everyone is starting from a different red dot. Some people have no belief system at all (which ironically is a belief system). A few may have some kind of church or religious history. Some may have an ongoing commitment or strong influence from a false religious belief system. Some are curious about the gospel. Others may be "believers," but they are all at different points of maturity. The ultimate destination is life with Jesus Christ, but the obstacles and next steps are unique depending on the person. Paul Johnson of the Canadian National Baptist Convention designed a helpful example of Stages[40] on a spiritual path. Understanding Stages has been important to church plants like Fellowship Pickering, Ontario. You'll hear more about them later.

Paul's discipleship process "helps disciple makers develop a strategy for investing in others." Stages is an incredibly practical tool that includes a downloadable app. One frequently asked question by disciple makers is, "How can I help people move forward spiritually?" Paul offers examples of concrete ways to help move people closer to Christ. His ideas will inspire other ideas for new church planters.

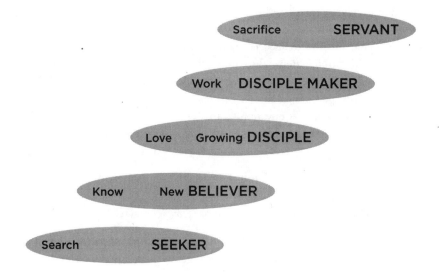

Process Thinking Is Awkward

The "speed" and multitasking required of a new church planter are staggering. Planters understandably struggle to set priorities and remain focused. Creating community through small groups makes sense and is on every planter's radar. But although some small groups will have some organic influence on making disciples, more intentionality is usually needed.

Have you ever bit off more than you can chew? This is the constant pressure experienced by planters. You may have experienced a parallel phenomenon at your local Walmart, Target, or other big-box retailer. Have you ever visited to pick up "a couple" of needed items? You think, "I don't need a buggy. I can go much faster without one."

On your way through the store toward the milk section, and then to the garbage bag section, something happens. You begin to notice other things that would make your home function more smoothly and your life improve.

The "grab now" rush intensifies with little view to either your original mission or your personal capacity. Before long you start to look like a disheveled Christmas tree with "helpful items" dangling everywhere from your person.

By the time you meander to the milk section, there is absolutely no place for the milk to fit. And you have not even approached the garbage bag section. The bottom line: your mission is an epic failure. Your noble yet ill-conceived craving for something more effective triggered you to randomly grab more than you could effectively carry.

For your mission to succeed, you needed a predetermined plan, a clear path, and intentional steps. But the random grab is more natural, and we all love organic, right? Clearly some things will not simply happen "all by themselves" in spite of our best intentions.

The most important question to answer in a discipleship process is this: "What kind of disciple should we be making?" For example, we should want to make a fruit-bearing disciple in three areas:

1. They engage people with the gospel (disciple maker).
2. They obey the commands of Christ (obedience).
3. They demonstrate Christlike character (character).

Now in a discipleship process you create environments and relationships that help people move through personal stages of growth. Your task is to create both a coaching environment and a teaching environment. As a spiritual coach you ask open-ended questions to help people determine where they are (where their red dot is located), what God is saying, and where they are going. For example:

Disciple Maker

- What relationships away from church are you cultivating for gospel influence?
- What is your next step in those relationships?

Obedience

- What areas in your life do you need to grow in obedience to Christ?
- What does God want you to do next?

Character

- What personal struggle in your life is the most urgent for you to address?
- How can you address that area?

The strengths of a discipleship process are preestablished targets and clear paths to get there. A commitment to the process means everyone can answer the questions: "How are we doing? What adjustments do we need to make more and better disciples?"

Design Your Own Process

Paul Johnson's Stages is one of many brilliant examples of a discipleship process. However, taking someone else's model does not always create needed ownership by a new church plant or take contextual idiosyncrasies into full account.

New church planters should design or determine their discipleship process early. Everything in your new church should support the process. From sermons to small groups, to core team meetings, the common language and focus should be your process for making disciples. Integration of this process beyond small groups and classes is absolutely critical.

Here are four simple questions to help you begin the process:

- What kind of disciple are we making? (Definition)
- How do we help them assess their own maturity? (Stages)
- What environments and relationships will we create in order to help them mature? (Steps)
- How will we measure and celebrate success? (Metrics)

The Back of My Camel

"G" coaches and mobilizes church planters in one of the most violent areas of a predominantly Muslim country. His story illustrates the need for a heart shift to multiply disciples in and from the harvest. In one of "G's" gospel conversations, a Muslim herder responded: "Your religion will not fit on the back of my camel. Why would I even consider it?"

The herder explained that he could take his prayer mat off the back of his camel and practice his religion anywhere, anytime, without needing help from anyone. He said that what he had seen of "Christianity" was that when someone converts they must go to church, attend meetings, and listen to others at prescribed times during the week. If he really wanted to be the best Christian, he would need to go far away from home to get training. It just would not fit on the back of his camel.[41]

Discipleship begins with the first conversation you have with a lost person. Your process should be so simple that he or she can understand and own it. A common mistake of new church planters is that they subconsciously view that disciples are made to support the church domain. But Sunday morning disciples are, at best, only making baby steps to becoming what God wants them to be. Discipleship processes are church supported and designed to be practiced in the personal world of each disciple Monday through Friday.

Coaching Questions

1. Who from your past had the greatest influence on your personal discipleship?

2. What is your plan to communicate stories of life change in your church plant?

3. What steps can you take to define or improve your discipleship process?

Chapter 29

A Process for Multiplying Disciples

For emphasis we like to say to "make disciple-making disciples" you need to inspire a vision for multiplication. But in the Great Commission (see Matt. 28:19–20), Jesus indicated you are not making real disciples if they are not disciple makers.

Disciple making is what Jesus' disciples do.

The Great Commission Path

Go—Make Disciples—Baptize—Teach

It seems like a prescription. Others might call it a path of obedience. If the path is followed, multiplication will happen. So the Great Commission, at its fundamental essence, is simply a call to multiply. The first core group of the Christian movement got its guiding directions from their Lord. Jesus' words stalwartly reinforce that disciples make disciples. The disciples' mission wasn't to produce satisfied consumers of the movement. What would obedience to the Great Commission produce? Only one thing: owners of the mission.

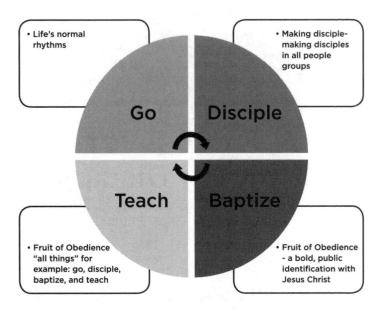

The Multiplication Mandate

If you look closely, you will discover at least four critical elements of supernatural multiplication from Jesus' words about the harvest.

> Then Jesus went to all the towns and villages, teaching in their synagogues, preaching the good news of the kingdom, and healing every disease and every sickness. When He saw the crowds, He felt compassion for them, because they were weary and worn out, like sheep without a shepherd. Then He said to His disciples, "The harvest is abundant, but the workers are few. Therefore, pray to the Lord of the harvest to send out workers into His harvest." (Matt. 9:35–38 HCSB)

Here is an important Kingdom fact: if you love the harvest, you will love other harvesters. If you are jealous of other harvesters, you simply do not love the harvest.

Why? Because the harvest is not about you. It's not even about your new church. It's not about your share. It's not about your personal capacity. It is about an urgent reality that is life or death with the eternity of others hanging in the balance.

Consider these realities of the harvest:

PART 7: MAKING DISCIPLES

209

It's Big

"Jesus went to all the towns and villages, . . . teaching . . . preaching . . . healing." The task was beyond His personal capacity. In a moment of possible compassion fatigue (remember, Jesus was fully human), He stopped to disciple His disciples.

The Workforce Is Limited

"But the workers are few." The number of workers is in the exact opposite proportion to the size of the harvest. Suddenly Jesus' focus mysteriously shifts from the great big harvest situation to a labor-shortage problem. Are the laborers more important than the harvest? In this case, yes. The natural laws of farming dictate that laborers must come before the harvest in order of priority.

Prayer Is Our First Strategic Step

Our success is not a product of human will or resourcefulness. I am not a mathematician, but it does not take a math wizard to tell you the numbers don't work. Big harvest plus a labor shortage equals a big problem. It doesn't add up, unless, of course, God does the math. Here's how God works it out.

The Workforce Is Unlimited

"Send out workers." The current reality is that the workers are limited. That is the bad news that we can do little to change. But there is some good news that God wants us to see. The potential workforce of harvesters is actually as big as the harvest itself. The harvest can immediately become coharvesters with us. So as we pray and ask that God's supernatural power is released on the harvest itself, we are praying for a harvest of harvesters. As they are harvested, God solves the workforce issues. It is not as complicated as we make it.

What part of our religious hearts does God need to capture so we might become willing to approach the harvest God's way?

The numbers are impossible in North America alone. The majority of these people are living in densely populated urban places that have little gospel exposure. The math adds up that in the US and Canada alone there are 259 million people who need to hear and see and taste and smell the gospel immediately.[42] They are all living on borrowed time.

We simply don't have enough "rock star" planters to build large harvest-gathering warehouses. I thank God for every one of the incredibly gifted leaders and communicators that lead large churches in North America. They're often doing more than their share of the heavy lifting. But from Jesus' instructions we see that North America will ultimately be won from His work within the harvest. New disciple-making churches must be started from a new harvest within the darkest places in our cities. But unfortunately, much too often we wait for the harvest to knock on our existing church's doors. And our results have been embarrassing.

To further complicate this, 81 percent of the North American population resides in metropolitan areas.[43] These same areas correlate with the geographies that have the least evangelical presence. Following a Pauline missiological principle, the North American Mission Board has strategically focused much of our church-planting energy and resources on thirty-two of these spiritually neglected cities of influence.

The Send North America[44] strategy is not prioritizing the people in these thirty-two metropolitan areas as *more* important than the rest. We simply believe they are not *less* important. Why should the bulk of spiritual resources and manpower be redelivered to areas that already have the bulk of spiritual resources and manpower? Moreover, why should the harvest that reflects both the greatest spiritual need and the greatest cultural influence continue to go unharvested year after year? We believe concentrating efforts on the most unharvested fields is the fastest and most efficient way to get the gospel everywhere.

But even with a strategic priority like Send North America, if God does not send harvesters, the fields will wither and die unharvested. We can't buy, strategize, or will our way into a greater harvest success.

But we can pray and work toward a greater workforce.

- Kingdom multipliers love the other laborers as much as laboring.
- Kingdom multipliers love the other witnesses as much as witnessing.
- Kingdom multipliers love the other disciple makers as much as discipling.
- Kingdom multipliers love the other church planters as much as church planting.

Next Step: A Heart Shift

The heart shift from addition to multiplication, from harvest to harvesters, is seismic for perfectly good reasons. We must shift from an "each one reach one" mentality to an "each one reach many." No longer is the metric how hard can I work *in* the harvest but how hard I can work *for* the harvest. Here are three illustrations that will give a framework for the colossal heart shift that is needed to move from adding to multiplying.

Farmer Versus Cook

When you pray to thank God before your next enormous holiday meal, I can predict most of your prayer content—no discredit intended. None of you will say, "Thank you, Lord, for the farmer from Idaho, who many months ago labored with great patience, worked long days, and took great risks to plant, nurture, and harvest these incredible mashed potatoes." Yet he spent many lonely days doing his part to put food on your table. On the other hand, some of you will say a version of "and bless the hands that prepared this meal." Grandma is likely the star of the enormous holiday meal show. As a colaborer, she gets instant gratification.

The farmer doesn't really care that grandma gets the credit or that he is seldom even a footnote. His ultimate goal is to feed the masses from the fruit of his labor. He plans, he searches for the best crop for the best field, he works, and he waits. He experiences disappointment because of variables he cannot control like wind, sun, and rain.

Multiplication is labor-intensive requiring patience, risk, and a healthy dose of humility.

Making Plays Versus Making Players

Players love to be in the middle of the action where blood, sweat, and tears are exchanged for glory, superstardom, and cheerleaders. Rarely in professional or college sports does a coach suit up and play. And when that does happen, it is even rarer that he succeeds at both. Both assignments require too much skill, energy, and focus. To a great coach, making players is much more important than making plays. Without multiple positions on a team being filled by passionate players, the mission of the team is already thwarted.

To make players, a player developer must surrender personal ambitions. Dreams must die. His dream of being in front of a packed home stadium receiving the Most Valuable Player award after winning the World Series must be laid aside. He now lives for the success of others.

Multiplication requires a high level of skill, energy, focus, sacrifice, and a healthy dose of humility.

Midwife Versus Mother

The mother experiences all the joy of giving birth. I am not minimizing the pain, risk, stretch marks, and all the discomfort involved (that would surely get me in trouble), but a mother has just personally and intimately participated in the most incredible miracle on earth. Yet the midwife has a unique helping role in the process.

God has planted a desire in the hearts of most women to be a mother. Having a baby is something she has dreamed about since she was a child. Giving birth is a dream fulfilled. Multiplication is likely to come for the mother, but that's not what she is thinking at the moment of birth. She is focusing on the future hopes and dreams of her new baby.

The midwife is seldom there for the first day of kindergarten, the senior prom, or the wedding. She moves on to the next person to help them realize their God-given dreams. Yet her role is indispensable.

Multiplication requires a helping spirit, an ability to celebrate other's victories, and a healthy dose of humility.

Lessons learned for the multiplier.

- *Multiplication is not about you.* Personal ambition, even for God's mission, is released.
- *Multiplication is about enjoying others' success.* "For now we live, if you stand firm in the Lord" (1 Thess. 3:8 HCSB).
- *Multiplication requires sacrifice.* Short-term addition is more self-gratifying, but long-term eternity is at stake for the masses.
- *Multiplication involves risk.* God absolutely honors obedience but not always in a "prosperity theology" way we subconsciously think. We must unconditionally surrender our personal agendas for the Kingdom.

Disciple-making Disciples Template

Matt and Arrica Hess moved their family from Memphis, Tennessee, to Pickering, Ontario, in 2012. Pickering had thirteen evangelical churches for a population of a hundred thousand people. Younger families and multiple ethnicities make up a spiritually curious city.

"You have to be willing to let God shape what takes place," Matt said. And this is exactly what they did. From the beginning they made the seismic shift from making disciples to making disciple makers. Their vision is to multiply groups and churches through the Pickering community beginning with Fellowship Church.

Engage Gather Disciple is a process they created to develop disciple-making disciples. More than a program or a class, Engage Gather Disciple (EGD) is about creating a disciple-making culture at Fellowship. The process is integrated into everything that is done in their new church with a focused mission to multiply disciples, small groups, and churches.

Sebastian Vasquez joined Matt's team in Toronto early in the process and wrote the EGD content manual. Seba posed these questions:

- What percentage of your non-Christian friends, family members, coworkers, and neighbors would go to a Bible study or church regularly if you asked?
- What's your strategy for everyone else?

If you go to their website,[45] you will see the foundation for developing disciple makers. Stages, explained earlier, creates a spiritual conversation starter for those new at making disciples by asking them to self-assess their own spiritual stage.

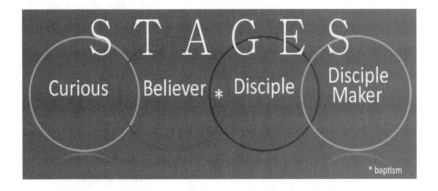

For Matt, the EGD helps create a culture to address the "Terrible Two" or the two biggest obstacles in making disciple makers:

1. *Am I capable of discipling someone else?* "Do I 'have it all together' enough to be a disciplemaker?" "Do I know enough?"
2. *Is the Holy Spirit moving and drawing people to the Father?* "Do people really want to hear?" "Will anybody respond?"

The EGD culture is not confined to a training tract (although one is included). But it's a part of ongoing strategic discussions within small groups, core team meetings, and with church-planting interns.

Matt explained that his church is constantly being challenged, both formally and informally, on how they are "building roads into the harvest." If they are not, then they help one another decide how they can engage and gather on a higher level.

The four major elements of EGD equip disciples as disciple makers:

1. Become a gospel conversationalist—being fluent in the real life implications of the gospel.
2. Map out your social fields—areas in your life where you are in constant contact with the same people.
3. Gather to engage or disciple—find an area of interest for people you are trying to reach and design a gathering around that interest.
4. Work a discipleship path: Stages—knowing spiritual stages and how to help people supernaturally work through them.

Although Fellowship is early in the process, Matt is encouraged by what God is doing. Of those who attend Fellowship, 70 percent are previously unchurched. They're now in the process of launching their second church. And the God stories are happening all around them. One example is James:

At the very first door I knocked on, a young man named James answered the door. As James and I began to talk, I realized he was extremely curious about God. James filled out the survey, and I followed back up with him the following week. At our second meeting I asked James if he wanted to know more about Jesus Christ and the Bible. He said yes. Over the next six months James was in our home probably twice a week either for a Bible study, a meal, or just to hang out with our family. James eventually gave his life to Christ, and I had the privilege to baptize him soon after! But the story continues. Probably four months after his salvation, James called me one day on the phone and said he needed to talk. He sounded nervous. He said, "I know this is going to sound weird because I'm a brand-new Christian and everything, but I really think God wants me to become a preacher." After I walked with James through his calling, I confirmed that he indeed is called to preach. He preached for the first time with me several months ago on a Sunday morning and did a great job. He is currently leading a LifeGroup in our church for singles, is discipling young men, and is preparing to coplant a church over the next eighteen months.[46]

The EGD process is a contextual strategy to help new church plants and everyday believers become disciple makers. If you are planting in a culture that is predominantly unreached and not even curious about the gospel, discouragement can come quickly. Fellowship Pickering's example can inspire your creativity and reinforce your mandate.

If your vision as a church planter is merely to make disciples, the road will be long. But if God gives you a path to making disciple-making disciples, then the Kingdom impact possibilities dramatically multiply.

Which leads us to the next phase on a movement cycle.

Coaching Questions

1. What is your prayer strategy for multiplying disciples?

2. What "heart shift" needs to take place in you to become a more effective multiplier?

3. How can you create a culture of multiplication in your church plant?

Part 8: **Multiplication**

There is a great and sad irony in the church-planting world that so much care and attention are devoted to instructing planters on "how to launch their church," and a comparatively insignificant amount of energy is invested in preparing that planter and his new church for Kingdom movement. The very process that leads a harvesting people to a multiplying harvest is often short-circuited with a return to addition, consolidation, and barn building.

In this section we will discuss: (1) What are the biblical, natural, and mutually beneficial reasons to become a multiplying church? (2) What are some self-serving myths we have believed to avoid multiplying, and what are some missteps we can sidestep? (3) What multiplication systems seem to work in secular environments? (4) How can we shape ourselves in such a way that if the Holy Spirit blows on our sails, we can be in the middle of a Kingdom movement?

Let's begin with a biblical rationale.

Chapter 30

Why Multiply?

It is an encouraging phenomenon to watch "normal" shift when the old normal felt so wrong. When I planted my last church, I was both deeply convicted and thoroughly convinced that this church would be seriously about multiplication. We proposed a God-sized vision that we would multiply twenty-five times over in the next two decades. I began to scour across North America in a search for brothers who had this same passion. They were hard to find. I found several who talked the talk but fewer who were willing to pay the price. I found a friend in Atlanta, another in Las Vegas, another in Dallas, one in St. Louis, one more in Tucson, and a small handful of others. We would gather together a couple of times a year for wisdom and encouragement (and to convince ourselves that we weren't nuts).

But normal seems to be shifting. More often than not, when I meet a new church planter, he talks multiplication in his first sentence. Often he points to a team member he is grooming as the heir apparent for their first multiplied plant. This is not the culture that was emanating from the postchurch-growth era. This is something far more Kingdom.

So, feeling compelled to convince fewer, let's look together at a few persuasive reasons multiplication should be a part of any healthy church-planting prospectus.

It Is Biblical

Where does church multiplication fit into our ecclesiology? And if it does, how central should it be?

Neither from the writers of the New Testament in general, nor the specific instructions from King Jesus, were Christians ever encouraged simply to reach to people with the gospel. From the beginning, believers were to be formed into assemblies called by a common purpose. Our English word *church* comes from a Greek word, *ekklesia*, meaning "the called-out ones." Following the pattern of the synagogue, the early believers were quickly called out and gathered into newly formed congregations (as is noted in Acts 2:41–47; 5:11; 13:1). This was the normative pattern found in the book of Acts.

Following the instruction of their King (Matt. 28:19–20; Mark 16:15; Luke 24:47–48; John 20:21; Acts 1:8), the book of Acts opens with an introduction to the first Jerusalem church and ends twenty-eight chapters later with the church of Jesus Christ multiplying all over the known world.

Every now and then someone will say to me, "Jeff, where in the Bible are we commanded to start churches?" My response is, "The entire New Testament!" It's the theme of everything. From Jesus' selecting, preparing, and commissioning His disciples to the testimony of their actions in Acts, to the letters and epistles sent to the newly planted churches, to the Revelation of John where Jesus encourages and corrects churches that were planted. On the essential gospel message Jesus established His church, a church designed for all people in all places. My question back is, "Where in the New Testament are they not planting churches?"

Luke provides us with one of his typical summary statements in which he refers to the church in a general sense. In this particular report Luke dispassionately describes the normal activity of the first-century church, which is instructive to this discussion of multiplication: "So the church throughout all Judea and Galilee and Samaria had peace and was being built up. And walking in the fear of the Lord and in the comfort of the Holy Spirit, it multiplied" (Acts 9:31).

What may be surprising to those who argue for a more consolidated slant to church is that this was never the mentality of the first-century church. Luke, as almost a parenthetical thought, jots down that in a season of peace the church was busy multiplying. It is surprising to us that the church was not readying itself with internal growth to help it withstand the certainty of upcoming persecution. Consolidation in a season of peace seems from a prudent perspective as steward and wise. Yet this first-century church refused to pause in order to consolidate. The winds of persecution would find certainly them, but their numbers would not be static and dug in but scattered and fanning out. Certainly one of the keys that moved Christianity from cultic Roman outlier to its dominant sacred force in less than three centuries was its proclivity to multiply. It's not that we want to imitate the early church in terms of all of its contextual ecclesiological forms—many of them have and should have changed. It's that we desire to learn from their obedience to Christ and the blessing that followed. The goal in the twenty-first century isn't necessarily literal first-century churches but churches that produce faithful disciples, just as faithful church planters have across all of church history. We want to imitate them insofar as they imitated Christ.

Squatting down cross-legged and dominating the turf became the revered fascination that followed this period of history. And with this massive effort of consolidation, the church finally gained notoriety and respectability. With this respectability many were joyous because on the surface it seemed like a noble victory. But wiser sages grieved, for they understood that with this newfound respectability the church had sold her soul. The Kingdom's increasingly spontaneous expansion of a spiritual movement was reduced to a much darker prescription of sterility and uniformity. The image of Jesus and His church could now be readily seen in art and architecture, but no longer was it visible in the priorities of His people. Pagan images were replaced with Christian ones, and the empire slowly chugged downward to the onset of the darker ages.

The multiplication of churches as witnessed in Acts offers several insights that demonstrate how the disciples lived out the propositional truths they received. Apparently many churches were planted in a short span of time, for we read that Paul and Barnabas appointed pastors in "every church" (Acts 14:23). Further, Paul traveled "through Syria and Silicia, strengthening the churches" (Acts 15:41). Paul obviously formed new believers into congregations wherever he went. In the final chapter of Romans, we find Paul giving personal greetings to numerous Christian leaders who led churches Paul had never visited. Second- and third-generation church multiplication had quickly begun to spin off of Paul's early pioneering work as the apostle to the Gentiles. Normal to the first-century church's sacred experience was the practice of sending out their best for the advancement of the Kingdom of God (Acts 13:1–3).

This is not to say that all church multiplication methodologies and applications are biblically sound or that all churches should be multiplied. One obvious evidence of the grace of God toward humanity is that some churches will never multiply. Multiplying a sacred expression of darkness is of no benefit to the Kingdom of God.

A biblical understanding of church multiplication requires a clear appreciation of the theological nature of the church. With a biblically solid ecclesiological perspective, the long-term intentions of the church should always guide any short-term strategy or vision. So what is the biblical intention of churches? What should be the substance of new communities of Christ? Certainly a biblical understanding of church would guide us to start new communities of:

- Regenerate children, born of God, and belonging to God (Rom. 1:7; 1 Cor. 1:1–2)
- Interdependent connection, living appreciatively and reliantly on the Holy Spirit's work through the entire community (Rom. 12:3–8; 1 Cor. 12:12–30)
- Humble believers amazed and propelled by grace and therefore living and breathing the gospel wherever they travel (Matt. 10)
- Incarnational disciples living transformed lives within the world, yet not isolated or alienated from the world (1 Cor. 6:12–20)
- Meek and unpretentious practices with an application of the gospel that is both accessible and understandable to an uninitiated world (book of Gal.; John 14:26; 16:13–15)
- Selfless and self-sacrificing followers emulating the lifestyle of their leaders who themselves embody a singular and primal desire to glorify God (Rom. 16:25–27; 1 Cor. 6:20; Phil. 1:20)
- Undiscriminating messengers without racial walls, national borders, or socioeconomic separation, and therefore missionary by their genetic code (Rom. 15:18–19)
- Reproducing emissaries obediently and skillfully taking the gospel to new places and from that commission multiplying new expressions of Christian community (Acts 9:31)

Clearly a straightforward reading of the New Testament can lead to no other conclusion than the normal state of a Kingdom-spirited congregation is to seek to provide opportunities for every person to come face-to-face with the good news of Christ. With this high and eternal motivation, the biblical record illustrates a church that radically focused on multiplication.

It Is Natural

Perhaps the least examined issue that is germane to all churches is an honest appreciation for its own natural, and, yes, temporal life cycle. Often, in a desperate attempt to distract itself from its own mortality, declining churches, in a self-indulgent binge, perform numerous cosmetic enhancements to hoist an illusion of youthful vitality. The thin plastic veneer usually fools few, and the church marches one step closer to its ignominious end.

Over the past few decades, one untested yet habitually echoed axiom has garnered an almost biblical standing in our evangelical easy-speak: *healthy churches grow (implication: continuously)*. It seems that despite both the evidence of church history and the overwhelming weight of self-sacrificial Kingdom themes within Scripture, it all really comes down to this singular, all-important metric: *do we have more sitting in our benches this year than last?*

For the majority of evangelicals, this new dogma is not an emboldening creed. According to the Leavell Center for Evangelism and Church Health,[47] of the more than forty-two thousand Southern Baptist churches in North America, fewer than 11.9 percent of them qualify with an unexceptional threshold of health defined by a modest annual baptism rate of one per thirty-five members. In other words, 88 percent of Southern Baptist churches have plateaued in their growth or are declining.

With 88 percent of churches failing to embody "health," as described by the school of church growth, we are faced with one of two possible deductions. Either the local church was not intended to eternally produce quarter after quarter of positive returns, or our ecclesiological assumptions are still plausible—just universally poorly executed.

The former seems to be a more honest conclusion from the facts.

For many it is an astonishing notion to consider that *every local church has a life cycle.*[48] To many it may seem cold to think of a church this way. But without exception every church has had a beginning, and it will have an end. The Kingdom advancement that emanates from a local church has an eternal effect, but the fact remains, no one can visit Paul's most impressive Philippi church plant. Its life cycle is long completed; yet its impact remains. Every church has a life cycle designed for eternal impact.

It is also noteworthy to consider that churches, like other natural organisms, *are designed to grow the fastest at the earliest stages of life.* A juvenile plant is called a "shoot" for a reason. This natural order found in plants, puppies, and people also seems to sync with a casual observation of the normative growth patterns of churches. The fastest growth is usually reserved for the front end of the life cycle. Zero to 75 percent of trajectory usually happens quickly and efficiently. The final 25 percent requires enormous energy and resources.

Also (and quite instructive), like other natural organisms *churches are designed to begin reproducing both soon and often.* Our recent Western norm of beginning families late in a parent's reproductive cycle is an aberration to the experience of nature and history. Normally reproduction happens early and continues through the majority of life. Wherever we see the Kingdom of God rapidly gaining ground, we always find disciples reproducing disciples and churches reproducing churches. With this the natural end of the life cycle of a particular local church is not quietly marked as a dooming failure but unashamedly celebrated because of an eternal Kingdom impact that is beheld by a sizable and appreciative family tree.

Every local church has a life cycle. Churches are designed to grow the fastest at the earliest stages of life. Churches are designed to begin reproducing both soon and often.

Finally, like all other organisms, *churches are not intended to continuously grow forever.* The natural rhythm of a church's life cycle is to grow quickly in the earliest stages, reproduce frequently during their maturing years, and hopefully assist as wise, generous, and loving grandparents during their final years.

There is great tragedy in that so many churches do just the opposite to what is natural in every other realm of God's creation. When they start to plateau, rather than ramp up reproduction, they often turn inward in a frantic and futile effort of self-preservation. Their metrics for this last gasp of church health has little to do with a Kingdom picture of new believers, new disciple makers, new churches, and a transformed community but instead revolve around bank balances and viable critical mass.

With Kingdom far from their thoughts, the natural act of multiplication is understood as a self-eroding action of creating internal competition. Fallen thinking ensues. "Doing church is difficult enough without organically creating new and feistier competitors grasping for the same decreasing market share." Sadly, when a church makes the unnatural choice of ecclesiastical birth control in order to preserve its accustomed lifestyle, the natural and exponential advance of the Kingdom of God ceases.

So, as a new church planter, help your leaders appreciate the brevity of life. The church you are about to start has an end date already fixed by a sovereign King. Compelled by that urgency, leverage this new church as a lethal Kingdom asset to a pervasive darkness that has enveloped your city.

Multiply yourself. Often. Create generations of dangerous disciples that will pick up the Kingdom mantle after your season is through.

Start from the beginning with the fascination of ordering your internal priorities in such a way that you just might shape a movement. Strategically set your sails so if the winds of Holy Spirit blow your way, there could be no other explanation but God. Humbly position yourself within His Kingdom for Christ to receive incredible glory through His church that He started through your yielded life.

To a darkened and dying world, this is utter madness.

To an illumined and living Kingdom, this is only natural.

It Is Beneficial

Every church plant, if it survives, becomes a church.

The length of time in which it crosses over from "church plant" to "church" is different in every case. But my wife, Laura, and I have both been able to identify the dreary day it happens. We have seen it enough. Some strange thing occurs within the spirit of a church plant that indicates we are now entering a new season of leadership. I have usually mourned on those days. It's not that it is an inherently bad thing in and of itself. It's just a church planter's realization that the sweetest days are behind us, and my leadership role has to shift.

When an effective church planter engages a community, he has an internal and compelling urgency directed squarely at the harvest. He is on a mission from God. Others can see it in his eyes. Soon the harvested become harvesters, and the whole thing takes on a life of its own. For a church planter these are the days that will never be forgotten.

But unfortunately, usually, you only get to live these days once. Things soon get more complicated because despite your planting methodology, organizational structures and systems must be constructed or everything that has transpired will soon evaporate. So the church planter is forced to simultaneously create an organization while inspiring that organization toward her Kingdom assignment.

Over time pioneers get replaced or outnumbered by settlers. And then one day it happens. For the first time you are publicly challenged about your preoccupation with this "outward vision." One boisterous (or courageous) sheep rises up and bleats a countervision: "We need to take care of ourselves before we go out trying to save the world!" You look into the eyes of the flock, and you can see a carefully hidden agreement by many. Several of your leaders stand and publicly affirm God's direction and rehearse all the signs of God's favor, but you know in your heart that things are now changed. You are officially a church. Your leadership must adapt.

For most church planters these are days mourned. A page has officially and forever been turned.

The next phase of leadership involves a moderation of his apostolic voice within a plant and a dialing up of his shepherding function. Even though every corpuscle of his personality screams "mission!" he correctly realizes that he cannot look at wounded sheep and then point to the mission and say, "limp faster." The flock needs a pastor.

Often this phase is when the founding church planter leaves. He was either not able to get past his sadness, or he wasn't equipped with sufficient pastoral patience and skills. Equally often, this is the phase where the flock chooses a replacement leader who majors on "pastor" and minors on "apostle." At this point the congregation focuses on internal matters, and what started as a missionary movement settles into becoming a nice, comfortable church.

Before any potential church planters jump off a bridge, let me share some good news. There is one way to gain back what was lost and much more. Only one. That one way is to turn down the tap of addition and open wide the faucet of multiplication. In the process of multiplication, you have both the opportunity to shepherd (disciple) the flock you steward but also corporately turn the flock outward toward the waiting harvest. By simultaneously caring for the wounded among you, and guiding the healed back out toward the wounded, you build a healthy environment that is being equipped for multiplication.

The following eight beneficial transferences occur when a church moves out of itself toward the Kingdom assignment of multiplication:

1. Multiplication helps churches move from a brand-expanding, self-centered incentive for continued ministry, to a *Kingdom-expanding, gospel-centered, harvest focus motivation* for ministry. The church becomes truly Kingdom, producing fruit that will withstand the day of judgment (see Matt. 25:31–46; John 15:1–11).

2. Multiplication helps churches move from a singular and homogeneous Kingdom door, to a *multilane Kingdom entrance designed to effectively engage numerous and diverse cultural and socioeconomic backgrounds.* The church becomes porous, able to engage and assimilate numerous people groups.

3. Multiplication forces churches to move from an overdependence on an established and staid leadership base to the *Kingdom multiplication*

assignment of discovering, developing, and deploying new and emerging leaders. The church becomes an ongoing incubator for leadership development, securing a Kingdom impact for the generations to follow.

4. Multiplication inspires churches to move from general and detached prayers for the lost to an *informed, passionate, and desperate prayer life for their harvest.* The church becomes personally responsible for the harvest that surrounds them, and the urgency of their prayer life correlates with that responsibility (see Mark 9:38; Luke 10:2).

5. Multiplication requires churches to move from an abstract evangelism training process to an actual, vigorous, *"just in time," on-the-job evangelism training for disciples caught up in new webs of evangelistic relationships.* The church leaders become less "evangelism promoters" and more "evangelism coaches," guiding disciples who are actively engaged in multiple disciple-making relationships.

6. Multiplication helps churches move from a nonintegrated and distant missionary understanding to an *integrated and personal missionary appeal within the congregation.* The church itself becomes a missionary agency as it actively calls out new missionaries within its numbers to bring the gospel to new places and people groups within their city and beyond.

7. Multiplication inspires churches to move from academic, curriculum-based, missions-education programs to a *personal, life-transforming, "flesh and blood, hands on" experience with missions.* The church becomes deliberate with its Kingdom assignment and builds church-planting engagement into its discipleship process.

8. Multiplication necessitates that churches move from an unlived (which, by definition, is unbelieved) theoretical faith, to a *living, breathing, faith-walking journey that is frequently punctuated and propelled by ongoing, miraculous "God stories."* The church becomes a peer community that mutually challenges one another toward living an obedient life of faith.

All church plants, if they survive, become churches. Not all churches become Kingdom expanders. By instilling the value for multiplication deep and early within the DNA of a new church plant, God will use your ministry to start a Kingdom reaction that will far outlast you and will ripple throughout eternity.

When Should a New Church Multiply?

Probably the most frequently asked question that I receive from new church planters is this, "Jeff, how big should we be before we think about multiplying?" I like this question because it usually demonstrates that the church planter is preparing his strategy to include the priority of multiplication. I often answer the question by asking a question of my own. "What size do you think that you need to be?" Almost universally the answer comes back, "I think that to be effective, we need to be ____." The blank is usually a tremendous year's growth larger than they are right now. If they are 75, the blank is 125. If they are 150, it is 250. And so it goes.

I like the question because it reveals that the planter is thinking about multiplication. Like most questions though, if it's not exactly the correct question that we're asking, the answer that comes back may not be that helpful. The question that we just asked and answered speaks to the bias of a church-centric missiology. What we are really asking is, "If we multiply, how negatively might it affect our growth trajectory?" "Can our assembly withstand the adverse impact of concentrating energies somewhere else?" These are all reasonable questions, but they are queries that demonstrate a prioritization of how a church is shaped, over what Jesus' church actually does.

If the question of multiplication were approached from a bias emerging from a Kingdom-centric missiology, how would things change? For one, the shaping of the assembly would not become mission-one. Lostness would take the seat of highest priority. The assembly's shape would accommodate strategies that would have the greatest ability to effectively reach into the lostness' density and diversity.

Suppose as a planter, under God, you took the spiritual responsibility that every man, woman, boy, and girl in a four block radius, would have the opportunity to hear and see and taste and smell and feel the good news of Jesus Christ, on multiple occasions, so that each can intentionally accept or reject the gospel. If you drew the circle on a map and said, "Under God, we take spiritual responsibility for these lives." How would that decision affect your strategy?

Probably very few planters would ask the question, "How large should we grow before multiplying?" Instead, you would begin to dig deeply into that community and start to understand what is needed for all to understand the gospel. You would discover language groups and cultural affinities that are currently untouched by anyone's strategy and who would be very unlikely to enter the doors of your new assembly. A new and better question naturally emerges. How does the gospel travel to these families? Who will go to them? (Rom. 10:14).

You would begin to earnestly and urgently pray (Luke 10:2) asking the Father to send very specific help. "Father we need someone to help us reach into a Vietnamese community. And a biker enclave. And all those Ukrainians. . . ." Your eyes are peeled for God's answer. Soon you've discovered leaders who have cultural ties to these groups—and you begin to invest your loaves and fish (Mark 6:41–42) into helping them bring good news to this community. Rapidly you have multiplied yourself into numerous locations and people groups.

The church-centric question of "how large" soon sounds very feeble to your ears when you consider the Kingdom impact that is taking place simply by asking a better question.

Multiplication is not typically and singularly a question of capacity, but rather of intent.

Coaching Questions

1. What multiplication principles from Scripture will be the most important to communicate?

2. How will the knowledge that your church has a life cycle influence your strategy?

3. What "beneficial transferences" are most important for your church plant?

Chapter 31

Multiplication Myths and Missteps

As we have noted, there are numerous *biblical, natural,* and corporately *beneficial* reasons to set up a new church on a trajectory for rapid multiplication. The image of dozens of new evangelistically effective churches branching off your family tree is likely spiritually intoxicating. Dreaming further to the spiritual impact of subsequent generations spawning off of the plants you led to establish can be overwhelming. It all seems so biblical, natural, and beneficial.

So, why does it seem to be so rarely attempted?

As in the first days of creation, Satan often seems to slither into our conversation and plant seeds of doubt toward Kingdom commands that are both clear and obvious. "Did God really say, 'Go into all the world . . . ,' or was that really just a metaphor?" One can almost hear the "hiss" in the background. The snake continues, "When Jesus said, 'Whoever would save his life will lose it, but whoever loses his life for my sake and the gospel's will save it' (Mark 8:35), surely He only said that to instruct you how you get into His Kingdom, not how you are supposed to live your lives in His Kingdom. That's asking way too much! Hiss."

And so, believing the little lies of a dark prince, much of the church has so "normalized" its practices and priorities that they now more closely mirror corporate America than they do the Kingdom of heaven. After decades of methodological malpractice that have become attached to distortions of the church-growth movement, we have so rationalized and contorted our understanding of Jesus' Commission, that our follow-through seems entirely contra Kingdom. We build organizational and operational strategies more on the basis of *Good to Great*[49] and *Execution*,[50] than we do the Sermon on the Mount (see Matt. 5–7) or the book of Acts.

The ensuing results that come from our business discipleship is that when we speak of the Kingdom subject of multiplication, we have been forced to recite the talking points found in our handbook of corporate mythology. Most of these talking points are carefully crafted to include a thin covering of both spiritual substance and stewardship wisdom, but with a few careful questions, the obvious heart issue surfaces above the pious veneer.

Myths of Multiplication

1. There Are Already Plenty of Churches in Our Community
(aka: Why would we want to create competition for ourselves?)

The argument that was used by other pastors, unpersuasively so, against starting your church in the community often becomes the battle cry of established church planters once they have carved out their own niche. We see new harvesters as competition, not help.

A planter would be wise to remind himself of a few important facts he once knew well. First, many of the churches you are driving past are plateaued or have been in a state of decline for many years. Second, the churches to population ratios of any urban area within the West are staggeringly low. Third, the majority of existing churches in your community are not set up to be effective harvesters; the lost are not coming. And fourth, without multiplying evangelistically effective churches in your city, the harvest will be lost.

The only leaders concerned about creating competition are the leaders fervidly competing for the same thin slice of the preconverted pie. It's not why you planted.

2. We Will Multiply Once We Grow Our Base to "X" People
(aka: Pastors are honored for bigger, not more.)

I have found that many planters have a fixed number in their mind that indicates when they're "large enough" to multiply. When this is the case, two things often happen. First, the number they choose is a number they will never reach. When we get to be five hundred people, or three hundred, or two hundred. What the planter is really saying is, once that I have established my kingdom, and it is safe, solid, and secure, then I'll begin to think about the Kingdom of God. So really, multiplication was never a truthful part of the plan.

The second thing that happens among "X first" leaders is "numbers creep." When a minority of them are able to hit their arbitrary "X," the "X" must go up because they are still not ready. They have set their church up on an *addition* plan, not a *multiplication* plan. Staffing needs are much different with addition.

The bottom line is that our evangelical subculture has celebrated addition over multiplication for too many decades. For too many years we have honored the pastors with the largest preaching audience over the pastors who have multiplied into the largest Kingdom gains, and that seems to be a difficult illness to shake.

3. If We Multiply, We Will Lose Our "Us-ness"
(aka: We have already made our friends.)

Something special happens when a team gathers around a united Kingdom vision and witnesses God's hand of blessing on them. A *koinonia*[51] happens among that team. For many it will be there first taste of the true nature of a Kingdom community. Deep bonds of friendship are built. It is unlike any previous experience. This is the good news. The bad news is that many will emotionally resist any move that will threaten their newfound fellowship. To some, multiplication will be seen as a threatening enemy to their cherished fellowship.

An important series of questions need to be answered at this point. Is this *koinonia* that is being experienced a result of the assembling of a special group of people, or is it a special work of the Holy Spirit? And if it is the latter, can it be found again in multiplication? And if it can, would it be right for us to keep this community *koinonia* to ourselves?

In life there are few gifts more precious than good friends. A sign of the spiritual maturity of a congregation is not only correlated with how voraciously they defend their unity but also with how freely they release it to others.

4. If We Multiply, We Will Lose Control of Our Branding
(aka: I may not get credit.)

As an effective church planter, you have worked hard on creating a brand. You might resist the word, but the fact remains that you have diligently crafted a corporate image, culture, vision, set of operational systems, and community reputation that distinctively sets you apart. This branding accurately reflects your calling, your passions, the context of your community, and the message of "your church" that you want others to know. It was not an easy task to move from nothing to where you are, and intuitively you know that one of your assignments as lead planter is to keep it on track. So the idea of multiplication suddenly becomes complicated.

The church you started is an amalgam that reflects both you (possibly your team) and your context. This unique amalgamation is never a "one size fits all" but is specific to an individual and a context. So how does multiplication work when you deploy a different personality into a different context? Obviously things will need to look and feel different. What will happen to our brand?

Many deaths come in Kingdom living. The one corpse that seems most difficult to stay buried is that of our religious ego. Multiplication and brand expansion[52] are opposite instincts in that they push and pull us in opposing directions. Multiplication pushes us into new forms, ideas, models, and methodologies because of the diversity of needs within the harvest. Brand expansion pulls us back into a conformity that we have created, appreciate, and control. For multiplication to occur, much of what we have developed as our "branding" will become an impediment to a different harvest. The Kingdom death a church planter must come to face is his own willingness to multiply into places and people groups where his name and brand will have little association.

On the journey of planting for the glory of God, our brands must sit quietly in the backseat.

5. We Will Never Be Able to Swing It Financially
(aka: We already paid the price.)

Faith never gets easier. It usually grows more difficult. As a single man, faith was pretty easy. I heard God's voice and obeyed. Done. When I got married, it was a little more difficult; now my bride would be affected if I got "faith" wrong. As our family grew, there was more at stake. We assumed our children liked to eat, so we really needed to hear God's voice correctly. Faith was getting harder. Once a new church was up and going, now there was far more at stake—not just my life, and my family's, but so many others. My faith became community. Every level of leadership you take, the consequences of faith have greater impact. Faith never gets easier.

There seems to be a point in many church planters' lives that faith is a principle of their past but not their present. Much faith had been used to bring them to the point where they now live, but now, with all that is at stake, new faith seems largely unavailable. A long time ago there was much talk about multiplication and movements, but in light of the risks, that seems like a distant memory. Questions that once irritated us coming from others now paralyze us within ourselves. Where will we find the cash? How will we afford to give up leaders? We are just barely making it now; why would we want to bite off more?

For church planters to become multipliers, there is a spiritual obligation to continue with faith. "And without faith it is impossible to please him, for whoever would draw near to God must believe that he exists and that he rewards those who seek him" (Heb. 11:6).

6. If We Multiply, We Will Slow Our Momentum
(aka: Addition has always been my plan.)

Momentum is the strength or force that something has when it is moving. It is the strength or force that allows something to continue or to grow stronger or faster as time passes. To a savvy church planter, momentum is one physics principle that is not to be trifled with. It takes a lot of sacrificial energy to bring a church plant from a static idea to a dynamic reality that begins to rumble with its own driving thrust. Momentum is our friend.

But before we rocket too far down the road with momentum, it might be wise to ask ourselves an important question: "All this speed is wonderful, but are we traveling in the right direction?" The ride might be thrilling, but the destination may not be the place of your dreams. Momentum is only good when it carries us to the places where we really want to be. This brings us back to our ultimate purpose, the Kingdom harvest.

If preserving momentum makes us prioritize *keeping* and *saving* in order to *add*, instead of *giving* and *sharing* in order to *multiply*, we might want to question our charted terminus. Momentum can be found wherever energy is applied. Can you imagine the momentous impact of your life given to a vision of multiplication? A momentum applied to a selfless Kingdom vision? A momentum that originates from the breath of God's Spirit and is applied to a vision inspired by that same Source? It is eternal.

If addition is your plan, then roll with the momentum you can muster. If Kingdom is in your sights, then be careful about the momentum you garner. Make sure it leads you deep into the harvest.

7. What If Our New Plant Outstrips Us?

(aka: My religious reputation might depreciate.)

It seems silly to even articulate this objection. It is a concern that no socially aware church planter would ever publicly admit to owning. But that doesn't mean it is not there. We are a complicated mixture of godly passions and broken cravings. Even though we have surrendered to our Father's call, we still easily identify with Paul's angst-ridden confession (see Rom. 7:13–25). And what often leads the parade in our multifarious muddle of motivations is our well-tended pride.

The fact that you are a planter, or are considering becoming a planter, likely means you have a pioneering, entrepreneurial, hard-charging kind of leader. You like to win. You hate to lose. And you don't often find yourself standing in anyone's shadow. You're a leader, and leaders lead. Here's the rub. If leading means winning to me, I will never become a leader of any Kingdom significance. Kingdom leaders value the objective more than their placement. They celebrate when others succeed; they mourn when others fail (see 1 Cor. 12:26). They are secure enough to surround themselves with other leaders more talented and capable than they. Why? Once again, the Kingdom harvest is their primary calling and passion. If every church that multiplies out of their efforts outstrips them by every measurement, the Kingdom leader rejoices with a full heart.

The flamboyant "atta boys" that come with a carefully managed sacred reputation mean far less to Kingdom leaders than the quiet "well done, good and faithful servant" (Matt. 25:23). To those whose hearts are in their Father's harvest, His sincere approval is ample.

8. Why Give More? We Are Already Giving 10 Percent to Missions

(aka: Kingdom sacrifice stops with us.)

Much in the same way many believers struggle with "tithing," many church planters struggle with the Kingdom concept of generosity. We want people to be generous toward our vision, but often that is where things stop. We become a *cul-de-sac*[53] on the road to generosity. As fleshly believers readily reveal the condition of the heart with the question, "Does tithing have to be *gross*, or can it be *net*?" (see Acts 4:32–37), so a church planter reveals his spiritual condition with his attitude toward Kingdom generosity (Matt. 6:21).

Allow me to be bold. For most potential planters you do not have enough money or enough people in hand to pull off the vision God is laying on your heart. That might frighten some of you. All you can see is lack. And that lack might drive some of you to grasp all you can. Here's another way to approach things. God has given you a vision. If it truly is God's vision, then its ultimately God's problem.

Instead of grasping with clenched fists, as if it were all up to you, try releasing the tension and live openhandedly. Kingdom first (see Matt. 6:25–34). Make an oath to your Father (and make it public in your core team for accountability) that every dollar and every life God brings to you, you will not see it as yours but as His. With open hands you ask, "Father, how do you want us to steward these blessings for your Kingdom?"

What you will learn and what you will teach just might be revolutionary. Be generous.

Multiplication Missteps to Sidestep

As you might have noticed, most of the myths that keep us from multiplication emanate from the spiritual condition of our darkened hearts. From that murky state we envisage addition as our sheltering ally and multiplication as our feared foe. But hopefully we do not stay in this condition for long.

Once we get clear of ourselves, multiplication becomes the obvious strategy to get at a wasting harvest. With new sense of urgency, we set off to the fields to gather all we can. But just as farming takes time to master, so does the task of multiplying for the harvest. Let me share a few missteps to sidestep, many of which I have painfully stumbled through personally. These are not necessarily mistakes of the heart (although they may be) but are more likely rookie mistakes of inexperience. We will look at the larger implication of these later when we discuss the options in multiplication systems.

1. Cloning

When you've done something well, it is normal to have a sense of satisfaction. Perhaps you have successfully planted in an area where few have experienced success. For that success you have learned important things about yourself and your context. The application of that knowledge led you to experience a church-planting victory.

Cloning, as a multiplication strategy, is problematic for two reasons: contexts vary and so do planters. Resist the temptation to franchise you.

Pour into up-and-coming planters the principles that guided your decision making, not the decisions themselves. When a new planter understands the "whys," he will powerfully own the "whats."

2. Naivety

The opposite oversteer from the heavy hand of cloning is the error of being too naïve. Often an effective church planter has an intuition in his methodology that cannot be taught. He approaches his work as a natural athlete. He sweats and works hard, but there is also a strange effortlessness to it. If this is likely to describe you, please capture this. You are a gift and not the norm. Expecting others to perform at your level is both naïve and unhelpful.

Often gifted planters, after hearing faith-affirming evidence of God's call on a new planter, will trust this new planter's strategic instincts. This is usually a mistake. Spiritual intuition doesn't seem to be a gift that is equally distributed. Do not assume other planters have it. By testing their ideas, you may save them a world of pain.

3. Inattention

With an impassioned call to multiplication, many planters will not strike a good balance between "how many" and "how well." With apostolic impulses they will start new churches without taking the time or attention to ensure that they are viable.

In constructing a church-multiplication system, striking the right balance between numbers and quality is vitally important. An overemphasis on numbers will lead to anemic plants starving for the nutrition they need to thrive. An overemphasis on quality will lead to an introspective faith paralysis that never leads to multiplication. Find a balance that requires both faith and the responsibility of proper parenting.

4. Entitlement

The opposite pole of inattention is entitlement. Just as a child becomes deeply damaged through overprovision, so a church plant will not likely survive when it is drowned with resources. Ed Stetzer noted: "I found in my own Ph.D. dissertation research (2003), that initial funding had no correlation with the survivability of a church plant. A later, larger study Warren Bird and I cite in *Viral Churches* showed the same thing. Funding is not the magic pill for church planting and in some cases it can be a poison pill."[54]

By taking away the walk of faith from a new church, you have robbed them of experiencing God for themselves. Leadership becomes superficial because there have been few opportunities to dig deep in faith together. What starts as a generous gift of love to a church plant often becomes the source of their undoing.

5. Autocracy

If a church planter does not have a sense of "ownership" of his work—if he perceives that he is a puppet carrying out the orders from the mother ship—he will unlikely give it his best or stay long. The responsibility of leadership has been hijacked from the outside.

Just as a good parent tries to walk the fine line between taking responsibility and giving responsibility, so a new church planter should be given as much ownership as he is capable of handling. If he is incapable of effectively owning responsibility, it likely means your process of assessment flawed. If you have assessed well, allow the planter and his local team to feel the burden for success. The more autocratic the parent is, the less likely the daughter congregation will succeed over the long term.

Multiplication, when it is done effectively, rigorously engages both the heart and the mind. It exposes our spiritual vulnerabilities and requires our best strategic thinking. By taking the risk of becoming a parent, you will learn more about yourself than you likely wanted to know and, at the same time, will become much more like your Father.

Coaching Questions

1. Which of the eight multiplication myths will be your biggest obstacle?

2. How can you lead your team and church plant past the myth?

3. What are your next steps to prepare for multiplication?

Chapter 32

Exploring Multiplication Systems

Since multiplication is really not optional behavior for churches that desire to be Kingdom first in all areas of their priorities, it follows that a new church would want to carefully think through the range of multiplication systems available. For full disclosure about the systems that we will be discussing, I have had personal connections using each of them in different seasons of ministry. Each has some advantages and some disadvantages. As you synthesize the ideas in this chapter with the ideas of models in chapter 10, you will likely come up with an ecclesiologically sound methodology for the multiplication of sustainable new congregations.

One thing to appreciate is that we are not debating a conversation that is relatively new to Christianity. This dialogue has had some thoughtful argumentation over the centuries. Certainly one of the most influential missiologists of the nineteenth century was England's Henry Venn, recording secretary of the Church Missionary Society. Venn developed his idea of mission in a series of pamphlets and policy statements, written between 1846 to 1865, where he sought to clarify the main goal of mission and the most effective means of realizing it. In collaboration with Rufus Anderson, the concept of the indigenous church emerged as the central construct of his mission theory. A church was judged to be indigenous when it was *self-propagating, self-financing, and self-governing*. This idea was later coined The Three Selves in popular expression.

Taking a position that was well out of tune with the sentiments of colonial England, Venn forcefully insisted that continuing in a pejorative approach to mission would be ecclesiologically harmful.[55] His theory, which is once again being widely challenged,[56] remains, in my opinion, one of the best ways to ensure generational advancement through sustainable church multiplication. Although few missionary societies followed his warnings against colonialization and dependence, his ideas continue to be constructive, especially to this subject.

If Kingdom movements of evangelistically effective churches multiplying and transforming the landscape of our communities is our goal, then developing indigenous multiplication systems that can carry us to that goal becomes critical. Although there are numerous approaches to reproducing, most methodological constructs fit into one of three general approaches.

1. Sending/Sponsoring

The term "sending church" is a little more precise than "sponsoring church," the term that has been widely used in the past. The idea of "sending" speaks to a higher level of involvement in the church-planting process that includes, but is not limited to, people and resources. The older term of a "mother-daughter" relationship better describes the commitment required in successfully parenting a new church plant to the destination of Venn's Three Selves.

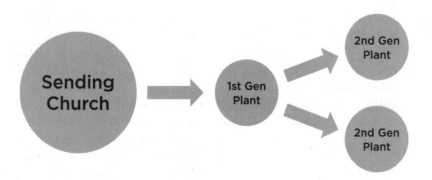

This is the model of church multiplication that most are familiar with. Plants are started, generally one or two at a time,[57] under the assistance and supervision of a sending church. The sending church, on varying degrees, takes the ownership/responsibility for success of the plant. Below is a table that describes four variables of accountability that is most often observed:

	Resources	Relationship	Commitment to Success
Fully Engaged	High Investment	High Investment	Completely Committed
Moderately Engaged	Medium Investment	Medium Investment	Mostly Committed
Minimally Engaged	Medium Investment	Low Investment	Partially Committed
Nonengaged	Low Investment	Zero Investment	Uncommitted

Fully Engaged

This is a sending church that is highly invested in both resources and relationships into the success of a new church plant. This sending church is as rare as it is valuable. Frequently the church planter is brought on staff in the sending church to provide the necessary time for proper research and development, core building, and, if necessary, partnership development. Members of the sending church are loaned or given openhandedly. Often planters are encouraged to recruit their core out of the sending church's membership. The church plant's budget is seen as the sending church's responsibility, and she either provides the necessary resources or works on the planter's behalf to help finance the plant through coalition building.

Weekly the church plant has visibility within the sending church's services through prayer emphasis, video reporting, guest preaching, and testimonies. The sending church leverages its assets to assist the church plant in leadership training, evangelistic outreaches, special events, and emergency response. The church planter is seen by the church as an extension of the sending church's staff and is included in staff development processes and leadership retreats. Often, as the church plant develops its own multiplication system, the sending church continues in relationship by joint venturing together in church planting. This sending church is a "mother church" in every sense of the word.

Moderately Engaged

This is a sending church that has mid-level investment in both resources and relationships into the success of the new plant. She is similar in spirit to the *fully engaged* sending church except to the degree of commitment.

Luxuries like bringing the planter on staff or considering him as an extension of their staff are generally not considered. Financial ownership of the plant's budget is usually not offered, but there is a healthy interest in working with the planter in securing the necessary financial investment. A *cart blanche* core-recruiting license is not usually offered, but with permission members are invited to join the launch team.

Spotlighting of the church plant within the sending churches is more sporadic but given enough attention that the members feel invested in their plant's progress. The planter annually returns to the sending church to preach and celebrate together what God is doing. Mission teams are sent to strategically help in tactical times within the church plant's development. When the church plant becomes self-sustaining, there is a joyous celebration service. This is a helpful and healthy commitment level that is accessible to a broader number of potential sending churches.

Minimally Engaged

This is a sending church that offers a medium investment in resources and low investment in relationships. Again, this sending church would be similar to those within the *moderately engaged* category, but with the exception of the relational equity that is offered. This sending church would not assume the responsibility of funding the plant's budget or aiding in a coalition building process but would generously offer what would likely become the highest financial investment within the group of partnerships that would be built.

The relational investment is largely uninspiring. Rarely is the plant celebrated within the life of the church, except perhaps at business meetings when the missions committee offers a report. Mission trips are an annual event, and the planter has to work hard to accommodate his strategy to what his sending church is offering. At the end of the financial commitment, the plant is unceremoniously forgotten, and the sending church moves on to other things. To date this engagement category may represent the largest number of sending churches within North America.

Nonengaged

This is a sending church with low investment in both resources and relationships. The word *sponsoring church* may better describe this relationship because it acts little as a "mother" or "sends" much of itself to its plant. Likely it entered into a church-planting relationship either out of spiritual compulsion or a sense of missional competition. Its heart and priorities are squarely consumed on itself, and like a self-absorbed parent the children pay the price.

The *nonengaged* sending church usually agrees to a token financial investment with no offer of leveraging its network for further help. It may visit its church plant as one if its "mission experience offerings" that it makes available to its membership, but it is not given priority. If the planter visited his sending church, he would likely find that many of the members wouldn't be aware of his church plant. This category of sending church represents the worst missional experience for both the church planter and itself.

The Sending Church model of multiplication, especially in the *fully* and *moderately* engaged categories, is a strong methodology to consistently see the multiplication of healthy congregations. With this methodology both the planter and the sending church can feel connected to each other and to the mission itself. In the *fully engaged* category, the sending church actually builds a reproducing culture within the churches it plants and sets the stage for movement. If this is your multiplication strategy of choice, by eliminating the lower two categories (which might have been modeled for you), you will set a new standard of engagement and investment for future generations to follow. A "new normal" will certainly advance the Kingdom of God.

2. Multisite

Somewhere around the turn of the last millennium, we began to notice the phenomenon of the multisite church gathering incredible momentum. Although early examples of this methodology have existed since the mid 1980s, with new advances in technology, the multisite sensation has recently enjoyed tremendous growth. Undoubtedly the most controversial of all multiplication systems,[58] multisiting seems to have attracted enthusiastic fans and equally fervent detractors.

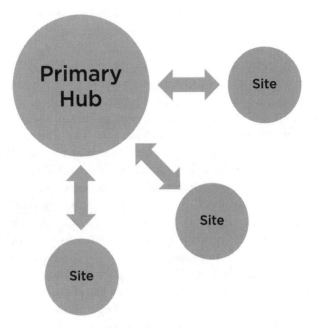

The strengths of multisiting as a multiplication methodology are many. The primary congregation usually has tremendous motivation toward the success of each site because it will be an expression of itself. The primary congregation has an opportunity to leverage skills, systems, and a culture that it has worked hard to develop. This leveraging often finds results, and they usually come quickly. It gives opportunity to engage the broader membership in the multiplication of itself in other locations, providing additional positions for new leaders to develop. It provides much safer opportunities to experience multiplication by requiring a less apostolic/entrepreneurial leader. By lowering the leadership threshold, an organic leader can quickly emerge from within the congregation. "Brand awareness" also becomes an advantageous asset as the primary congregation enters new neighborhoods as an understood entity. Finally, there can be an avoidance of redundancy by scaling personnel over multiple sites. There is no need for every congregation to "own" every ministry specialty, and therefore diffusing leadership over many locations can drastically reduce costs.

With logistical strengths like these, it is no wonder that multisiting has become the preferred multiplication methodology of many churches over the last decade. However, with great strengths come some inherent weaknesses.

Skipping past the ecclesiological issues[59] many have articulated, you soon come to realize that multisite is not a multiplication model at all but a model for increased addition. Rarely will you find examples of multisite that have a plan for their sites to multiply themselves. It is usually a spoke-and-hub organizational pattern with primary leadership emanating from the hub. This can create and guide a strong network but leaves little opportunity for multiplication. Another weakness, usually reserved for multisite churches employing a video feed, is the lack of development available for pastoral leadership. By leveraging the gifting of a celebrity communicator, few next-generation communicators are being prepared. However, many nonvideo-driven multisite churches have addressed this problem through a teaching team approach.[60] A final, major critique of the pure multisite model is that, unless it is affinity based, it is often difficult to reproduce when removed from its original geography. Perhaps with the exception of the Bible Belt, it seems that religious celebrity doesn't travel well. I can think of three renowned multisite churches that have attempted to journey to Toronto, and none successfully made the trip. This observation has been similarly pointed out in numerous cities across North America.

The multisite model offers tremendous advantages of leverage that will assist strong congregations in starting new, near cultural expressions that can thrive in a community. The strengths can outweigh the weaknesses, especially if the planter from the beginning has a strategy to overcome them.

3. Church Planting Incubator

This might appear as a strange moniker to some, but it aptly describes a highly intentional church-multiplication strategy that is borne out of a local church. Other titles that have been used are church-planting centers, church-multiplication centers, multiplying church centers, and, I'm sure, a few other variations on the theme. Despite their assorted names, effective church-planting incubators have three key elements in common: (1) a church-planting candidate *assesses in*, and then he is, (2) in context, *discipled up*, and finally he is, (3) *commissioned out* to plant. Let's look briefly at these three elements.

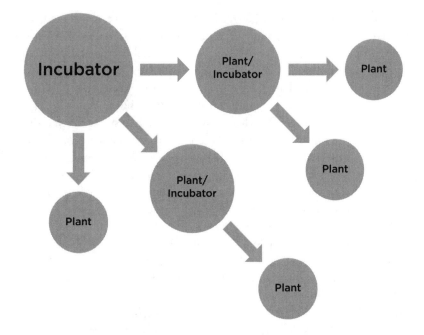

1. Assesses In

A church-planting incubator often initiates an indigenous network of planting, and so a proper assessment becomes critical. Whether the planting candidate is developed from within the congregation (this tends to happen with great regularity) or he is an outside leader caught up in the gravitational pull of their vision, assessment is a nonoptional requirement.

Assessment usually centers on two different aspects of the church planter. First, the normal considerations are carefully studied. Does the candidate have a clear call to this ministry? Does he have the gifting and leadership capacity necessary? Is his family sharing this sense of calling? Is the order of his life something you would want to replicate?

But a secondary area of assessment is unique to planting within a symbiotic network—the character of the leader. Is he teachable? Do you like being with him? Can you imagine linking arms with this leader for years, perhaps decades? Do the other planters within the network trust him? One proud spirit can do much damage in an interdependent network, so experienced church-planting incubators screen carefully for character.

2. Discipled Up

Potential church planters that work through the systems of a church-planting incubator have incredible missiological advantages over planters who plant on their own. From the beginning they are watching a contextually appropriate model of ministry being lived out before their eyes. When removed from the realm of theoretical, planting candidates get hands-on experience with the practicalities of ministry.

Habits of church-planting effectiveness are taught, watched, and measured for progress. One large series (network) of church-planting incubators that I interact with speak a common language and measure common progress on: (a) Is the candidate effectively reaching new believers? (b) Is he able to produce disciple makers? (c) Is his commitment to multiplication likely to extend beyond lip service? This—among other nuanced instruction on doctrinal integrity, contextual communication, and leadership development—becomes core to a discipling process that is pretuned for multiplication.[61]

3. Commissioned Out

When the leaders within a church-planting incubator deem that a planter candidate is ready and prepared to effectively plant a new church, he is commissioned and sent out. This sending has great strength because it comes packed with tremendous relational equity. The time spent in an internship not only prepares a planter with the necessary skills for a contextually appropriate strategy but also knits him into a brotherhood that synergistically tackles a common geography as an apostolic team.

Often networks convene in regular celebration gatherings for testimonies that inspire, create community, and further cast vision. The ultimate goal is that each planter that is sent out would himself create a multiplying system from his new church. Although this rarely happens at 100 percent success rate, if assessments were thorough, the majority of plants become church-planting incubators themselves. If the character of the leaders walk in humility together, this can become exponential quickly.

A further benefit of this multiplication system is one that comes with an interconnectedness of gifts. Often, because of the different passions of leaders, different strengths and emphases develop between congregations. These strengths can be leveraged across a network of interdependent churches to create a much higher degree of strength, health, and evangelistic effectiveness.

The three most common multiplication systems: (1) the sending church, (2) multisiting, and (3) a church-planting incubator all have advantages that can fit the passions and personalities of almost any leader whose Kingdom vision exceeds his own personal reach. By planting with multiplication squarely in your sights from the beginning, you can lay a foundation that will far exceed both your greatest dreams and your leadership capacity.

Coaching Questions

1. Which multiplication system makes the most sense to you now?

2. What steps will you take to implement this system over the next ninety days?

3. Which multiplication system would you like to attempt in the future?

Chapter 33

Shaping a Kingdom Movement

We have been on quite a journey. We started with an understanding of what Jesus might have meant for His church to be *Kingdom first*. From there we delved into a practical look at the *character* of a leader that is necessary for Kingdom advancement. Third, with an understanding that *contexts* radically differ, not only from region to region but also from neighborhood to neighborhood, what is a Kingdom-first approach that is respectful to the communities we will serve? Fourth, we examined *communication* and gained an appreciation for what "grace" and "truth" might sound like to our varied audiences. Fifth, we investigated the kind of *teamwork* necessary for effective Kingdom collaboration. Sixth, we sought perspective on how a church might *make a difference* in the geography it takes responsibility for. Seventh, from that responsibility we tackled building a Kingdomesque *disciple-making* road map for groups to journey. Finally, after we have considered the Kingdom implications of systemic multiplication, we investigated what it would mean for the church itself to become a *multiplication* system. The whole process was a practical application of what it might mean to plant a church that was truly Kingdom first.

Now, in this closing chapter of this book, let's briefly look together at some practical steps for a church planter to implement in a Kingdom-first approach to his task. The following seven steps, although not infallible, are progressive suggestions that would lead a new church from mind-set to missionary.

1. Model a Kingdom-First Mind-set

Shape your people's perspective. The five-year trajectory of a new church is usually established in her first six months. This is the precise reason most missiologists so urgently emphasize the prenatal period of church development. Once the baby is born, you've got your hands full.

With a Kingdom-first mind-set shaping your direction, let its rationale and applications leak out from you at every opportunity. If your strategy calls for preview services, take an offering and give it away equally to a ministry serving a social fault line and to your first church plant. Let people know this. Let people in on your heartbeat. In your church-planting preaching, let the second, corporate application (see chapter 16) speak to the Kingdom nature of your assignment.

Most importantly, model the Kingdom yourself. Fully appreciate that your life, lifestyle, and priorities will become the model others will mimic. With great humility invite your people to imitate you as you imitate Christ (see 1 Cor. 11:1). Make a pledge, make it publicly, that every person and dollar that God makes you steward of will always be His; He decides how it is invested in His Kingdom. You, as His people, will listen and obey. Change everything about church that is empty or self-serving.

2. Model Multiplication at All Levels of Church Life

For any church multiplication system to be effective, every system that supports it needs to become a multiplying system. Disciples must become disciple makers. Leaders must become leadership developers. Pastors must become indigenous staff developers.

To do this a church planter has to shift from a marines mentality to an army mentality. In the early days of a church, you work like marines. Almost everyone can do almost everything. If the radio guy goes down, the closest one picks up the radio and keeps moving. The army is filled with singular specialists. As the church develops, things need to change from marines to an army approach. The early core, full of servant-hearted leaders, needs to multiply itself into new leaders being developed. This multiplication thinking happens at every level and in every ministry.

When your Kingdom assignment is not a church but a lost city and a lost world, you can never come to a place when you have enough leaders. Multiplication moves from a nicety to a strategic necessity.

3. Model Partnership and Teamwork with Local Churches of Your Tribe and Beyond

The more insular you become, the narrower and more unusable you grow. It is easy to observe spiritually immature Christians, who understand theology better than any who walked before them, create theologically constricted categories of approved association. The more they talk with one another, the tighter the categories become. Soon, in cult-like fashion, they lay claim to sole perspective of orthodoxy and all truth. They disassociate themselves (shun) from any who also look through a glass dimly (1 Cor. 13:12), as they do, and dare to come to different conclusions.

While of course it is important to maintain the highest standard of biblical orthodoxy. Hubris does not need to be part of the package of tenets. There is too much to be done to maintain a self-aggrandizing and insular posture of spiritual isolationism. The harvest is waiting in the fields unharvested.

Become an answer to Jesus' prayer and partner for the harvest (see John 17:20–21). Link up with other churches and new church plants in important Kingdom ventures. Let a lost world see that you are not in competition with Christ but with an insidious darkness that is smothering and suffocating their community.

4. With Creative Redundancy, Advocate for Church Planting

Part of effective vision casting is growing in the skill of creative redundancy. Simply listing "church planting" as one of your core values does not make it so. It becomes a core value when it is integrated into the discipleship process of your church and spoken about with frequency.

Many founding pastors have discovered that church planting easily falls off the shelf of church priorities. When it's budget time, more pressing issues at home always need priority. When it's time to send out leaders, it's rarely the best that are asked to go (see Acts 13:1–3). Part of our fallen constitution seems to always cry, "Us first."

The task of the planting team is to consistently keep the vision of multiplication before the congregation. The minute you assume it's there is the moment it's gone. It takes a courageous leader to consistently advocate for the harvest instead of capitulating to a more soothing message desired by idle harvesters. Cast the vision a thousand different ways, and then cast it again.

5. Become a Sending Church and Plant a New Church (with a High Resource/High Relationship Model)

The first step into multiplication should probably be as a sending church. Prayerfully seek out a potential church planter who has both tremendous capacity and humility. Work through an assessment process with your eyes wide open. Construct a coaching path that will properly develop any areas of weakness and fan the flames of his passions and strengths.

Take responsibility for him, his family, and his team. Join hand in hand in a partnership development effort. Model for him what you would want him to model for the next generation. Become a fully engaged sending church that is completely committed to the success of this first plant.[62]

Work with him in developing a core. Help him wisely select leaders from your congregation that will be valuable to the tenuous first days. Spend time each week with him as a mentor and coach. Help him learn lessons you learned the hard way. Pray that this church plant will grow incredibly dangerous to darkness. And then celebrate with great frequency. Weekly update your congregation with God stories and victories that come from this first iteration of multiplication.

6. Disciple a Cohort of Potential Church Planters

Here is a word from experience: if you make multiplication a priority of vision and practice, potential church planters will gravitate to you. Some will come from the outside that have serendipitously discovered you. Others will come from within, hearts fully captured by the vision, ready to change careers, sell homes, dip into savings, do whatever is necessary for the Kingdom. They're simply following your example.

Here is your opportunity to set the stage for rapid multiplication. As the founding pastor, take these leaders under your wing. Spend time formally and informally with them, collectively and individually. Speak into their spirits as to what you see the Father doing in them and through them. Give them opportunities of significant leadership around you. Guide their steps with feedback and encouragement.

This is the season when you begin to prepare and construct the final phase of your discipleship strategy. You are about to go viral (Matt. 13:33).

7. Become a Church-Planting Incubator

With all of the preparation, vision casting, experimentation, and experience, you are ready to prepare leaders to start multiple congregations. You have shaped values, priorities, and infrastructure to see a Kingdom movement become a reality. You assess in, disciple up, and commission out fully prepared Kingdom disciples for the harvest.

Spiritual warfare will increase at an exponential rate so prepare yourself for battle. You have obediently positioned yourself for maximum Kingdom impact, so engage your prayer warriors to fight with you.

And perhaps, like never before, pray like this: "Our Father in heaven, hallowed be your name. Your kingdom come, your will be done, on earth as it is in heaven. Give us this day our daily bread, and forgive us our debts, as we also have forgiven our debtors. And lead us not into temptation, but deliver us from evil" (Matt. 6:9–13).

Coaching Questions

1. Which of the "seven practical steps" can you get the most traction with now?

2. What steps can you take to move forward in that step?

3. What step will be your greatest challenge?

NOTES

1. C. Peter Wagner, *Church Planting for a Greater Harvest* (Ventura, CA: Regal Books, 1990), 11.

2. Jeff Christopherson, *Kingdom Matrix: Designing a Church for the Glory of God* (Boise, ID: Elevate Publishing, 2012).

3. Ibid.

4. I'm indebted to years of friendship and collaboration with Gerry Taillon, a fellow church planter and executive director of the Canadian National Baptist Convention. These four metrics are fruit of that partnership.

5. ἁμαρτία *(hamartia)* is a self-originated ethical failure of hitting God's prescribed target for living. *Strong's Concordance* gets to the point with "missing the mark."

6. Again, John 1:14, the perfect picture of God's glory.

7. *Merriam-Webster Online*, s.v. *husband*, "one that plows and cultivates land: farmer." See http://merriam-webster.com.

8. www.flourish.me is an equipping community for wives of planters and pastors. Kathy Litton, who has experienced both incredible achievement and deep tragedy, gives direction to this culture-creating ministry. By introducing your wife to this ministry, you may be helping her thrive as she walks with other planters' wives and shares common experiences in the planting process.

9. Mac Lake and Brian Bloye are incredible Kingdom collaborators with the Send City Network Team I lead at the North American Mission Board. Church-planting networks across denominational lines are currently using their systems. See www.launchstrong.com.

10. Brian and Amy Bloye, *It's Personal: Surviving and Thriving on the Journey of Church Planting* (Grand Rapids, MI: Zondervan, 2012), 73–83.

11. We do not know how long it was before Paul appointed Ephesian elders. This verse indicates he stayed three years with them in Ephesus and then gave this charge as he headed toward Jerusalem.

12. Planters can build multiple planting scenarios on a Church Planting Growth Projector that will help them zero in on a realistic financial approach to a church-planting strategy in context. The tool can be found at www. plantingprojector.com.

13. As far as I know, no tool exists for "likeability." But when that ethereal quality is not there, there is usually no church plant to follow.

14. The math of this example is: 150 people x $18 per person x 52 weeks = $140,400.

15. 120 people x $9.00/week x 52 weeks = $56,160 annually.

16. J. D. Payne, *Missional House Churches* (Milton Keynes, UK: Paternoster Publishing, 2007), 36–44.

17. Barry Whitworth leads the Multiplying Churches Team at the Baptist Resource Network of Pennsylvania/South Jersey. Barry has extensively researched North American church multiplication and is developing a growing network of Church Multiplication Centers. See MC², Multiplying Church Network, http://pennjerseycp.com/our-roots.

18. Helpful statistical data for the US can be found at United States Census Bureau, http://www.census.gov; United States Census Bureau, American Fact Finder; http://factfinder2.census.gov; or in Canada, Statistics Canada, http://www12.statcan.gc.ca/census-recensement/index-eng.cfm.

19. Following dozens of coffee-shop napkins, this concept was originally documented in *Kingdom Matrix,* chapter 13: "Kingdom Design."

20. Chapter 24 is dedicated to understanding the concept of *social fault lines*. In short, social fault lines are generally recognized areas of social brokenness or concern within a given community.

21. As opposed to *convictional secularization*—a firmly held ethical belief system that is derived apart from, and in opposition to, any religious worldview. Convictional secularists compose a small minority of most secular societies. The vast majority tends to be cultural secularists, people who share secular values but have few underpinning reasons as to why.

22. Gary D. Chapman, *The Five Love Languages: The Secret to Love that Lasts* (Chicago, IL: Moody Publishing, 1994).

23. For more on church planting and preaching, skip to chapter 16.

24. The whole contrived simulation is reminiscent of Elijah's imprudent pride when he declared that he was the only one fully devoted to God. See 1 Kings 19:10, 19.

25. A French term that has migrated to become an English colloquialism, literally translated as our "reason to be."

26. Ed Stetzer, *Planting Missional Churches* (Nashville: B&H Publishing Group, 2006), 301.

27. Ibid., 300.

28. Ibid.

29. Stephen Gray, *Planting Fast-Growing Churches* (Saint Charles, IL: Churchsmart Resources, 2007).

30. Eric Swanson and Rick Rusaw, *The Externally Focused Church* (Group Publishing, 2004).

31. See "LoveLoud" North American Mission Board, http://www.namb.net /loveloud.

32. For an overview of poverty in the United States from 1966 to 2012, see "Living in Near Poverty in the United States: 1966–2012," http://www. census.gov/prod/2014pubs/p60-248.pdf, accessed December 19, 2014. Note that widowed women experience the second highest poverty rates, only behind pre-high school children; see p. 5.

33. See Amy Florian, "Serving Widowed Clients Whatever Their Age," Financial Advisor, accessed December 19, 2014, http://www.fa-mag.com/ news/serving-widowed-clients-whatever-their-age-14829.html.

34. See "Senior Poverty: Action Needed to Address a Growing Problem," NSCLC: National Senior Citizens Law Center, accessed December 19, 2014, http://www.nsclc.org/wp-content/uploads/2011/02/NSCLC-Senate-Aging-Statement-030414.pdf.

35. Roland Robertson, "The Conceptual Promise of Glocalization: Commonality and Diversity" (Seoul: Proceedings of the International Forum on Cultural Diversity and Common Values, 2003), 76–89.

36. Thomas Friedman, *The World Is Flat, 3rd ed.* (Picador, 2007).

37. Bob Roberts Jr., *Glocalization: How followers of Jesus Engage a Flat World* (Grand Rapids, MI: Zondervan, 2007).

38. Paul David Tripp, *Instruments in the Redeemer's Hands: People in Need of Change Helping People in Need of Change* (Phillipsburg, NJ: P&R Publishing, 2002), 63.

39. Rick Warren, *Purpose Driven Church* (Grand Rapids, MI: Zondervan, 1995).

40. Paul Johnson, Canadian National Baptist Convention, http://cnbc. ca/new-disciple-makers/stages.

41. Interview with Neal McGlohon, *The Cypress Project*, December 22, 2014.

42. "Why Send" video, www.namb.net/sent-cities.

43. Ibid.

44. "Send North America," North American Mission Board, http://www.namb.net/overview-why-send.

45. See Stages, Fellowship Pickering, http://fellowshippickering.ca/stages.php.

46. Personal Interview, December 2014.

47. See Paul F. South, "NOBTS Study: Eighty-Nine Percent of SBC Churches Not Experiencing Healthy Growth," New Orleans Baptist Theological Seminary, http://www.nobts.edu/publications/News/LeavellCentersidebar3-09.html.

48. A friend and colleague, John Worcester, has been a pioneer in numerous new methodologies in church planting. He has influenced many to think strategically about maximizing their life cycle for the Kingdom of God.

49. Jim Collins, *Good to Great: Why Some Companies Make the Leap . . . and Others Don't* (New York: Harper Collins, 2001).

50. Larry Bossidy and Ram Charan, *Execution: The Discipline of Getting Things Done* (New York: Crown Business, 2002). Note: This is in no way to diminish the value of the leadership principles that can be learned from *Good to Great, Execution*, or a myriad of other helpful and well-written business books but simply to remind ourselves that corporate success and Kingdom obedience often move in diametrically different directions.

51. *Koinonia* is a transliteration of the Greek word Κοινωνία, which generally means "communion or mutual participation." It is often used to describe the state of unity and fellowship that should exist among believers in a church that desires to live as the body of Christ.

52. A more comprehensive look at the problem of brand expansion can be seen in Jeff Christopherson, *Kingdom Matrix: Designing a Church for the Kingdom of God* (Boise, ID: Elevate Publishing, 2012), 111–16.

53. *Cul-de-sac* is a French phrase that literally translates "bottom of the bag." It is ironic that without a Kingdom perspective on finances, we often see ourselves as containing and holding instead of channeling and giving Kingdom resources.

54. See Ed Stetzer, "Plan by Multiplication, Not Funding: Viral Churches, part 6," *CT: Christianity Today*, http://www.christianitytoday.com/edstetzer/2012/march/plant-by-multiplication-not-funding-viral-churches-part-6.html?paging=off.

55. Dana Lee Robert, ed., *Converting Colonialism: Visions and Realities in Mission History, 1706–1914* (Grand Rapids, MI: Eerdmans, 2008), 14–15.

56. Henry Venn and Rufus Anderson's prescription for indigenous planting (self-financing, self-propagating, and self-governing) has been criticized because of many examples cited of nonindigenous churches being established that are clearly marked with Venn's three characteristics. As this is obviously true, it does not diminish the effect that the "three selfs" have on propelling an indigenous movement forward.

57. The exception to this is often a large church that is minimally engaged/invested in their plant's success. Often they attach their church's name to numerous plants as one of many investing partners.

58. See "Multi-site Churches: May–June 2009," 9Marks, http://9marks.org /journal/multi-site-churches. This website has a series of helpful essays that express viewpoints that are both pro and con on multisiting.

59. See Jonathan Leeman, "Twenty-Two Problems with Multi-site Churches," 9Marks, http://9marks.org/article/twenty-two-problems-with-multi-site-churches.

60. Kensington Church, founded by a humble Steve Andrews, is now found across greater Detroit in huge numbers. Kensington is an excellent multisiting example of a large church propelled by an uncelebrity-driven approach to leadership. From their first days, leadership development was primary as Pastor Steve was busy constantly developing a teaching team. Kensington is also a great example of a growing trend in a hybrid approach of both multisiting and multiplication through church planting. Learn from these guys. See Kensington Church, https://www.kensingtonchurch.org.

61. Specific church-planting models are rarely prescribed or enforced. Many church-planting incubators see the benefits of numerous models to reach a varied audience. However, often church plants from an incubator tend to follow the pattern they have observed to be effective.

62. See chapter 32, "Exploring Multiplication Models," referring to the *fully engaged* category.